Windows® 7
FOR
DUMMIES®
*e*LEARNING KIT

Windows® 7

FOR

DUMMIES®

*e*LEARNING KIT

by Jennifer Fulton

WILEY

John Wiley & Sons, Inc.

Windows® 7 For Dummies® eLearning Kit

Published by
John Wiley & Sons, Inc.
111 River Street
Hoboken, NJ 07030-5774
www.wiley.com

Copyright © 2012 by John Wiley & Sons, Inc., Hoboken, New Jersey

Published by John Wiley & Sons, Inc., Hoboken, New Jersey

Published simultaneously in Canada

For general information on our other products and services, please contact our Customer Care Department within the U.S. at 877-762-2974, outside the U.S. at 317-572-3993, or fax 317-572-4002.

For technical support, please visit www.wiley.com/techsupport.

Wiley publishes in a variety of print and electronic formats and by print-on-demand. Some material included with standard print versions of this book may not be included in e-books or in print-on-demand. If this book refers to media such as a CD or DVD that is not included in the version you purchased, you may download this material at http://booksupport.wiley.com. For more information about Wiley products, visit www.wiley.com.

Library of Congress Control Number: 2011939651

ISBN 978-1-118-03159-9 (pbk); ISBN 978-1-118-09902-5 (ebk); ISBN 978-1-118-09903-2 (ebk); ISBN 978-1-118-09904-9 (ebk)

Manufactured in the United States of America

10 9 8 7 6 5 4 3 2 1

WILEY

Dedication

To my husband Scott, without whom nothing is possible.

Author's Acknowledgments

My thanks to Amy Fandrei and Nicole Sholly who helped bring this project to fruition. My thanks as always to my friends at Microsoft for their continued advice, support, and guidance on Windows 7.

About the Author

Jennifer Fulton, Senior Partner of Ingenus, LLC and iVillage's former "Computer Coach," is an experienced technical writer with more than 20 years in the business. Jennifer has written and edited hundreds of online course materials for both college and middle school audiences, and authored more the 150 best-selling computer books for beginner, intermediate, and advanced users.

Jennifer is also a computer trainer for corporate personnel, teaching a variety of classes, including Windows, Microsoft Office, Paint Shop Pro, Photoshop Elements, and others.

Publisher's Acknowledgments

We're proud of this book; please send us your comments at http://dummies.custhelp.com. For other comments, please contact our Customer Care Department within the U.S. at 877-762-2974, outside the U.S. at 317-572-3993, or fax 317-572-4002.

Some of the people who helped bring this book to market include the following:

Acquisitions, Editorial, and Vertical Websites

Senior Project Editor: Nicole Sholly

Acquisitions Editor: Amy Fandrei

Senior Copy Editor: Teresa Artman

Technical Editor: Keith Underdahl

Editorial Manager: Kevin Kirschner

Assistant Project Manager: Jenny Swisher

Quality Assurance: Josh Frank

Editorial Assistant: Amanda Graham

Sr. Editorial Assistant: Cherie Case

Cartoons: Rich Tennant (www.the5thwave.com)

Composition Services

Project Coordinator: Nikki Gee

Layout and Graphics: Melanee Habig, Andrea Hornberger, Jennifer Mayberry

Proofreaders: Lauren Mandelbaum, Mildred Rosenzweig

Indexer: BIM Indexing & Proofreading Services

Special Help: Leah Cameron, Becky Huehls, Jennifer Riggs, Brian Walls

---

Publishing and Editorial for Technology Dummies

> **Richard Swadley,** Vice President and Executive Group Publisher

> **Andy Cummings,** Vice President and Publisher

> **Mary Bednarek,** Executive Acquisitions Director

> **Mary C. Corder,** Editorial Director

Publishing for Consumer Dummies

> **Kathleen Nebenhaus,** Vice President and Executive Publisher

Composition Services

> **Debbie Stailey,** Director of Composition Services

Table of Contents

Introduction

*I*f you've been thinking about taking a class online (it is all the rage these days), but you're concerned about getting lost in the electronic fray, worry no longer. *Windows 7 For Dummies eLearning Kit* is here to help you, providing you with an integrated learning experience that includes not only the book and CD you hold in your hands but also an online version of the course at www.dummieselearning.com. Consider this Introduction your primer.

About This Kit

Each piece of this eLearning kit works in conjunction with the others although you don't need them all to gain valuable understanding of the key concepts covered here. Whether you pop the CD into your computer to start the lessons electronically, follow along with the book (or not), or go online to see the course, this kit teaches you how to

- ✔ Log on, choose strong passwords, and navigate the Windows 7 interface.
- ✔ Launch programs, organize files, use a file manager, and keep track of your libraries.
- ✔ Play music and videos on Windows Media Player, organize your photos with Windows Photo Viewer, and share files online through a Windows Live Account.
- ✔ Set up a home network, share your devices, and build a homegroup.
- ✔ Browse the Internet and discover everything you ever wanted to know about e-mailing.
- ✔ Set up an admin account, perform routine maintenance, use parental controls, and stay safe on the Web.

How This Book Is Organized

This book is split into six lessons, which I describe here:

- **Lesson 1: Getting Started with Windows 7** This lesson details the basics: You will learn how to log on to your Windows machine, safely shut down or log off your computer, create and switch between user accounts, and become familiar with navigating the Windows 7 user interface.

- **Lesson 2: Playing with Programs, Folders, and Files** Windows 7 offers many tools and features to help you move among your programs and files quickly and easily. In this lesson, you discover how to work with several of them so that you can manage programs through the Start menu and taskbar, organize files, and keep track of your libraries.

- **Lesson 3: Organizing Your Pictures, Movies, and Music** If you're like many people, you'd like to organize your photographs, listen to music, and watch DVDs — digital media tasks that are possible in Windows 7. It just takes some organization and learning the ins and out of making that magic happen. Windows 7 — and this lesson — comes armed with plenty of tools and methods for you to organize and share your photos, music, and movies.

- **Lesson 4: Networking Your PCs** From connecting your PC to a Wi-Fi router and securing your files to setting up and managing your router, this lesson aims to help you with home networking. You will learn to manage your Internet and network connections, create a homegroup, share files and devices with that homegroup, and stream media.

- **Lesson 5: Playing on the Internet** Whether you're researching a paper, looking for entertainment, or sharing photos, this lesson will help you in all online endeavors. You start by exploring Internet Explorer 9 and then venture into tabbing, bookmarking Favorites, setting a home page, and using e-mail like a pro.

- **Lesson 6: Staying Safe and Secure** In this lesson, you will set up an admin account, perform routine maintenance, secure your computer, manage how your kids use the computer, stay safe while surfing the Web, and troubleshoot disasters.

- **About the CD appendix** The appendix briefly outlines what the CD at the back of this book contains and what you'll find in the online course (available at www.dummieselearning.com). The appendix also contains a few technical details about using the CD and troubleshooting tips, should you need them.

How This Book Works with the Electronic Lessons

Windows 7 For Dummies eLearning Kit merges a tutorial-based Dummies book with eLearning instruction contained on the CD and in an online course. The lessons you find in this book mirror the lessons in the course, and you can use the two together or separately. Both the book and the course feature self-assessment questions, skill-building exercises, illustrations, and additional resources. In each lesson in the book, you'll find these elements:

- ✔ **Lesson opener questions:** The questions quiz you on particular points of interest. A page number heads you in the right direction to find the answer.
- ✔ **Summing Up:** This section reiterates the content you just learned.
- ✔ **Know This Tech Talk:** Each lesson contains a brief glossary.

Conventions Used in This Book

A few style conventions will help you navigate the book piece of this kit:

- ✔ Terms I truly want to emphasize are defined in Lingo sections.
- ✔ Web site addresses, or URLs, are shown like this: www.dummies.com.
- ✔ Numbered steps that you need to follow, and characters you need to type (like a user ID or a password) are set in **bold**.

Foolish Assumptions

I assume you know what eLearning is, need to find out how to use Windows 7 (and fast!), and want to get a piece of this academic action the fun and easy way with *Windows 7 For Dummies eLearning Kit.* You need a PC, loaded with Windows 7. You also need the Internet Explorer 9 browser (which should come with Windows 7), but I show you how to update to that version if you need. And you need an online connection.

Icons Used in This Kit

The familiar and helpful Dummies icons guide you throughout *Windows 7 For Dummies eLearning Kit,* in the book and in the electronic lessons, too.

The Tip icon points out helpful information that's likely to make your job easier.

This icon marks a general interesting and useful fact — something you probably want to remember for later use.

The Warning icon highlights lurking danger. When you see this icon, you know to pay attention and proceed with caution.

In addition to the icons, you also find these friendly study aids in the book that bring your attention to certain pieces of information:

- **Lingo:** When you see the Lingo box, look for a definition of a key term or concept.
- **Go Online:** Serving as your call to action, this box sends you online to view Web resources, complete activities, or find examples.
- **Extra Info:** This box highlights something to pay close attention to in a figure or points out other useful information related to the discussion at hand.
- **Coursework:** Look to this box for homework ideas that help you further hone your skills.

Class Is In

Now that you're primed and ready, it's time to begin. If you're altogether new to Windows, this course starts at the beginning (see Lesson 1) and helps you get comfortable using all aspects of Windows 7. If you're already familiar with earlier versions of Windows and have upgraded to 7, you can speed through the basics to dive into more advanced techniques. Whichever path you choose, you can use the book in tandem with the online course — the content of one reinforces the other.

Lesson 1
Getting Started with Windows 7

- Prevent unauthorized use of your programs and files by creating a unique Windows login password for each person who uses your computer.

- Shut down the computer safely without losing any work by logging off properly.

- Adjust the monitor contrast and resolution, and change the relative size of text and objects to see small text and objects more clearly.

- Make selections and perform other tasks by clicking, dragging, or double-clicking with the mouse, touchpad, trackpad, or touchscreen.

- Move, resize, and arrange windows however you like.

*W*indows 7 is your computer's *operating system*. You can think of Windows 7 as the taskmaster of your computer — you tell Windows 7 what you want to do, and it directs your computer to do it. You don't typically talk to your computer to get it to do something (although a few grumbles now and then don't hurt); instead, you make selections from what you see onscreen using the computer's mouse or keyboard, or both.

What's nice about Windows 7 is that it brings a certain commonality to everything you do with the computer. You might compare learning Windows 7 to learning to driving a car. After you figure out how to start a car, switch gears, apply the gas and the brake, and turn the steering wheel, you have the basic idea and can apply these same concepts to any car you want to drive.

With this book, you learn how to "drive" Windows 7 and then apply that knowledge to anything you want to do on the computer, whether that's writing a letter, adding up a bunch of numbers, listening to a CD, or browsing the Internet. This lesson gets you started by showing you how to log in and off Windows 7, set up and manage user accounts, work with the interface elements, and adjust Windows 7 to match your wants and needs as a computer user.

Logging In and Off Windows

When you turn on your computer, Windows pops up and asks you to log on. *Logging on* identifies you to the computer while simultaneously preventing people from using your computer without your permission. Logging off is basically the opposite — *logging off* prevents further access to the computer (essentially freezing it) until someone logs back on. To get this kind of protection for your computer, you need to provide Windows with some information to compare against at login. You do so by setting up a username and password (which when combined make a *user account*) that Windows uses to verify your right to access the computer.

When you start Windows for the very first time in *your* life, it may or may not be the first time in your *PC's* life as well. If your PC has never run Windows, you may see a dialog box marked "Set Up Windows." It will ask you to enter your name, and this will be the username for Windows whenever you log on later. You type your name into this box. This isn't a form you're filling out for Microsoft; it's a way to gain entry to your PC for the first time. Below that may be a box that asks you to name your PC, and as you're typing your name, you'll note Windows comes up with a suggested PC name for you based on your own name. If that's a fair enough name, you can leave it; otherwise, you can replace it with something that sounds cooler.

Your username can be your full name, your first name only, or a nickname. Hey, it's your computer and your choice about what you want Windows to call you. By the way, the username can contain a space between the first and last names, if you go with your full name.

If you don't establish a password the first time you log on, someone can log on to Windows by simply pressing the Power button. Even if you live all alone, if someone comes to visit, or breaks in and steals your computer, believe me, you want your stuff protected with a password.

After you click Next, Windows may lead you through the process of whatever your PC needs to start it for the first time — generally, it's not a long list. Your PC may restart itself at least once; then Windows will ask you for the password you want to use for your account. You *do* want a password; you do not want to skip this step. In a few pages, I'll tell you more about what you need to know to choose a good password. Just this once, you'll need to type the password twice because Windows won't show you what you're typing (in case someone's looking over your shoulder).

On the other hand, Windows may not only have been set up on your computer, but it may have been used one or more times before. (It may have been someone else's PC first.) In that case, when you start up your PC, it will look something similar to Figure 1-1. If you've logged onto Windows before, the login screen appears, along with an *icon* (a small picture) with your chosen username below it.

Types of user accounts

If you don't see an icon with your name (refer to Figure 1-1) when you turn on the computer, you might see an Administrator, Guest, or Standard icon, which represent types of user accounts. Each type of account has certain rights and responsibilities:

✔ **Administrator:** Has the most control over the computer. Anything the Administrator tells the computer to do, it does, even if it's something stupid like deleting system folders, letting a program install itself so it can send private information to hackers over the Internet, or messing with other users' setups. Specifically, the Administrator can install and uninstall programs, change computer settings (including parental controls), set up new user accounts, and manage the Guest account.

✔ **Standard user:** The account that many Windows 7 users have. A Standard user can perform many of the same tasks as the Administrator by entering the Administrator's password and following prompts. But mostly, Standard users use the installed programs and hardware devices (such as the printer), add and delete files (that aren't password protected), and access shared files.

✔ **Guest:** A Guest account can use computer resources, such as installed programs and hardware devices, as well as add and delete files (with the same restrictions as a Standard user). The Guest account can't access shared files or manage the Guest account — that's for someone who can get Administrator permissions.

Figure 1-1

When you click an Administrator or a Standard user icon, you'll probably see a login screen like in Figure 1-2. Hopefully at this point, you know the password.

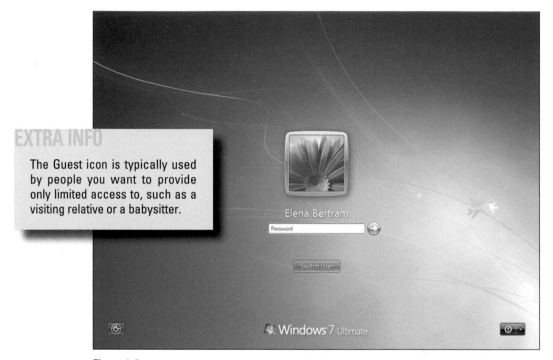

Figure 1-2

If you see only Administrator and Guest when you login for the first time, click the Administrator icon because it has permission to make changes to the computer. And you need this power to create a personal account and icon for yourself.

If your computer is set up with only one account, that account is the Administrator. As grand as that might seem, being the Administrator is not all it's chalked up to be; after all, ultimate power comes with the potential for ultimate screw-ups. So, set up an actual Administrator account and then change your account to the generic Standard user level. That way, when you're logged in under your own account and ask the computer to do something stupid, it asks you, "Do you really want to remove the Programs folder?" while providing you with the means to say no. When you really need to do something dangerous, you can log off your regular account and log in as the Administrator to do it.

Making a good password your key

Logging in to Windows is like turning the key in the ignition of a car. Without the right key, you can't start the car. After you have the key, it starts right up. The same is true with Windows.

To start using Windows, log on, typically by typing a password, which is a series of letters, numbers, and other characters that are hopefully hard to guess, such as `Coffe$lavE32`.

To prevent someone from simply sitting there, typing random passwords and maybe getting it right, make sure that your password is something that's hard to guess but easy for you to remember. For example, base the password on the initials of your old high school sweetheart or the name of a favorite book, movie, or television character.

A good password:

- ✔ Uses a combination of upper- and lowercase letters, plus some numbers or special characters like @, $, or <.

- ✔ Is at least eight characters long (Microsoft recommends a password of at least 14 characters).

- ✔ Does not contain your name or any other full word. For example, instead of using HarryPotter as a password, try H@rrYP0tr, which combines upper- and lowercase letters with numbers and special characters. You can use spaces in passwords, too, so you could use H@rrY P0tr.

If you decide that your password is pretty lame and easy to guess (for example, your first name), you might want to change it by following the steps in the section, "Account Maintenance."

I don't recommend writing down your passwords, but if you must, at least keep them in a place that's hidden and not obvious. (The drawer of your computer desk is a pretty poor hiding place. So is your wallet.)

Making Windows more usable

Windows provides many ways in which you can make it easier to use, especially if you have problems seeing, typing, or holding your hands steady. Some changes can be made right before you log on, so that even from the get-go, your experience with Windows can be a good one. Follow these steps from the logon screen:

1. **Click the blue Ease of Access button on the far left of the login screen (refer to Figure 1-1).**

   The Ease of Access options appear, as shown in Figure 1-3.

2. **Select the options you want, and then click OK or press Enter.**

   You select the option(s) you want by selecting the check box to the left of a particular option. Check out Table 1-1 for explanations of the Ease of Access options.

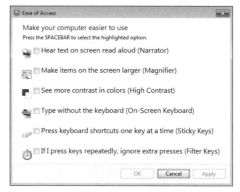

Figure 1-3

Even if you have no problems using a mouse or keyboard, or reading tiny text, it might be worth your while to try some of the Ease of Access options, just to see what they do. I like using the Magnifier from time to time, especially on some Web pages where too much minuscule type is crammed into too small a space. The High Contrast option is useful on my laptop, especially when I'm sitting next to a window and catching the glare.

TIP

You have to use the Windows Aero theme to use the Magnifier in any mode other than the Docked mode. You find out how to change Windows themes in an upcoming section, "Making the boring desktop just a little less so."

LINGO

A Windows **theme** combines a coordinated set of icons, colors, sounds, desktop background, and screensaver for a unified look.

Table 1-1	Windows Ease of Access
Option	*What Happens When It's Selected*
Narrator	Windows scans onscreen text and reads it to you. Windows also reads error messages that pop up so you'll know immediately if something happens on your computer.
Magnifier	The mouse pointer becomes a magnifier that enlarges text or images when the mouse moves over them. Magnifier runs in three modes: Full-Screen (magnifies the entire screen and enlarges the area around the mouse pointer even more), Lens (magnifies only the area around the mouse pointer), and Docked (this default mode magnifies a large section of the screen around the mouse pointer).

Option	What Happens When It's Selected
High Contrast	The colors onscreen change so that there is more contrast between them, making objects and text easier to distinguish.
On Screen Keyboard	A keyboard appears on the screen, and you can use the mouse or other pointing device to simulate typing instead of using the regular keyboard to type.
Sticky Keys	Keyboard shortcuts, such as Ctrl+F, work when you press each key separately. Without this option, you must press and hold the Ctrl key down while pressing F.
Filter Keys	Windows ignores keys if they're pressed more than once in rapid succession.

Logging on to your account

After you set up a password-protected user account and adjust Ease of Access options (as needed), you're in a great place for logging on to Windows 7 whenever you want. Here's what you do to log on.

1. Press the Power button to turn on the computer.

After a few seconds, Windows displays the logon screen, as shown in Figure 1-4.

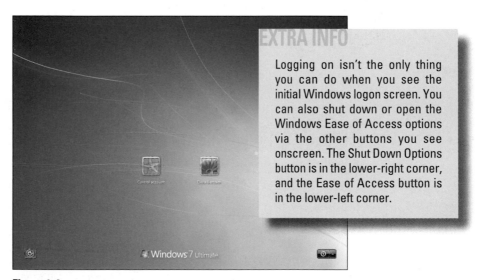

EXTRA INFO

Logging on isn't the only thing you can do when you see the initial Windows logon screen. You can also shut down or open the Windows Ease of Access options via the other buttons you see onscreen. The Shut Down Options button is in the lower-right corner, and the Ease of Access button is in the lower-left corner.

Figure 1-4

2. **Click the icon with your username or the Administrator icon (if you plan to change computer settings or set up user accounts).**

   After you click a logon icon, the icon picture enlarges and a Password box appears just below it, as shown in Figure 1-5. If you click the wrong icon, don't panic; instead, click the Switch User button to click a different icon.

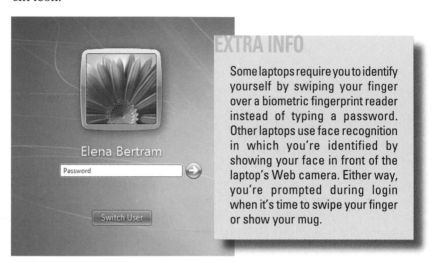

Elena Bertram

EXTRA INFO

Some laptops require you to identify yourself by swiping your finger over a biometric fingerprint reader instead of typing a password. Other laptops use face recognition in which you're identified by showing your face in front of the laptop's Web camera. Either way, you're prompted during login when it's time to swipe your finger or show your mug.

Figure 1-5

3. **Type your password into the Password box and press Enter.**

   After you type a password and press Enter, Windows appears, and you can start working (or playing). If you accidently type the wrong password, simply try it again. If your daughter (who's grounded for the third time this month) tries to log on to your computer without your knowledge but can't come up with the proper password, she can't log in and Windows remains frozen at the login screen. That'll teach her.

Logging off your computer

When you're through working in Windows, log off. You have a boatload of options on exactly how to log off, and the choice depends on whether you're coming back to the computer soon and exactly how much power you need to save in the meantime (especially on a laptop). Your choices include shutting down, logging off and possibly switching users, locking the computer down, restarting it, or sending the computer into sleep or hibernation.

You'll probably have an occasion to choose any of these options, as shown in Figure 1-6, as follows:

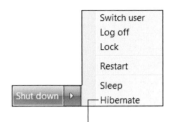

You may not see the Hibernate option.

- ✔ **You'll be away from home for the weekend and want to power off the computer.** In this case, save any open files that you're working on, close your open programs, and choose Shut Down.

Figure 1-6

Windows can close your programs for you during shut down, but if you haven't saved your files yet, you may lose data. Sometimes, a program will temporarily halt the shutdown process to warn you that you haven't saved your files, but most times, you get no warning at all. So save your files before attempting to shut down.

- ✔ **You plan to go to work and won't be back on your home computer for nine hours.** Again, save your files and close your programs, but this time, choose Log Off. Logging off is similar to shutting down except that the computer and monitor are not actually powered off.

- ✔ **Your best friend is visiting and wants to check her e-mail.** In this instance, you can simply leave your work as is and choose Switch User. Windows saves your work in progress to the hard drive and freezes your open programs in their current state. The Switch User process, by the way, displays the login screen so a different user can log on.

In Windows, each user account has its own programs, files and such, and a unique desktop for working. So when you switch users, the computer may present you with a different desktop background and set of programs.

EXTRA INFO

Before you even think about shutting down a computer, it's important to understand a little bit about how things work so you won't accidentally lose something you've worked hard on. To work on something (such as a photo or letter you want to edit), Windows copies that something into **memory** — the computer's work area. When you tell a program to save some changes to a file, the program copies the entire file to the hard drive. Any changes that have not been saved are still in the computer's memory, and as long as the computer has power, that data is safe enough. Should the computer lose power (because it's shut down or there's a power surge or something), unsaved changes (those that haven't been saved to the hard drive) are lost. So be sure you save your files often so you don't accidentally lose the changes you make to them.

✔ **You need to check the mail, fill your coffee cup, or do a couple other quick chores.** Because you won't be gone long, you want your programs to continue humming away doing whatever work you left them to do. (For example, Outlook can continue to pick up e-mails for you.) Choose Lock to lock down the computer so you can walk away and still return right to what you were doing without worrying that someone used your computer while you were gone.

✔ **Your computer is running sluggishly, you updated a program, or for some other reason, you want to clear your computer's memory.** Save your documents, close programs, and choose Restart. The computer starts the shutdown process, but instead of leaving your computer turned off, Windows reboots the computer, refreshes memory (so programs and data are cleared out of memory and the computer can start anew), and brings up the login screen again.

✔ **You plan to stop work on the computer, go to lunch, and perhaps make a stop at the drugstore.** In this case, you're probably interested in saving power, so you can choose Sleep or Hibernate. Sleep saves your work in memory so that you can nudge the computer out of sleep quickly. Not all PCs have the Hibernate option — typically only laptops have it. Hibernating saves more power than sleeping because it dumps the contents of memory to your hard drive and then powers down memory. It also takes a bit longer to reawaken than sleep because all the programs and data that were running are restored to memory from the hard drive.

Laptops are typically set up so that if you shut the lid, they automatically go into Sleep mode. In addition, computers often put themselves to sleep after so many minutes of inactivity to save power. You can adjust these settings to suit the way you want to use your computer. See Lesson 6.

To shut down or perform some other variation, follow these steps:

1. **Click the Start button.**

2. **Click the Power button to perform the action listed on it (which is typically Shut Down); otherwise, click the arrow on the Power button to see the pop-up menu.**

   Additional shutdown-type options appear on the pop-up menu, as shown in Figure 1-7.

3. **If you are not shutting down, choose a different option from the menu.**

   What happens next depends on the option you choose. See Table 1-2 for a rundown of the options available from the Power button.

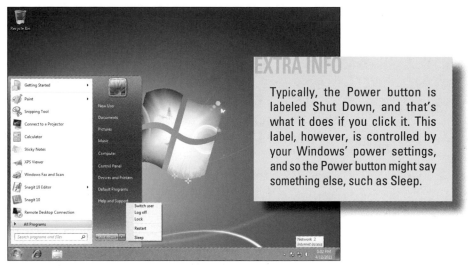

Figure 1-7

EXTRA INFO

Typically, the Power button is labeled Shut Down, and that's what it does if you click it. This label, however, is controlled by your Windows' power settings, and so the Power button might say something else, such as Sleep.

Table 1-2	Power Button Options	
Option	*What Happens to the Computer*	*What Happens to Your Work*
Shut Down	Windows performs an orderly power-off procedure.	Some programs may warn you that you have unsaved data and give you a chance to stop. Click Cancel to stop shut down so you can save your data.
Switch User	Windows presents the logon screen so a different user can log on. You can log back in, too, if you didn't mean to switch users.	Windows puts your data and programs in memory so you can easily return to your work when you log back on.
Log Off	Windows closes programs and displays the logon screen. Use it to log back on to work on the computer again.	Some programs may warn you about unsaved work, but be diligent and save your work before you log off.
Lock	Windows displays the logon screen so you can log back on when you return.	Your programs and data stay just as you left them.

continued

Table 1-2 *(continued)*

Option	What Happens to the Computer	What Happens to Your Work
Restart	Windows starts to shut down by clearing everything from memory; then it restarts and presents the login screen.	Again, some programs may warn you about unsaved data and give you a chance to cancel the restart.
Sleep	Windows appears to have shut down, but not really. To log back on, lightly press the computer's Power button. On some computers, you can also move or click the mouse, or open the laptop lid to wake up the computer.	Sleep stores data and running programs in memory.
Hibernate	Windows takes a few moment to save the contents of memory to the hard disk before turning off the power.	The current state of your PC is copied onto the hard disk, so that when you re-engage the PC (whenever that might be), you can pick up work exactly where you left off.

Logging off automatically

Your logon password stops people from using your computer without your permission. But if you've already logged on for the day, what's to stop Tom from stealing your hard-earned sales leads off your laptop while you're grabbing that extra cup of coffee? You can set up Windows to display a screensaver (a simple animation) whenever the computer is inactive for a bit of time, and to display the logon screen whenever someone tries to stop the screensaver and start using the computer again. Without a password, no one can use your computer after the screensaver starts.

LINGO

A **screensaver** is a program that keeps an image moving onscreen so a static image can't burn itself into the screen. On older CRT monitors, screensavers helped preserve them from damage. Screensavers aren't needed for today's flat-screen monitors, however, and may wear them out more quickly. Instead of using a screensaver, adjust the Windows power settings to turn off the computer and its monitor.

WARNING!

Actually, with today's modern flat-screen monitors, a screensaver possibly does more harm than good because it can increase the amount of *backlighting* (which is how a flat screen is lit). If you use a flat-screen monitor, consider logging off automatically by using the Windows power settings instead of starting a screensaver. See Lesson 6 for help.

To set up the screensaver so it starts after a period of time and then logs you off, follow these steps:

Figure 1-8

1. **Choose Start➪Control Panel.**

2. **Click Appearance and Personalization and then click Personalization.**

3. **In the lower-right corner, click Screen Saver to see the Screen Saver Settings dialog box, as shown in Figure 1-8.**

4. **Choose a screensaver from the Screen Saver drop-down list.**

5. **Select the On Resume, Display Logon Screen check box.**

   This option tells Windows to display the logon screen when the screensaver runs, and then someone returns to the computer and wiggles the mouse.

6. **Set other options as desired and click the Apply button to test the screensaver.**

   • *Wait:* Click the up and down arrows to set the Wait time, which is the amount of inactivity that must transpire before the screensaver kicks in.

   • *Settings:* Click the Settings button to set special options for some screensavers. For example, with the Photos screensaver, you choose the folder containing photos you want Windows to use.

7. **Click OK to save your changes.**

Managing Accounts

After starting your computer, you log on to Windows using your account's password. Windows then presents you with your desktop — yours, not your spouse's, not your kids'. Your desktop sports the Windows theme or desktop background you may have selected, gadgets you've installed, and icons you've saved to the desktop. If more than one person uses the same computer, each user can be set up with a different account, so when a user logs in, she is presented with her own desktop and setup, not yours.

Every user can personalize his account with a unique photo and name, making the process of choosing the right account to log on with much more fun (and easier). In addition, each user can protect his desktop, setup, and files by creating a login password that keeps other users from logging on with his identity (while also preventing non-users from logging on at all).

Giving your account a new face

Windows picks the icons associated with an account pretty randomly, which may leave you scratching your head about what the icon has to do with you. Do you feel like a fish, butterfly, or flower? If you don't like the icon Windows chose for you, choose an icon that represents you or your interests.

1. **Choose Start⇨ Control Panel.**

2. **Click User Accounts and Family Safety, and then click User Accounts.**

3. **Click the Change Your Picture link.**

4. **Click a picture to use with your account, as shown in Figure 1-9, and then click the Change Picture button.**

Figure 1-9

Choose a picture.

To use a photo of your own as your new icon, click the Browse For More Pictures link, select a picture file, and then click Open. The User Accounts pane reappears, so you can make other changes to your account.

5. **Click the Close (X) button to close the Control Panel.**

By the way, the image you select for your account picture appears as your login icon and at the top of the Start menu!

Changing your password

Here's an account element you might want to change regularly: your password. For example, you may decide that you need to make your password harder to guess, or you may have reason to think that someone's figured out your password. Either way, you want to change it to something new.

1. **Choose Start⇨ Control Panel.**

2. **Click User Accounts and Family Safety, and then click User Accounts.**

3. **In the User Accounts pane that opens, click Change Your Password.**

4. **Type your current password and then your new password (twice) as prompted.**

   To change your password, you need to know your current

Type your new password twice.

Figure 1-10

one. Type your current password in the Current Password box. Then, type the new password first in the New Password box and again in the Confirm New Password box.

5. **(Optional) Type a hint.**

   If you want to display a hint to help you remember the password each time you log in, type that hint in the Type a Password Hint box. Remember that anyone who tries to log on sees this hint (they may not know what it means, but they'll see it).

6. **Click the Change Password button.**

   The password changes, and you have to use the new one the next time you log in to Windows. You return to the User Accounts pane.

7. **Click the Close (X) button to close the window.**

Giving your account a new name

Suppose you buy a new computer, take it home, and discover that although the store employees set up the computer all nice and pretty, they didn't bother to ask your name and instead set up everything under User 1, Owner, or What's His Name. I'm guessing that you don't answer to any of these names, so you might want to change the name for the account to your real name.

You need to be logged in as the *administrator* (the one in charge, as far as Windows is concerned) to change the name associated with an account. After logging on as the administrator, follow these steps to change an account name:

1. **Choose Start➪Control Panel.**

2. **Click User Accounts and Family Safety, and then click User Accounts.**

3. **In the User Accounts window (see Figure 1-11) that appears, click Change Your Account Name.**

4. **Type a new account name in the New Account Name text box and then click Change Name.**

   Your new account name can include spaces, upper- and lowercase letters, and even numbers, if you like.

   The account name changes and you return to the User Accounts pane so you can make other changes to your account.

5. **Click the Close (X) button to close the window.**

EXTRA INFO

You might think that a simple solution is to set up a new account under your name and then to delete the dummy account the store set up. Don't do that. You see, after the employees at the store set up the User 1 account (or whatever they called it), they then installed your programs (such as Microsoft Office) under the User 1 account. So if you remove the User 1 account, you can't run your programs because they're set up to allow only User 1 to access it. The smart thing is to simply change the name on the User 1 account to John Smith or whatever so that Microsoft Office and the other programs think, "Oh, now we're owned by John Smith, so I'll let him start us up. We are so over that User 1 person."

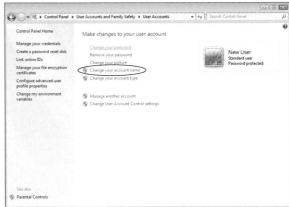

Figure 1-11

Adding new accounts

To keep your computer secure, set up an account for each person who will use your computer, rather than letting them use your account to log on. Initially, Windows is typically set up with two accounts — your account (which has Administrator rights) and a Guest account. Again, being the Administrator means you can basically make any change you need to the computer; being a Guest allows you to use programs and the printer, and to add and delete files as long as they aren't password-protected. Guests, however, can't change computer settings.

The Guest account may not be activated at first, so if you plan on letting your guests use it to log in, you have to turn the Guest account on:

1. **Choose Start⇨Control Panel.**

2. **Click User Accounts and Family Safety, and then click User Accounts.**

3. **In the User Accounts window, click Manage Another Account.**

   The accounts on your computer appear. If the Guest icon says that it's currently turned off, you need to turn it on to use it.

4. **Click the Guest icon to see the Turn on Guest Account window.**

5. **Click Turn On.**

   The Guest account is activated and appears as an option when you log on to Windows.

To set up a new account on the computer (assuming the account you're using has permission):

1. **Choose Start⇨ Control Panel, click User Accounts and Family Safety, and then click User Accounts.**

2. **Click Manage Another Account.**

   The accounts on your computer appear.

3. **Click Create a New Account to see the Create New Account pane, as shown in Figure 1-12.**

Figure 1-12

4. **Type a name for the account in the New Account Name box.**

5. **Select the account type and click the Create Account button.**

   You return to the User Accounts pane.

6. **Click the Close (X) button to close the window.**

Setting Up a Good Work Environment

Okay, call me Princess, but I like things — including Windows — to work the way I want. If I can't see the text clearly, I want Windows to make it bigger; if I can't remember what day it is, I want Windows to tell me; and while I'm working so hard, if Windows can entertain me with a cool desktop background or interesting gadgets, that's even better.

Say hello to Windows!

After you log on, you see the Windows desktop environment, with several standard features, as shown in Figure 1-13.

Desktop

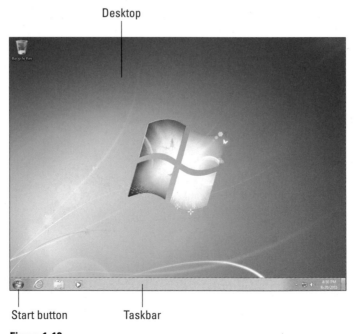

Start button   Taskbar

Figure 1-13

Think of this environment as a starting point for you to decorate and arrange your own Windows workspace. The environment consists of

✔ **Desktop:** Takes up the entire screen and is similar to your own office desktop. On it, you find the tools you need to get things done. Eventually, like a real desktop, the Windows desktop will also become cluttered with the flotsam and jetsam of computing life. You're likely to gather shortcuts to software programs, files you create while working in those programs, and various gadgets — perhaps a traffic report or weather monitor. Later in this lesson, you learn how to remove stuff from the desktop that you no longer need.

✔ **Start button:** Sports the Windows logo and is located in the lower-left corner of the desktop. This button provides you with many selections for starting programs and making changes to your computer. When you click the Start button, it brings up the Start menu, which is divided into left and right panes. On the left, you find icons for your favorite programs. On the right, you find links to *libraries* (gathering places for shared folders of the same type, such as photos) and to the different parts of your computer, such as its hard drives, printers, and settings.

✔ **Taskbar:** Contains icons for programs you use most often, such as Internet Explorer, Windows Explorer, and Windows Media Player. Figure 1-14 shows the Start menu and taskbar.

✔ **Recycle Bin:** Acts as a kind of Windows trash can. Things you delete go in this bin, and every once in a while, you have to empty it.

Recycle Bin

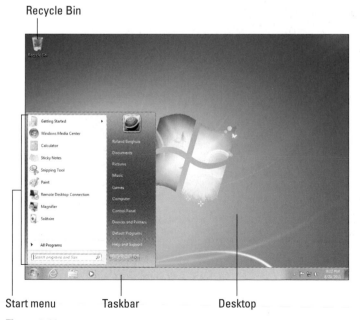

Start menu   Taskbar   Desktop

Figure 1-14

On your desktop, you can work with more than one program at a time. And true to its name, Windows presents programs in separate windows, or boxes, onscreen. For example, you might have an e-mail program, Microsoft Word, and a photo-editing program all open and running at the same time. You can resize and arrange these windows however you want so you can work with all your open programs easily.

Adjusting your monitor(s) so you can see

Here's an important task to do when you sit down at your computer for the first time: Adjust the monitor so you can see. Obviously, try to position the monitor so the sun doesn't shine directly on it. The sunlight can cause an irritating reflection that makes the monitor almost useless. After adjusting the monitor's position to reduce glare, you may need to compensate for the lighting conditions by adjusting its brightness and contrast.

✔ **For desktop monitors,** brightness and contrast adjustments are typically done using external controls or knobs on the front of the monitor, or through an onscreen menu. Look for a button with a sun symbol to adjust brightness, and a black and white circle to adjust the contrast. To bring up a menu, you typically press a button marked Menu or something similar.

✔ **For most laptops**, you don't find external monitor controls. Some laptops allow you to adjust the display brightness (contrast is something you typically can't adjust) by pressing the Fn key to display a series of icons and associated function keys, and then pressing one function key (such as F6) to increase the brightness, and a different function key (such as F7) to lower brightness.

You may be able adjust the brightness (the amount of *backlighting*) of a monitor using Windows:

1. **Choose Start⇨ Control Panel.**

   The Control Panel window appears, as shown in Figure 1-15.

2. **Click Hardware and Sound.**

3. **In the Hardware and Sound window, click Power Options.**

   The Power Options pane appears, as shown in Figure 1-16.

Figure 1-15

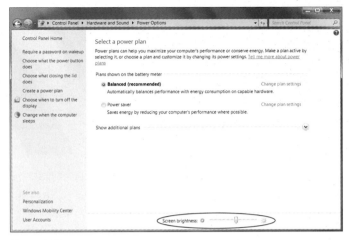

Figure 1-16

4. **Drag the Screen Brightness slider at the bottom of the Power Options pane to adjust the amount of backlighting.**

   If the Screen Brightness slider isn't present, you can't adjust screen brightness this way. If the slider is present, drag it left to make the screen darker or right to make it brighter.

5. **Click the Control Panel window's Close button (the X in the upper-right corner).**

LINGO

Backlighting is created by a florescent light located behind the surface of the screen, which lights it from behind. Without backlighting, some monitors would still display data, but that data would be dark. With backlighting, the data is brightened and easier to see.

Adjusting the size of stuff onscreen

Monitors are capable typically of very high *resolutions,* which increases the amount of detail it displays. Unfortunately, using a high resolution also makes everything, such as icons and text, much smaller. You can compensate for the smaller text. To change your monitor's resolution

1. **Right-click the desktop, and from the pop-up menu, click Screen Resolution.**

   The Screen Resolution window appears, as shown in Figure 1-17.

2. **Click the down-arrow button beside Display — the one that shows the current resolution (such as 1024 x 768).**

3. **Select the resolution you want from the Resolution drop-down slider; just drag the slider up or down.**

TIP

Text looks sharpest if you set your monitor to its optimum resolution. As you drag the slider, watch for the notation, recommended, which indicates that the selected resolution is the one the manufacturer recommends.

4. **Click the Apply button.**

The screen changes to the selected resolution. If you like the new resolution and want to continue using it, click Keep Changes. To change back to the original resolution, click Revert.

5. **Click the Control Panel window's Close button.**

LINGO

A computer screen is made up of a series of colored dots. The more dots, the more color variation and the more detail the monitor can render. The higher the **resolution** a monitor uses, the more dots in its display. Thus, if you increase your monitor's resolution, you see more detail. In addition, because higher resolutions use more dots, those dots are smaller so more of them can fit in the same space; because the dots are smaller, onscreen items are smaller as well, although you can compensate for that.

If you increase the screen resolution, what you see onscreen appears smaller. And so, you may want to adjust the size of some other onscreen items, such as text, icons, and gadgets. After you change the resolution of your monitor, the Display window reappears, as shown in Figure 1-18. This makes it pretty easy for you to change the size of onscreen text.

Figure 1-17

Choose a text size.

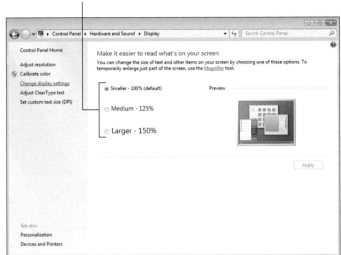

Figure 1-18

Try these adjustments:

✔ **For text, choose one of the options you see in the Display window:** Smaller 100%, Medium (125%), or Larger (150%), and then click the Apply button. Restart the computer and click Log Off Now or Log Off Later (if you need to close programs and save your open files).

You can increase onscreen items temporarily using the Magnifier. See the earlier section, "Making Windows more usable."

✔ **For icons, choose from the following:** Right-click any open spot on the desktop. In the resulting pop-up menu, choose View and then select Large Icons, Medium Icons (the default size), or Small Icons.

If you change your monitor to a high resolution, you may want to increase the size of the mouse cursor. See the later section, "Taking the mouse cursor out of hiding."

Setting the right date and time

Who needs a watch when the time and date are clearly displayed on your cell phone? And if you're working at your computer, it has a clock and a calendar as well. You find them at the right end of the taskbar in the *notification area*.

Of course, it does you no good to depend on your computer's clock if the thing isn't set properly. But you can make sure that the clock is set for your current time zone and has the correct date. Follow these steps:

1. **Click the time and date in the taskbar's notification area.**

2. **In the small window that appears (see Figure 1-19), click the Change Date and Time Settings link.**

3. **In the Date and Time dialog box (see Figure 1-20), click the Change Time Zone button.**

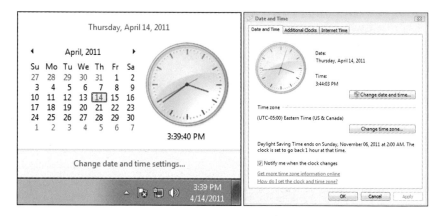

Figure 1-19   **Figure 1-20**

4. **In the Time Zone Settings dialog box that appears, select your time zone from the Time Zone list and then click OK.**

   If you live in an area that adjusts its clocks for Daylight Saving Time, select the Automatically Adjust Clock for Daylight Saving Time check box, as shown in Figure 1-21.

5. **From the Date and Time dialog box, click the Change Date and Time button.**

6. **In the Date and Time Setting dialog box that appears (see Figure 1-22), select a new date from the calendar and click OK.**

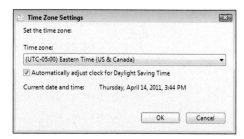

Figure 1-21

7. **Click OK again to see your adjusted date and time in the notification area.**

Arranging, hiding, and removing icons

Figure 1-22

Tiny pictures, or icons, fill most Windows' desktops. Each icon represents a different program or a file, and if you double-click an icon, that program or file opens so you can begin working.

Whether you opt for few or many desktop icons, you can still keep them neat and tidy by arranging icons in neat groups, hiding the icons when you need a clearer desktop, and removing icons you don't use.

WARNING!

When you install programs, most of them ask whether you want them to place an icon on the desktop. Don't let those icons pile up on you — pay attention when you install programs and deselect the option to add a desktop icon for the new program if you don't want one.

Windows places certain icons of its own on your desktop, although you can remove them if you don't use them. Here's how:

1. **Choose Start⇨Control Panel.**

2. **Click Appearance and Personalization and then click Personalization.**

3. **In the left pane of the Personalization window, click Change Desktop Icons.**

The Desktop Icon Settings dialog box (see Figure 1-23) allows you to select which icons you want showing on your desktop:

EXTRA INFO

Most icons (except for the Windows ones) are actually **shortcuts** to programs or files, so deleting an icon doesn't do anything but remove the shortcut — the associated program or file is left alone. To remove a non-Windows icon, right-click it and choose Delete from the shortcut menu that appears. Confirm that you want that puppy gone by clicking Yes in the dialog box that pops up.

- The Computer icon provides fast access to your computer's drives.

- User's Files provides access to your private files on the network.

- Network displays the various computers on the network.

- Recycle Bin contains deleted files awaiting removal from the system.

- Control Panel provides access to the computer's settings.

Figure 1-23

4. **In the Desktop Icons section, deselect the check boxes for the icons you want to keep off your desktop.**

5. **(Optional) Prevent a new Windows theme from changing how the Windows icons look by deselecting the Allow Themes to Change Desktop Icons check box.**

   Normally, you want this check box selected because if you choose a Monopoly theme for example, you want Windows icons such as the Recycle Bin to change, too (to Mr. Moneybags, maybe).

6. **Click OK.**

   The selected icons appear on the desktop.

To arrange the desktop icons, simply drag and drop them wherever you want them to be. For example, arrange icons manually around the edges of the photo that you're using as the desktop background.

TIP

If you like dragging icons to arrange them, you may notice that when you drop an icon, it seems to adjust its location to some kind of invisible line. This is the way the desktop was designed to behave, and it helps you align icons in neat columns without a lot of fuss. If you're a free spirit and don't care a fig for making neat rows, right-click an open area on the desktop and choosing View➪Align Icons to Grid to turn off that option.

To let Windows rearrange the icons, follow these steps:

1. **Right-click any open spot on the desktop.**

2. **From the menu that appears, choose Sort By and then choose from the following:**

- *Name:* Alphabetical

- *Size:* From small to large

- *Item Type:* Programs first, followed by files in alphabetical order, based on the name of the associated program

- *Date Modified:* From newest to oldest

The preceding steps are great for arranging desktop icons, but it's a one-time only thing. If you want Windows to arrange desktop icons automatically, right-click the desktop and choose View➪Auto Arrange Icons. One note: When you turn on Auto Arrange, it locks the icons on the desktop so you can't drag them around to arrange them manually.

Temporarily hide desktop icons by right-clicking any open spot on the desktop and then choosing View➪Show Desktop Icons to turn off the option. The icons on your desktop disappear from view. To redisplay them, repeat these steps to turn on the Show Desktop Icons option.

Making the boring desktop just a little less so

As shown in Figure 1-24, the Windows desktop is a gathering place for icons, dialog boxes, the taskbar, and gadgets. If you apply a Windows theme to the desktop, that theme may affect the way the icons look, the color of window borders, and even the sounds your computer plays.

EXTRA INFO

A Windows theme gives a unified look to the pictures, colors, and sounds your computer uses. A theme may change how the Windows icons, desktop background, screensaver, and the border surrounding windows look. Most Windows themes are classified by the marketing term **Aero**, which in Windows refers to transparent, glasslike window borders and animated window effects. Figure 1-24 shows the Nature theme, which changed the background and added a colorful, transparent border around all the windows and the taskbar. Windows has many built-in themes.

Figure 1-24

Follow these steps to apply a Windows theme:

1. **Choose Start⇨Control Panel.**
2. **Click Appearance and Personalization and then click Personalization.**

    The Personalization pane appears, as shown in Figure 1-25.

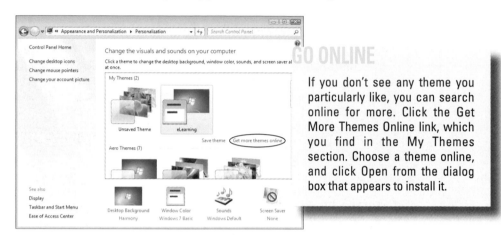

GO ONLINE

If you don't see any theme you particularly like, you can search online for more. Click the Get More Themes Online link, which you find in the My Themes section. Choose a theme online, and click Open from the dialog box that appears to install it.

Figure 1-25

3. **Choose a theme from the list.**

    The desktop, open windows, and icons change to match the theme you chose. In addition, one of the Windows' sounds plays. If you don't like the new theme, simply choose a different one.

Fine-Tuning Your Desktop

For people with less than perfect eyesight, the number one complaint centers around onscreen text and how hard it is to read — Windows has help for that.

Using two monitors may seem a bit selfish at first, but honestly, you might use it more often than you think. For example, with two monitors, you can easily compare two documents — by simply displaying one on each monitor.

If you like desktop icons, you'll probably love *gadgets*. They are more than a shortcut to something else; gadgets have their own functions, such as showing you the weather. And you can change your mouse pointer's look and feel, maybe so you can *find* it better on a large monitor.

Turning on ClearType to read more easily

You've already seen how you can increase the screen resolution and text size; both help improve your ability to read text easily. ClearType is just one more tool you can use to improve the text clarity. ClearType works best on flat, LCD monitors although you might want to try it even if you have an older CRT monitor.

You must be logged in as an administrator to turn on ClearType. Assuming you're an administrator, follow these steps to turn on and adjust ClearType so it works best with your monitor:

EXTRA INFO

Each dot, or pixel, on a screen is a combination of three light sources — red, blue, and green. By mixing these three colors in various amounts, all sorts of onscreen colors can be displayed. ClearType makes fine adjustments to the colors in each pixel, resulting in clearer, sharper text.

1. **Choose Start⇨Control Panel.**

2. **Click Hardware and Sound and then click Display.**

3. **In the left pane of the Display pane, click Adjust ClearType Text.**

4. **In the ClearType Text Tuner that appears, select the Turn On ClearType check box and then click Next.**

ClearType works best if your monitor resolution is set to the optimum setting for your monitor, so Windows checks the current resolution setting. Follow the prompts (changing the resolution, if needed).

5. **From the series of text samples that appear (see Figure 1-26), select the best sample and click Next.**

6. **Repeat Step 5 three more times as you compare all four sets of samples.**

Figure 1-26

7. **Click Finish.**

After turning on ClearType, you might want to use fonts designed to be used with it (although you can use any font). The fonts designed for ClearType include Constantia, Cambria, Corbel, Candara, Calibri, and Consolas.

Hooking up two monitors

Suppose you have a desktop computer with a big clunky CRT monitor, and you want a wider, higher-resolution LCD flat screen. You don't need to replace the clunky monitor — you can use both and increase the size of the Windows desktop (and the amount of stuff you can display at one time). Or you might have a laptop that you want to attach a larger desktop monitor to. Using both the laptop screen and a desktop monitor can also double your onscreen workspace.

Whether you can actually attach two monitors to a computer depends on whether there's an available plug for the second one. Most laptops made today do have this second plug. After you connect multiple monitors to one computer, the same desktop image appears on them all. Follow these steps to spread the Windows desktop over both monitors, as shown in Figure 1-27.

1. **Choose Start⇨Control Panel.**

Figure 1-27

2. **Click Hardware and Sound and then click Display.**

3. **From the list on the left, click Change Display Settings.**

   The Screen Resolution window appears, as shown in Figure 1-28. Both monitors appear as icons at the top of the window. The monitor labeled "1" is the main monitor — where the Windows Start button and taskbar appear. The "2" monitor becomes an extension, either to the left or right of the main monitor depending on which you prefer.

4. **Click the Identify button.**

   Windows displays a large number on each monitor so you can match it with the numbered icons in the Screen Resolution window. Drag these icons so that their location within the pane matches the matching monitor's location on your desk. For example, if the window shows that the monitor labeled 1 is on the left, but physically located on your right, just drag the icon marked 1 to the right within the window and drop it.

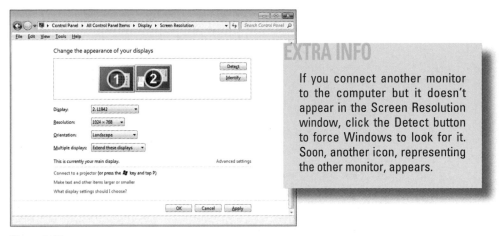

EXTRA INFO

If you connect another monitor to the computer but it doesn't appear in the Screen Resolution window, click the Detect button to force Windows to look for it. Soon, another icon, representing the other monitor, appears.

Figure 1-28

5. **Click the icon for the monitor you wish to make the main monitor and select the Make This My Main Display check box.**

   Again, the main monitor is the one on which the Start menu and the taskbar appear. Also, program windows typically appear on the main monitor when they're first started.

6. **Click the icon for the second monitor and select Extend Desktop to This Display from the Multiple Displays drop-down list.**

   The Windows desktop is extended, or widened, so that part of it appears now on your second monitor. You can now drag windows, icons, and gadgets between your monitors to arrange your desktop how you like.

7. **Repeat Step 6 for all your monitors (except the number one monitor).**

8. **Click Apply.**

   The desktop displays across all your monitors. If you like what you see, click OK. If you don't, make alternate selections and then click Apply so you can preview them.

There's nothing more you need to know about working with two monitors, but here are a few tips:

✔ **Make the cursor larger and signal its location:** With all that new real estate, it's easy to lose the mouse cursor. Make the cursor proportionately larger so you can see it and turn on the option that helps you quickly locate the pointer. See the upcoming section, "Taking the mouse cursor out of hiding."

✔ **Mismatched resolutions:** Each monitor can be set up with the resolution that's best for it (according to the manufacturer), but that may mean you end up with one monitor that uses a fairly high resolution (and small icons and text as a result) and another that uses a lower resolution. If this bothers you, you can adjust the resolutions of each monitor slightly and also adjust the size of onscreen items (see the earlier section "Adjusting the size of stuff onscreen") to produce a more uniform look.

✔ **Desktop background:** Windows allows you to use a picture as your Windows desktop. When you use more than one monitor, the same background appears on each monitor. You can, however, get Windows to display the one image across all your monitors if you want.

✔ **Screensavers:** Don't worry about obtaining some special *screensaver* that works with multiple monitors. All the ones in Windows do, and they appear on each monitor (simultaneously, of course).

Adding and removing gadgets

Gadgets are really fun — some are useful, such as the clock and calendar, whereas others are just nice to look at, such as a picture slide show. After adding gadgets to the desktop, you can move, resize, and customize them.

1. **Right-click an open space on the desktop and choose Gadgets from the menu.**

2. **In the Gadget Gallery that appears, click a gadget you want to add to the desktop and then click Show Details.**

   The details for that gadget appear, as shown in Figure 1-29. If you've installed a lot of gadgets, you may need to scroll through them by clicking the left or right arrows on the Page control, which appears at the upper left of the Gallery.

3. **Double-click a gadget to add it to the desktop.**

After a gadget is installed, hover the mouse pointer over it to display its toolbar, as shown in Figure 1-30. The buttons on the toolbar vary by gadget, but most of them have a Close, Drag Gadget, and Options. Here are some things you can do with gadgets:

Click to page through gadgets.

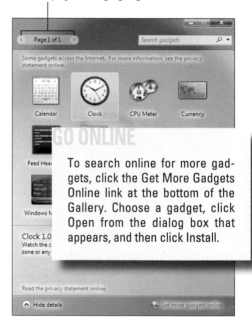

GO ONLINE

To search online for more gadgets, click the Get More Gadgets Online link at the bottom of the Gallery. Choose a gadget, click Open from the dialog box that appears, and then click Install.

Figure 1-29

✔ **Some gadgets have options that you can use to customize them.** Click the Options button to display the options associated with that gadget. Choose the options you want and click OK.

✔ **If you click the Close button, the gadget is removed from the desktop.** To get it back, open the Gadget Gallery and double-click the icon for the gadget. If you restore a gadget, you need to set its options again. The gadget will not remember how you had set it up.

A gadget's toolbar

Figure 1-30

✔ **To move a gadget, just click and drag it.** You can't click some gadgets without starting some action. For those, you must drag the gadget by its Drag Gadget button. You notice that when you drag a gadget near the edge of the screen or near another gadget, it snaps instantly to the edge or alongside the other gadget (like it's being pulled by an invisible magnet). This behavior allows you to line up your gadgets easily.

✔ **You can set a gadget to be visible always.** If you want a particular gadget to always be visible, right-click it and choose Always On Top from the menu.

✔ **Gadgets that display on top of windows and other gadgets end up partially obscuring them.** To be able to see a gadget and yet still see your work, make the gadget semi-transparent. Simply right-click a gadget, choose Opacity, and then choose a value from the menu that appears. A 100% value means that the gadget is fully opaque or not transparent at all. A 20% value makes the gadget almost completely see through, but with just enough color so you can read its display.

EXTRA INFO

Move a gadget by small degrees by right-clicking it, choosing Move from the menu that appears, and then using the up-, down-, left-, and right-arrow keys to move the gadget in that direction.

Quickly hide all your gadgets by right-clicking an open space on the desktop, choosing View, and then choosing Show Desktop Gadgets. To redisplay all the gadgets, repeat these steps.

Taking the mouse cursor out of hiding

On monitors that use high resolution, everything appears fairly small. You can compensate for this somewhat by increasing the size of onscreen text and icons (see the earlier section, "Adjusting the size of stuff onscreen") and by increasing the size of the mouse cursor. If your monitor has a lot of glare, you might prefer to use an *inverted cursor* (dark on light backgrounds, and light on dark backgrounds).

Follow these steps to make mouse-related adjustments:

1. **Choose Start⇨Control Panel.**

2. **Click Hardware and Sound and then click the Mouse link under Devices and Printers.**

3. **In the Mouse Properties dialog box that appears, click the Pointers tab.**

   The Pointers options appear, as shown in Figure 1-31.

4. **Select the mouse pointer set you want to use from the Scheme drop-down list.**

   Each set lists a relative size, such as Large and Extra Large. Preview it in the small preview pane to the right of the list, and select a different size if needed.

Figure 1-31

5. **Select or deselect the check box options.**

   - *Enable Pointer Shadow:* Windows 7 has a 3-D look, placing shadows behind windows and the mouse pointer. However, if this shadowing interferes with your ability to see the mouse pointer when needed, turn it off.

   - *Allow Themes to Change Mouse Pointers:* If you don't want a theme to change your mouse pointers set here, deselect this check box.

6. **Click the Pointer Options tab (see Figure 1-32) and, under the Visibility section, select the following check boxes:**

   - *Display Pointer Trails:* Another way Windows can help you keep track of the location of the mouse pointer is to leave a short trail behind the mouse as it's moved. Adjust the length of the trail by dragging the slider.

- *Show Location of Pointer When I Press the Ctrl Key:* With this option enabled, simply press the Ctrl key, and Windows points out the mouse pointer onscreen by surrounding it briefly with white rings.

7. **Click the Apply button.**

   Your selections from both tabs are applied to the mouse pointer. If you like them, click OK. If you don't, make some other selections and then click Apply again to try them out.

8. **Click OK to make your selections permanent and close the dialog box.**

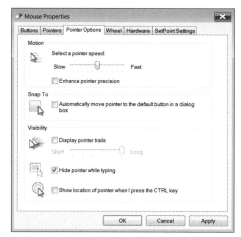

Figure 1-32

Getting Control of All Those Windows

Think about a TV remote control. Remotes rarely look alike but typically contain the same basic set of controls for On/Off, Volume, and Channel Up and Down. The same can be said of windows and the boxes in which programs, files, and other stuff appear. Although programs may utilize their windows in unique ways, they all contain a similar set of controls.

Control *what you're doing* (using a program) *to what* (a file or Web site, for example) and *where* (within the window). Some programs operate within one window, and everything they do takes place there. Other programs operate within multiple windows. Microsoft Word is a good example of a program that uses multiple windows: Each open document is a separate window that's contained not by a single workspace but by the desktop itself, as shown in Figure 1-33.

EXTRA INFO

Windows can overlap each other, and even cover other windows beneath. You often have multiple documents and other things going on simultaneously — each in some kind of window. For instance, you might be sending e-mails to your friends while updating the Christmas card list and scouring the Internet for bargains. To see all your work, you may need to move windows, resize them, or temporarily get one or two out of the way.

The "front" window is the active one.

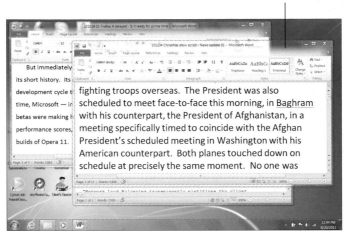

Figure 1-33

The place that windows inhabit is aptly called the *desktop* because there, they work like pieces of paper. The window at the top of the stack is active. To activate a window, click it (any part of it — the inside, the border, or whatever, as long as you don't click one of the controls along the frame of the window, like the Close box.) The other windows are all still open, and the programs inside them are still running. But Windows 7 gives the active window a bit of a glow along the frame and a longer shadow, helping your eyes detect that it's in "front" of the others.

Mastering the mouse or mouse replacement

To control all the windows running on the Windows 7 desktop, you commonly use your computer's mouse or other pointing device. Pointing, clicking, and dragging are not difficult, but they are skills that are important for communicating your choices to Windows.

The way you perform basic mouse-like tasks (such as pointing, clicking, and dragging) varies by the device you use. Many computers nowadays don't have a mouse; instead, they have trackpads, touchpads, trackpoints, and other funky devices like touch-sensitive screens.

A computer mouse typically has two buttons, a left and a right.

✔ **Clicking:** Point with the mouse and press the left mouse button. Clicking typically selects the item, which means that it's highlighted somehow, and Windows knows that you want to do something with it.

✔ **Right-clicking:** Pointing at an item and then right-clicking (pressing the right mouse button instead of the left) brings up a *context menu*, which is essentially all the stuff you can do with/to *this thing*. If you're set up for left-handed usage, click the left button instead (the opposite button you use to click).

✔ **Dragging:** The action you perform to move or select a group of things onscreen is dragging. For example, you might drag your icons around the desktop to arrange them. To drag using a mouse, point to the item, press the left mouse button, hold the button down as you move the mouse, and release the mouse button to drop the item when it's where you want it. When you click and drag over text, grab those characters and spaces to select the text, as shown by the highlighted text in Figure 1-34.

✔ **Double-clicking:** This mouse operation typically activates something, or makes it "run" or "go." To double-click, press the left mouse button twice rapidly, like tap-tap. You might double-click a program's icon on the desktop, for example, to start (run) that program.

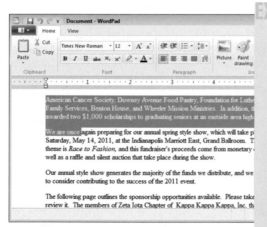

Figure 1-34

The altered states of windows

A typical window has three states, controlled by the buttons at the right end of the window's title bar, that set how much of the screen the window inhabits.

 ✔ **Maximized:** A window takes up almost all the screen space (except for the taskbar, which is typically always visible). Maximize a window when you want to concentrate on the program or document in that window and nothing else. Shown in the margin, the button you use to maximize a window looks like a single box, and it's located between the other two buttons at the right end of the window's title bar.

✔ **Restored:** A window shares screen space with other windows on the desktop. A window can be open, but not inflated to full size. For example, you might resize a window so you can see part of its contents while also viewing some of the contents in another window. Windows remembers this custom size so that if you maximize the window, you can later return it to that custom size. You restore a maximized window to normal with the same button (the one in the middle of the set of three), except that the button changes when it's in a maximized window so that it looks like a box on top of another box (as shown here).

 ✔ **Minimized:** A window moves off the screen without closing or exiting its program. The window is not closed; it's just not visible. Minimize a window by clicking the button in the upper-left corner that looks like a low, flat line (the first button on the left in the group of three).You can tell that a minimized window is still operating by looking for its icon in the taskbar.

 The X button (shown here) on the far right of the title bar is the Close button. On the active window (the one in front), the Close button appears bright red. Clicking a window's Close button starts a shutdown process for the document or program running in that window.

> **EXTRA INFO**
>
> When you click Close and the window contains changes to a file that have not been saved, the program typically asks you whether you *really* want to close the window. Click Yes if you don't care about saving anything new. Click No if you realize, oops, you want to save your changes first. If you click No, the Close operation is stopped, and you return to the program.

Controlling a window's size and position

Perhaps the most useful part of a window is the frame itself. In Windows 7, a window's *frame* is glassy and semi-transparent. Almost every part of this frame does something:

✔ **A window's title bar acts like a handle.** Click a window's title bar to drag the window anywhere onscreen. See Figure 1-35.

✔ **A window's frame acts like a rubber band.** Drag any side of the frame to stretch or shrink the window in that direction. Drag a corner to retain the window's proportions.

Except on a touchscreen (where a pointer may not appear), when you move the mouse pointer over a window frame, it changes to a pair of opposite-facing arrows, pointing in the direction you can stretch or shrink the window.

Drag a window by its title bar.

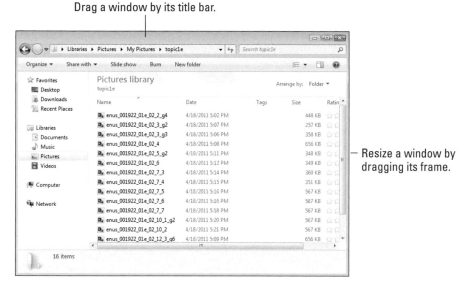

Resize a window by dragging its frame.

Figure 1-35

Scrolling a window's contents

If the contents of the window frame aren't fully displayed (because the window's been made smaller), scroll bars and boxes appear along the frame and/or bottom edge of the frame, as shown in Figure 1-36. You can then drag these — up and down or left and right — to see the rest of the content in that window.

✔ The scroll box represents the relative position of the displayed contents to the entire contents of the window. In Figure 1-36, for example, the position of the circled scroll box tells you that you are looking roughly at the middle of the list of files.

✔ To display a portion of the window that's hidden, drag the scroll box up or down (vertical scroll bar) or left or right (horizontal scroll bar). The direction you drag the scroll box is the direction you want to move, so to go down in the document, you move the scroll box down.

✔ To move the contents just a bit, click the arrows on either end of the appropriate scroll bar.

✔ To move through a document page by page (or by some other set amount), click anywhere in the space above or below the scroll box.

Scroll arrow

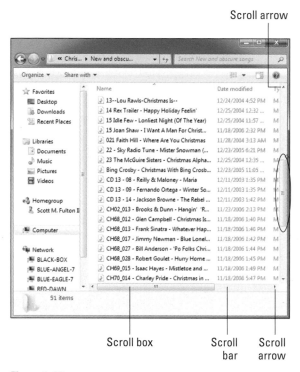

Scroll box   Scroll   Scroll
                     bar   arrow

Figure 1-36

Snapping a window in place

As you grow more accustomed to working with Windows, you frequently do things with more than one document or program. For example, you might send an instant message to your boss as you frantically search for the latest department expenses in the current budget spreadsheet, while leaving a Web page open along with a slide show you were working on when your boss pinged you. From the PC's perspective, it's multitasking; from your point of view, you're doing a job, and it doesn't matter how many programs or files you have to open to get it done.

Windows programs work the way you do — each one knows it's not the center of the universe, so each communicates well with others. For example, you can often drag data from one program's window to the other. If that's not possible, you may be able to cut and paste some of the data from one window to another, certainly if the programs in both windows recognize the format of that data — for instance, a paragraph or a picture.

When you work with multiple windows, sometimes you need to arrange two of them so that they share the screen equally, one on the left side and one on the right. Follow these steps:

1. **Drag the first window by its title bar handle, all the way to either the left or right side of the screen, and then drop it.**

   Windows automatically resizes the window to fit that half of the screen.

2. **Drag the second window by its title bar to the opposite side of the screen.**

   Windows snaps the second window to the other half of the screen, as shown in Figure 1-37.

3. **When you're done with those two windows, drag them by their title bars off their respective sides, and Windows restores them to exactly the size they were before.**

To snap a maximized window, drag it by its title bar to the top of the screen, or double-click its title bar.

Figure 1-37

Arranging multiple windows

Open windows (not minimized) can be arranged quickly so you can view them all. Open all your windows as long vertical or horizontal strips side by side, or stagger them slightly, one on top of the other, like a deck of cards fanned out.

✔ **To arrange open windows side by side vertically,** right-click the taskbar and choose Show Windows Side by Side.

✔ **To arrange open windows side by side horizontally,** right-click the taskbar and choose Show Windows Stacked.

✔ **To fan open windows down the screen from the upper left to the lower right (as shown in Figure 1-38),** right-click the taskbar and choose Cascade Windows. If you later right-click and choose Undo Cascade, those open windows return to their earlier positions onscreen.

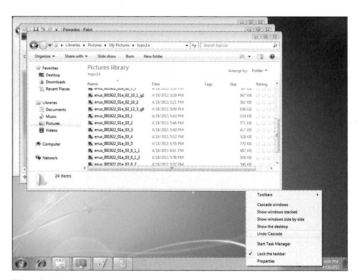

Figure 1-38

If you use a dual-monitor system and choose Cascade Windows, windows fan out on each monitor, depending on the monitor they're displayed on. Likewise, if you choose Show Windows Side by Side or Show Windows Stacked, the windows are arranged on the monitor they're displayed on.

Getting all windows out of the way

Something that's especially helpful when you have a handful of windows open at once is to get them all out of the way. On the taskbar, to the right of the clock, you see an almost invisible bar-shaped button, as shown in Figure 1-39.

 —— The Show Desktop button

Figure 1-39

This button is the Show Desktop button; hover over it, and in a moment, your open windows fade out, leaving ghostly outlines, as shown in Figure 1-40. Don't worry, the open windows are not gone. This is just a preview of coming attractions — or, more accurately, departing ones. If you click the Show Desktop button, the open windows really disappear (they're minimized to the taskbar), and you have a clean desktop.

COURSEWORK

There's another way to get rid of the zillion windows that clutter your screen, but leave behind just the one you want to work on at the moment. In other words, you can quickly minimize everything *except* the active window. It's surprisingly simple, and you'll want to practice this one a few times just to see it in action. First, open a few windows and scatter them around your screen. Click within one of the open windows to make it the active window. Then pick up the window by its title bar by clicking the title bar and holding down the mouse button, and then quickly shake the window back and forth a few times. If you do this right, all the other windows are minimized quickly except for the one you shook. To restore your other windows to precisely where they were before, pick up and shake your active window exactly the same way again.

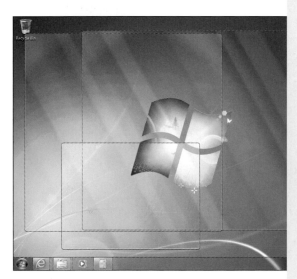

Figure 1-40

What's the deal with dialog boxes?

From time to time, Windows or a program will ask you a question that has a simple answer, generally yes or no. "Do you really wish to exit?" is common. Other times, you may need to choose from related options before a program or Windows can carry out whatever action you initiated.

The tool that's used for this purpose is the *dialog box.* The simplest ones you see ask you to confirm something important that you wouldn't want to ever happen by accident, such as deleting a file or closing a program. Typically, you confirm such actions by clicking a button in the dialog box, such as OK or Yes, as shown in Figure 1-41. The

Figure 1-41

button that means, "Ah, forget it" is usually Cancel. Sometimes you see an Apply button that means, "Commit these changes now, but don't go away because I have more changes to make."

A more complex example of a dialog box is one where you can make a bunch of choices, such as dialog box shown in Figure 1-42. To make these choices, you use a variety of controls and dialog box elements:

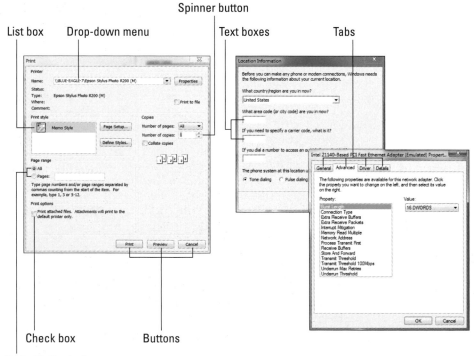

Figure 1-42

✔ **A check box** works just like on a tax form. When it's selected, it's like saying "yes" to a question. If a check box is deselected, click it to check it; click it a second time to change your mind and deselect it. If there are multiple check boxes in a grouping, select as many as you want.

✔ **An option button (also dubbed a radio button)** is a filled-in dot, such as an answer on an SAT test. An option button is used only in multiple-choice situations (and thus, you can choose only one), so if you click an option to fill it in and turn it on, any option in that same grouping that was already filled in turns off.

✔ **A text box** is a control that allows you to type text, perhaps by first changing the existing text.

✔ **A list box** is like a menu, displaying a list of choices. Typically, you can choose only one item from a list box; when you do, the item is high-lighted so you can tell it's chosen. To choose an item from a list, scroll until you find the option you want and click it. If you can have more than one choice, hold down the Ctrl key while clicking each choice.

✔ **A drop-down list box (also dubbed a combo box)** is probably the kind of list box you see most often. A drop-down list box looks like a text box that dis-plays the currently selected item, but has an arrow to the right that opens the entire list. Sometimes you can choose something else by typing it in the text box-like thing, but more often, you simply click the arrow to display the list and choose the option you want.

✔ **A spinner** is a text box that has an up-and-down arrow button on the right, for increasing or lowering the value displayed.

✔ **Tabs** are used in dialog boxes to divide them. You click a tab to switch between partitions. The dialog box remembers the settings you've made in the earlier tab, but it doesn't commit those set-tings until you click OK.

> **EXTRA INFO**
>
> A button other than OK or Cancel in a dialog box may be used to bring up another dialog box. Such buttons are labeled with an ellipsis (for example, Options . . .) that tell you something else is following — in this case, an Options dialog box. These "dialog boxes within dialog boxes" come with their own controls for choosing options and of course the typical OK and Cancel buttons. After clicking OK or Cancel in one of these deeper dialog boxes, you often return to the original dialog box to click OK (or Cancel).

Typically when a program, such as Word or Photoshop, displays its own dialog box, it suspends all input to anything else in that program until you click OK or Cancel, or something similar.

What you find in application windows

The most important programs in Windows where you do the most work are *applications.* Typically when you give an application a command, such as Save or Print, you use some form of a menu.

Recently, Microsoft's Office applications display commands on a Ribbon (see Figure 1-43) rather than a menu where the commands are hidden until the menu opens. On the Ribbon, each menu category becomes its own tab; click the tab to display the commands in that category and then click the command you want to apply (commands are displayed on the Ribbon as buttons, lists, and other familiar dialog box controls).

Figure 1-43

Most programs adjust the commands on a menu or Ribbon to coincide with the item you're working with. If you're using the Paint tool in a photo editor, the Edit menu may display only commands related to that tool, or non-related commands will be grayed out so you can't select them. In Office, the buttons on the Ribbon and even the tabs change slightly depending on whether you're selecting text, a graphic, or a chart.

 # Summing Up

In this lesson, you learned the basic information you need to get started using Windows, such as how to start your computer safely and how to shut it down. You also learned how to work with windows and to adjust the Windows environment to suit your specific needs, such as making things larger and easier to see. Here are the key takeaways for this lesson.

✔ Log off your computer when you leave it so someone can't use your computer without your permission. Click the Power button and choose Log Off (you intend to return fairly soon) or Sleep/Hibernate (you don't).

✔ To increase the resolution on a monitor so more items fit onscreen, go to the Change Display Settings window and choose a resolution from the Resolution list and click OK. It's best to select the recommended resolution for your monitor.

✔ After increasing the resolution, items appear smaller onscreen, so make them larger by selecting Medium or Large in the Display pane that appears after you change resolution.

✔ To hide a window, click the Minimize button. To restore the window after minimizing it, click its icon on the taskbar. To make the window as big as possible, click the Maximize button. To close a window, click the Close button.

✔ You can resize a window by dragging its borders. Reposition a window by dragging the window by its title bar.

Know This Tech Talk

account: The method Windows uses to associate individual users, such as yourself, with the people who use the computer, in order to maintain distinctions between personalized settings as well as to aid in security

active window: The window in which you are working

ClearType: Software included with Windows 7 that uses coloring tricks to make onscreen text easier to read, especially at small point sizes

context menu: A menu of related commands that appears when an item is right-clicked

Control Panel: A central location in Windows for settings related to managing the PC, devices attached to your PC, or Windows itself

dialog box: A window with special controls that allow a user to make choices

dragging: Pressing and holding down the left mouse button while dragging an item onscreen

Ease of Access: A set of tools, including Magnifier (for showing screen contents close-up), Narrator (for reading text aloud), and On-Screen Keyboard, that may enable many features of Windows to be more usable, especially by people with disabilities

gadget: A small program that sits on the desktop and performs a simple function, such as displaying the time or the weather

hover: To move the mouse over an item and leave it there a second or two until something happens, such as a ScreenTip appearing

icons: Small pictures that represent files or programs

instance: A single copy of a running program

mouse pointer: The onscreen object, usually an arrow, that indicates the object that will be activated or "pressed" when you click a mouse button

operating system: A collection of programs and resources that enable a computer to be usable by people

password: A series of letters, numbers, and special characters that when typed in the proper sequence, allows a user to log on

pointing: Moving the mouse pointer over an item onscreen

Ribbon: A method used in some applications (such as Microsoft Office 2010, and Paint in Windows 7) that replaces the menu bar with groups of more pictorially represented commands

right-clicking: Clicking the right mouse button while the mouse pointer is pointing to an item

save: Storing data being created with a program

title bar: Located across the top of most windows; displays the name of the program and/or file contained in that window

Lesson 2
Playing with Programs, Folders, and Files

✔ Create a panel that rapidly takes you to the things you do most frequently with your computer, separate from what any other user of your PC does or uses.

✔ Control multiple open programs, switching between them with ease and moving data from one open program to another.

✔ Build custom storage folders for your own documents accessible through your personal account.

✔ Search for programs or files with partial matches and a sophisticated search index.

✔ Create libraries for documents, song tracks, pictures, and videos stored all over your computer or home network that you can access and sort easily.

1 'm going to be blunt here. What you really should know about

Windows organization is this: You're going to be using programs, and most of those programs will be applications — the kind that help you to do your own work. You launch these programs using a set of tools that include the Start menu, the desktop, and the taskbar. Which tool you use for which purpose will eventually depend on what's the most convenient for you. Some tools are easier to access than others, but if you were to place every application you own on the taskbar, for instance, it will become cluttered and not so easy to use anymore.

The products of applications are documents. These documents are placed in a filing system, which happens to be the same filing system that maintains the files that constitute your programs. So partitions in the filing system keep your documents separate from your program files, and the most obvious and important among these partitions are the folders.

Now it's time to get started.

Launching Programs

The first thing it's very important to note about this Start menu is that it belongs to you personally. Your name is on it as a reminder to you that this is your personal account, so you're using this computer *as you*. This way, Windows can fetch *your* documents, *your* videos, *your* sticky notes, *your* desktop. You launch *your* applications from *your* Start menu. You do not have to create special folders or places to store your spouse's files, or your kids' drawings. Because each Windows 7 user has his or her (or its) own account, those partitions are created for you.

In earlier versions of Windows, the Start button — which brings up the Start menu — was labeled Start. However, in Windows 7, the Start button is a round, blue button in the lower-left corner of the screen, sporting the four-color Windows logo. (If you have two monitors, you see it in one or the other screen, not both.) When you hover your mouse pointer over the Start button, it glows proudly and a little Start tooltip appears, as shown in Figure 2-1.

Figure 2-1

TIP

Unless you're using a very old keyboard, your keyboard likely has at least one, maybe even two, Windows keys with the Windows logo. Just press one of those keys to open the Start menu.

Launching a program from the Start menu

Launching a program from the Start menu is easy: you open the Start menu and click just once on the program you want to launch. For instance, to start the Paint program (which is Windows' all-purpose doodling tool), just point to it and click. That seems simple enough. Pinned programs appear on the top of the Start menu, as shown in Figure 2-2, and recently opened programs below the partition.

These programs are pinned.

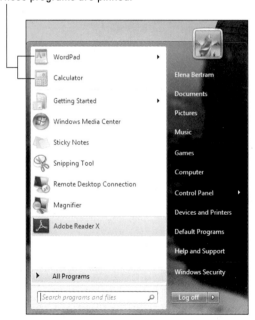

Figure 2-2

Pinning and re-arranging programs on the Start menu

As you use programs in Windows 7, the contents of this menu may shift during transit. On a never-before-used system, the Start menu shows a list of fairly ordinary programs that belong to Windows, such as Sticky Notes and Paint. As you install *real* programs on the computer, the Start menu rearranges itself to show the programs you use most frequently. However, you can tell Windows which programs you want to appear at the top of the Start menu every time you open it — a process called pinning.

For example, suppose you know that you use Paint more often than other programs, and you don't want Paint to shift around. You want its menu item to stay on top so you can find it again, and if you don't use it for a while, you don't want Windows to bury it in some odd location.

To pin a Start menu item to the top of the menu, follow these steps:

1. **Click the Start button to open the Start menu.**

2. **On the left pane of the Start menu, right-click the entry you wish to pin to the top.**

    A drop-down list appears.

3. **Choose Pin to Start Menu.**

    Immediately, the item is sent to the top of the Start menu. Now, when you want to launch that program, you know where you can always find it; and you simply open the Start menu and click the item once to launch it.

4. **To rearrange multiple items that have already been pinned to the top of this menu, click and drag any pinned item to a new position.**

    Notice in Figure 2-3, as you're dragging, Windows shows a black wedge. This represents the spot where the entry will be wedged when you release the pointer. (The black wedge may become invisible if you drag toward the very top of the list, but it doesn't mean you can't drag a pinned program to the top.)

Denotes where program will be pinned.

Figure 2-3

You can pin as many programs as you want on the Start menu. As long as there's room, Windows will continue to partition the Start menu so that the lower part shows programs you've recently or more frequently run.

If you change your mind and don't want a program to appear at the top of the Start menu, you can right-click it and choose Unpin from Start Menu. This doesn't delete the program. In fact, you can't delete or uninstall a program via the Start menu — uninstalling a program in Windows 7 is a *very* deliberate, multi-step act with plenty of safeguards, so it's nearly impossible to do so by accident.

Launching programs from and pinning programs to the taskbar

In Windows 7, you will likely use some programs every time you turn on your PC. Microsoft has guessed at three of these and placed launch icons for them on the taskbar: Internet Explorer (a Web browser), Windows Explorer (the file manager program that brings up a folder window), and Windows Media Player. The glowing tile effect around a taskbar icon represents a program that has been launched. When an icon lacks this effect, you can click it to launch the program. In Figure 2-4, for instance, the taskbar indicates that Adobe Reader is running and IE, the file manager, Media Player, and Microsoft Word are pinned but not running.

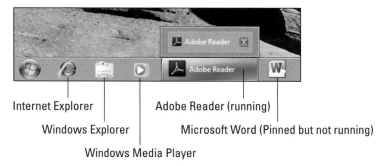

Internet Explorer

Windows Explorer

Adobe Reader (running)

Microsoft Word (Pinned but not running)

Windows Media Player

Figure 2-4

I recommend you pin to the taskbar only those few programs you use virtually all the time. I write for a living, and I use Microsoft Word every day. Word is on my taskbar along with Outlook for managing my e-mail and calendar. On occasion for creating an illustration, I use CorelDRAW. It's *not* pinned to my taskbar, but instead to my Start menu.

If you're a fan of pinning entries to the Start menu, you'll love how you pin stuff to the taskbar:

1. **Click the Start button.**

   The Start menu, ironically, is the place you find most of the programs you want to pin to the taskbar.

2. **Click All Programs.**

   If the program is already pinned to the Start menu, you probably don't want to also pin it to the taskbar (which would just be redundant), unless you want to unpin it from the Start menu first.

3. **Right-click the program, and in the drop-down list, choose Pin to Taskbar.**

   Immediately the item appears at the tail end of the menu.

By default, icons on the taskbar appear in the order in which they were originally pinned. If a newly pinned program is more important than another, however, you can click and drag it to a different location.

You launch a program that has been pinned to the taskbar by clicking its icon once. After the program is running, the taskbar places a glowing glass tile on top of the icon at the same spot.

To avoid confusion, you may prefer to have no programs pinned to your taskbar at all. This way, only running programs appear in the taskbar. In that case, remove the programs that Microsoft already pinned to the taskbar as follows:

1. **Right-click the icon you want to remove.**

   The taskbar displays the jump list for the program, which I discuss in the following section, "Using jump lists in the taskbar."

2. **Choose Unpin This Program from Taskbar.**

   The icon disappears. Of course, this does not delete the program, or any other shortcut to this program elsewhere.

EXTRA INFO

If you pin more than the usual handful of programs to the taskbar, when many other programs are running, the taskbar becomes full. In such cases, the taskbar's only option is to subdivide itself. A rocker switch appears in the taskbar, such as the one shown in Figure 2-5, whenever all the icons don't fit on one row. It's not the most obvious switch in the world, so remember to look for it on those occasions when your PC is very, very busy.

Rocker switch

Figure 2-5

Using jump lists in the taskbar

When you click a right arrow next to a program's name in the Start menu, a jump list appears. You also find jump lists, like the one shown in Figure 2-6, in the taskbar when you right-click a program's taskbar icon.

LINGO

The **jump list** is a new feature in Windows 7. Not all applications use it yet. For an app that does, the jump list typically contains documents most recently in use. With some others, you may also see a list of tasks you can have the program perform. For example, a Web browser may show you a list of pages you've seen recently, but a separate list of pages you view most frequently.

Figure 2-6

When finding a convenient and memorable place to pin programs, take into account that many of the bigger and better applications you'll be using everyday use jump lists. So in cases where it would be very handy for you to have a list of current projects, such as presentations or ledgers, pin the application associated with these items in a convenient spot where you can get to its jump list quickly.

The most frequent use of jump lists, both in the Start menu and the taskbar, is to reopen a recently viewed document. In Internet Explorer, however, the jump list is mainly used to open Web pages you visit most *frequently*, instead of most recently.

In the typical jump list, you may be able to do the following:

- ✔ **Pin items to a jump list:** You can pin a recent item to the top of this list to make it a frequent item. In the Recent list, right-click the entry, and from the drop-down list, choose Pin to This List.

EXTRA INFO

Not all programs make good use of jump lists, but some programs specifically created for Windows 7 do. You quickly discover when a program does *not* use a jump list when you right-click its icon in the taskbar, and the only two meaningful entries that pop up are a duplicate link for launching the program and the command Unpin This Program from Taskbar.

✔ **Start a common program task:** Other programs endow their jump lists with tasks that a program can do, typically in preparation for starting something new. With Outlook, for instance, the jump list lets you begin a new e-mail message, appointment, contact, meeting, or task.

 ✔ **Close a window or exit a program:** Several years ago, the way to exit an application was to choose File⇨Exit. Today, not all apps have File menus, so some folks resort to simply closing each window using its close button (the red "X" shown in the margin). Surprisingly, jump lists have solved the problem of programs not having common exit commands: At the bottom of each application's jump list is Close All Windows (or just Close Window if only one is open), which begins a shutdown sequence for all windows belonging to the application. If you have unsaved information in an open document, the app may give you a warning.

Switching among open programs

Whenever you launch a program, its icon appears in the taskbar. As you now know, Windows 7 can run many programs simultaneously, and many programs run in multiple windows. But the operating system maintains a kind of parliamentary procedure in which only one window has the floor and is "recognized." This active window is the one that's lit up a little bit along the outside frame, with a 3-D effect that makes it look closest to you.

You can click any visible part of a program window to bring the window to the front, so you can use that program or enter data into the document that's open inside that program. But sometimes, when the title bar or other identifying elements of one window are hidden by another that's in front of them, you won't know what you're clicking until you've clicked it. The taskbar solves this problem.

Although a program may use more than one window on the desktop, in Windows 7 by default, a program has to have only one icon in the taskbar at any time. In such a case, the taskbar creates a *stack* that looks like clear *mah-jongg* tiles. Figure 2-7 shows several such stacks. When two windows are open, the icon tile shows a stack of two. When you have three or more, however, the taskbar shows only a stack of three. (Perhaps Microsoft was afraid that if it stacked tiles too tall, they might fall over.)

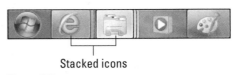

Stacked icons

Figure 2-7

Making any window the active window is an easy, three-step process.

1. **Click the program icon on the taskbar.**

   If the program has one window open, the window is restored to the front. If more than one program window is open, however, the taskbar reveals thumbnail images of up to seven windows. Labels help you identify what's in those windows.

   If you have more than seven windows open, the taskbar reveals a vertical list of the names of each one, without thumbnails.

2. **Hover over a thumbnail or label.**

   Windows reveals the corresponding window's identity and location to you by temporarily hiding all the other windows on the desktop. This way, you can browse all the open windows one at a time without closing, reopening, or shuffling them around.

3. **Click the label for the window you want to restore.**

   The hidden windows reappear, but the one whose label you clicked comes to the front.

Finding a program to start (or a file to open)

As you use Windows, the Start⇨All Programs menu becomes somewhat cluttered, and finding a program you don't use often and haven't pinned to the Start menu or taskbar can be time-consuming.

Instead of hunting through the All Programs menu for whatever program you want, search from the Start menu. This search feature is one of the most useful things you may ever see in Windows 7.

If you know what program or file you want, but don't know where it's located, you can type a few letters from its name. Here's how this works:

1. **Click the Start button.**

   The Start menu appears.

2. **In the Search Programs and Files box, type a few letters or numbers that may appear in the program's name.**

   The Start menu reveals the names of shortcuts, programs, or files that include the characters you typed. If you have Microsoft Office installed, this list may also include documents that may contain these characters inside, as opposed to in their filenames. If the results list is long, Windows may subdivide the results list by type or location, as shown in Figure 2-8.

3. **If you type a perfect match for an item, press Return to launch it immediately, or if you see what you're looking for in the list, click that item to launch it.**

   If you chose a program, the program is launched; if you chose a document, Windows launches the program associated with the document and then loads the document into that program.

You can type just part of the program or filename that you're looking for into the Start menu's Search Programs and Files box and still see results. The following examples illustrate how the search box conjures results for you to choose from using partial matches:

Figure 2-8

✔ **When you know the first part of a filename:** Suppose your husband is named Joan, and you've used Microsoft Word to create a document that you've named `Why is my husband named Joan.doc`. (Sadly, you can't use a question mark in a filename.)
If you click the Start button and type **Why**, this document will likely appear at the top of the list. If you continue to type **Why is my husband**, that document is certain to be at the top. If you press Return when that document is at the top of the search results, Windows opens your document in Word.

✔ **When you know any word in a filename:** You don't need to know the first word of a program or file to search for a partial match. Any part of the filename will do. So, if you needed to search through all your files to look for something pertaining to your husband Joan, you could type **Joan**. If you mention Joan by name many times in this document, it will likely appear at the top of the list.

EXTRA INFO

Windows 7 is comprised of hundreds of concurrently running programs, dozens of which may be operating at any one time. Many of these programs fit the category of *services* — programs that don't bother you unless they have to and are under the control of Windows rather than you. One of these is the Indexing Service, which runs almost all the time. Its job is to compile an index of the files you create so that you can search for items through the Start menu and the file manager.

✔ **When you've created files with similar names:** Now, if by some chance you've also created a document `Why is my husband a Martian.doc` (again, sorry about the missing question mark), when you type **Why is my husband**, Windows pulls up both documents in the list, and you can click the correct one to open it.

✔ **When your search word is similar to other terms in your files or filenames:** Say you've had a memory lapse and you think your husband is named John. (Perhaps, in the alternate universe, he is.) If you were to type **john** into the search box, documents whose filenames or contents contain John will take precedent over those with Joan. (Not capitalizing the "J" isn't a problem; Windows doesn't pay attention to capitalization.) If there are many documents on your computer, the search box may not pull any Joans at all. However, if there aren't a lot of Johns on your list, you might actually find Joan located more toward the bottom.

✔ **When you know (or want to use) only part of a search term:** Here is where that question mark comes in handy: If you type **jo?n**, you find files pertaining to both Joan and John. Here, the question mark is a wildcard that takes the place of a single character, telling Windows that you know there should be one character there, you just don't know which one. Similarly, if you were to type **j*n** with an asterisk in the middle, Windows searches for files that have a word starting with "j" or "J," ending with "n" or "N," and any number of other characters in-between.

LINGO

A **wildcard character** is something you type into a search pattern that acts as a symbol representing something else. The reason you can't use a question mark, an asterisk, or other characters, such as forward- or backslashes, is because Windows recognizes them as symbols rather than parts of the actual filename.

Finally, suppose you wake up one evening and realize, oh for heaven's sake, it's your wife who's named Joan! If you type wife into the search box, Windows won't pull up any of the files you're looking for. Windows 7 is not like Google, so it won't search on semantic relationships (such as husband/wife), only character patterns. If that's frustrating to you, it won't be as frustrating as when Joan walks in to tell you she's left you for hunky Welsh screen star Ioan Gruffudd — which could be the subject of your next thrilling document, "Why is Joan's new husband named Ioan." (And why can't you end a filename with a question mark?)

Windows includes a bare-bones raw text editor: Notepad. One of the nicest things about this little program (which otherwise has very few features of its own) is that its title is made up completely of single consonants separated by single vowels. This makes *Notepad* relatively easy to type. So you can launch this program entirely from your keyboard. Just find one of the Start keys (in the vicinity of your spacebar), press it, type **notepad**, and press Enter. Or if you want to leave a sticky note on your desktop, press the Start key, type **note**, and press Enter. You see, **note** matches Sticky Notes before it matches Notepad, so when you press Enter, you launch the #1 match in the list. This also teaches you something about pattern-matching: For Windows to launch Notepad instead of Note, you need to type at least **notep** before pressing Enter.

Organizing Your Files

Windows Explorer is a file manager that arranges files and directories. You open a folder window in Windows Explorer when you're looking for something. Each window represents a folder although it can be divided into two panes: The right pane reveals the folder's contents, and the left pane shows the folder's relative location in the directory.

When you open Windows Explorer, you're looking for a file of some sort — to use it, move it, or make a copy of it. You're typically faced with one of the following scenarios:

> **EXTRA INFO**
>
> Windows Explorer is the name Microsoft gave at one time to the file manager program. Another program in Windows is confusingly called Explorer: Internet Explorer (a Web browser). Windows 7 actually uses the term Windows Explorer less and less, so you might also see it referred to as the folder window or the file manager.

- ✔ **You know where the file is:** Handling this case is a matter of launching at the appropriate spot, and moving through the right folders to get to the file or files that you know are there.

- ✔ **You don't know where the file is:** In this case, Windows offers tools you can use to search for the right location quickly so that you don't have to go hunting blindly through folders back and forth.

The following sections walk you through the steps of opening Windows Explorer, using its search tools, and taking various actions with your files.

Opening Windows Explorer (the file manager)

Windows, by default, gives you two main ways to fire up Windows Explorer:

✔ **Choose Start⇨Computer:** The file manager shows the names of all the addressable storage devices connected to your PC, as shown in Figure 2-9.

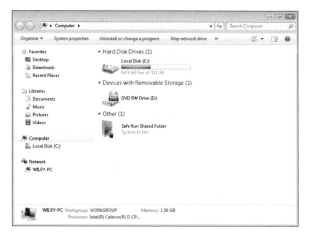

Figure 2-9

✔ **Click the folder icon that's pinned to the taskbar:** When you click the folder icon (shown in the margin), the file manager starts at the Libraries list, as shown in Figure 2-10. The Libraries list groups data files of like types, such as documents and media.

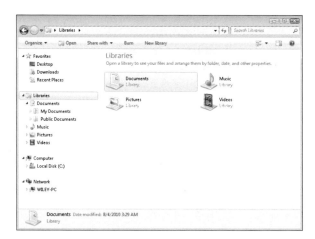

Figure 2-10

- Network takes you to the list of addressable devices on your network from your PC.

- Pictures pulls up the Pictures library, which includes all the folders with pictures in them that you are entitled to see from your account. This often includes pictures you've imported from your digital camera.

- Music takes you to a library with folders containing MP3 tracks, WMA tracks, and other songs or tunes that you can play with Windows Media Player, or sync to your MP3 player device.

- Video shows a library with folders containing videos you may have downloaded from the Internet or imported from your camcorder.

- Games is a little special: It brings up the Games console window. You launch games from this window the same way you would launch any program from a folder window or from the Desktop: by double-clicking its icon. On the left pane of this exclusive window are not only games, but ways to get more games. As you install new games on your system, their manufacturers will probably take up the invitation to install links to their catalogs in the Game Providers list.

EXTRA INFO

The Computer window is unique because it doesn't list folders but instead lists storage devices. Many types of addressable storage devices are available, such as built-in hard disk drives, external hard disk drives, solid-state drives, network-accessible drives, thumb drives, optical discs (CD-ROM and DVD-ROM), and something from the Dark Ages called a floppy disk drive. The icons that Windows gives each one may not look like what they are. For example, in Figure 2-9, I know for a fact that drive C: is an internal storage device; its icon makes it look like an external one. You just have to forgive Windows in this case for not being able to judge the book by its cover.

Figuring out what to do with a file manager

The center of any application window that you'll use in Windows 7 is called its workspace. With the folder window, you use the workspace in the middle to gather files and reveal information about them that's useful to you by sorting and displaying them in a relevant manner.

When you can see what you're looking for and gather it together in one place, you can do the following things:

✔ **Create exclusive storage locations** for files based on their subject matter. My Documents can mean anything; you'll find it easier to create personal folders like Family Budget, Julia's Allowance, Kids' Grades, and Really Weird Songs — folders whose name and location automatically denote their meaning.

- ✔ **Back up duplicate copies** of files to offloaded storage containers, such as DVDs.

- ✔ **Delete stuff you no longer need**, such as scans of grocery receipts from two years ago, or e-mail attachments that contain the biographies of the cast and crew of *Car 54, Where Are You?*

- ✔ **Launch programs** that use documents of a given type. I know, I know, you're shouting, "Another way to launch programs?" But when you find a song and you want to hear it, rather than launch a media player and load the song, wouldn't you rather just. . . double-click the song and hear it?

- ✔ **Build archives** of information you collect, either from work or by going online, that you may need for your research or business — documents of many types that you'll sort through and search for regularly.

Finding out what's where

On a shopping mall directory map, you usually find a point that's marked, "You are here." So where are *you* in the file manager? In the Navigation pane on the left side, the highlighted bar designates the folder you're looking at now, and its relative location in the directory.

- ✔ The Navigation pane on the left maps not only every storage point on your computer, but also every possible way of addressing that point. For example, you find your My Documents folder under both Computer and Libraries. It's the very same folder; it hasn't been duplicated.

- ✔ The Contents pane on the right lists the things that are included in the item you've indicated in the Navigation pane on the left. So when you click on a folder on the left, you'll see the files inside it on the right. When you click on a library on the left, you'll see the folders, files, and possibly other devices that comprise that library on the right. When you click on the name of a computer sharing the same network with you on the left, you'll see the names of shared folders from that computer on the right.

> **EXTRA INFO**
>
> Although Windows maintains many special folders — dubbed **system folders**, such as My Documents — with their own distinct purposes, the manila folder icon always distinguishes folders from files.

As shown in Figure 2-11, the Navigation pane is divided into the following five groups:

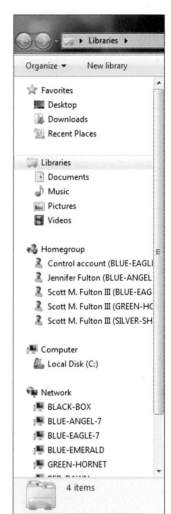

✔ **Favorites** contains shortcuts to folders you may access frequently. Some parts of Windows took the liberty of creating short-cuts for you, such as Downloads (Internet Explorer) and Recorded TV (Windows Media Center).

✔ **Libraries** are collections of files with similar types and purposes. You've already seen those that Windows creates for you, and you can make new ones. (See the later section "Managing Libraries.")

✔ **Homegroup** appears when you have more than one PC in your at-home network. Homegroup lists the recognized users in your Windows 7 network at home, along with the libraries of all similar files stored throughout your network in various places that are acces-sible to the people who use the computers in that network. In other words, Homegroup is a directory of all files at home that everyone in the network can access now.

✔ **Computer** shows the storage devices that are accessible to your PC by their single-letter code and name, assuming they have names. If a program is installed on your computer, it appears somewhere under Computer, prob-ably in the Program Files folder of the desig-nated system device. If a program is installed on someone else's computer, it will *not* appear on your PC. So if one of your housemates has Photoshop but you don't, there's no way for you to run it from your PC because you can't see it from the Computer window.

Figure 2-11

✔ **Network** shows all those storage locations throughout the network that are expressly permitted to be shared with you. If they're not being shared with you, you don't see them here. Each location is sorted under the network address name of the computer on which it's stored.

Conceivably, a well-shared folder may appear in as many as five places on the same folder window. Which one you use not only depends on what you're looking for, but why.

After you choose a location from the Navigation pane, the contents of that location appear in the Contents pane on the right.

If you see the file you want right away, you can just double-click the file to open it. If a file you're looking for is contained within another folder, you open the folder first. There are three ways to do that:

- ✔ Double-click its icon in the Contents pane.

- ✔ Click its entry in the Navigation pane on the left.

- ✔ Click its name on the path line at the top (to move *back* to a containing folder).

Along the top edge of the window is a path that shows the steps between the root level of the section of the folder window you're currently viewing and your current location, as shown in Figure 2-12. For example, one path to the My Documents folder leads from Libraries through Documents. The complete path — Libraries > Documents > My Documents > OneNote Notebooks > Work Notebook — appears on the path line at the top.

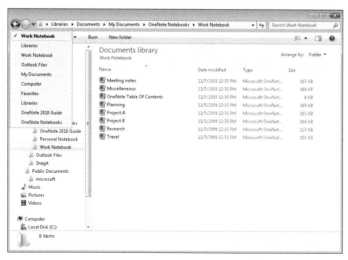

Figure 2-12

There are three ways to *back up,* or close a folder and move back one step:

✔ Click the entry for its containing folder in the Navigation pane.

✔ Click the step on the path line that's just before the current folder. When you point to it, Windows 7 lights it up like a bright blue button.

✔ Click the round, blue Back button, which as a left-pointing arrow, in the upper-left corner of the window. Just like a Back button in a Web browser, this button takes you to whichever folder you had open just before this one. That might be the folder that contains this one, and it might be some other location in the directory. Whenever you click Back, the Forward button (which has the right-pointing arrow) lights up, meaning you can use it to scoot the other direction toward the folder you just left.

TIP

If you want to see the entire sequence of folders you've browsed since you opened the window, click the blue down-arrow just to the right of the Forward button. A menu drops down like the one shown in Figure 2-12, showing all your steps thus far; click any one of them to return to that folder.

Creating a new folder

You may want to create a new folder for files with a common characteristic or purpose. Creating a new, empty folder with a new name is a very easy process, no matter which process you actually choose — and there are several. I show you three techniques. The first uses the command bar along the top:

1. **Open the folder where you want the new folder to appear.**

2. **Click New Folder on the command bar, as shown in Figure 2-13.**

   All new folders are named New Folder, but the name is highlighted so you can type a new name.

Figure 2-13

3. **Enter a new name and press Enter.**

   Type a new, unique name — one that doesn't appear elsewhere in this folder (although it may have been used for other folders).

The second method involves the context menu for the open folder. Most things that you right-click reveal a menu of all the things that can be done to or with them. Adding a new folder is one of the actions that an existing folder welcomes, so you find that action in its context menu:

1. **Open the folder where you want the new folder to appear.**

2. **Right-click an open spot outside of any files.**

3. **Choose New⇨Folder from the context menu that appears, as shown in Figure 2-14.**

   A folder appears in the window, with the temporary name New Folder.

4. **Enter a new name.**

This last method involves folders in the Navigation pane, which feature context menus. You can add a new folder to an existing folder you haven't even opened here:

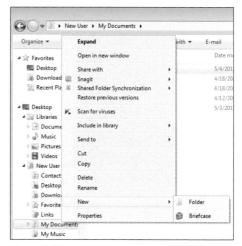

Figure 2-14

1. **In the Navigation pane, right-click the folder that you want to contain the new folder.**

2. **Choose New⇨Folder, as shown in Figure 2-15.**

   The New Folder entry appears in the Navigation pane.

3. **Enter a new name.**

Searching for files

Figure 2-15

Earlier, I mention that when using Windows Explorer, you either know what you're looking for or you don't.

For the latter circumstance, Windows Explorer gives you a search box to find files accessible from your PC. The search box shows you files whose names, properties, or even contents match or closely resemble the criteria you type into the box. Much the same way you'd search for something on the Internet and, to your delight, manage to find it, you can search for files on your computer based not necessarily upon where you think they might be located (if you knew the folder, you probably wouldn't be searching), but what they may be named or contain.

When Windows retrieves a list of files based on search criteria — the query you provide — it arranges them as though they share a common library, such as the example in Figure 2-16. The search results list can give you a peek into the contents of files that contain text, such as word processor documents and e-mail messages. (Windows can't decipher the lyrics of songs on an MP3 track, unfortunately.) Once retrieved, you can organize and sort the search results in this window using the same tools you use for arranging, sorting, and grouping folders and libraries.

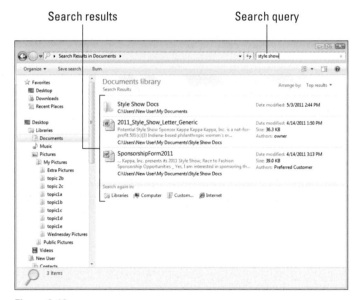

Figure 2-16

To search for files based on something you believe they may contain, here's what you do:

1. **Open the folder from which you want to base your search.**

   You can search your entire PC by clicking Computer in the Navigation pane. However, be advised that this particular search may be as slow as tax relief, especially if your PC has multiple storage devices. The Windows Indexing Service, which facilitates searching, may not index the contents of removable devices, such as thumb drives and optical discs. In fact, if too many devices on your PC can't be indexed, the search process won't even start — it'll sit there helpless and silent like the help desk at an electronics store.

To get better results, you can search the contents of all your libraries by clicking Libraries first. If you believe you know the folder that may contain the file(s) you're looking for or the folders that have them, use the Navigation pane to click that folder first.

2. **Enter your query in the search box.**

The search box explicitly lists the starting point for your search — the one you just clicked in the Navigation pane. In this box, type the data that you think best describes the files you're looking for — most likely data that belongs to the filename, but maybe characters that these documents you want are likely to contain. This search criteria constitutes your query — what you're asking your computer for.

3. **Press Enter and wait for the results.**

Libraries that contain files from all over the network may take longer to search. However, Windows will present results as it finds them, so when you start to see results, don't get too disappointed if there aren't too many just yet — more may be forthcoming. By the way, Windows won't "ding" you when it's done; it'll just sit there and stare into space like a teenager with homework.

Deleting files via the Recycle Bin

Like dead characters in *Star Trek,* deleted files are rarely, truly dead-dead. Instead, the act of deleting a file from a folder moves it into the Recycle Bin, which is a container from which you can restore the files and folders contained therein to the location(s) they were before, or truly remove these items from your system. In fact, every user account has its own Recycle Bin, so stuff that you intend to delete doesn't suddenly become visible to other folks who also intend to delete stuff.

Sending files to the Recycle Bin

Deleting is the act of sending files to the Recycle Bin, just to maintain a high level of drama. You can choose from a couple easy methods for deleting files. Here's one:

1. **Open the folder window containing files you wish to delete.**

2. **Select the files to delete.**

3. **Right-click any one of these files and choose Delete.**

   Or press the Delete key.

   A dialog box appears asking you
   to confirm that you want to send
   these files to the Recycle Bin, as
   shown in Figure 2-17.

Figure 2-17

4. **Click Yes.**

If you prefer to drag and drop files, check out the following steps for sending
files to the Recycle Bin:

1. **Open the folder window containing files you wish to delete.**

2. **Select the files to delete.**

3. **Click and drag the files to the Recycle Bin, as shown in Figure 2-18,
   and then release the mouse to drop them.**

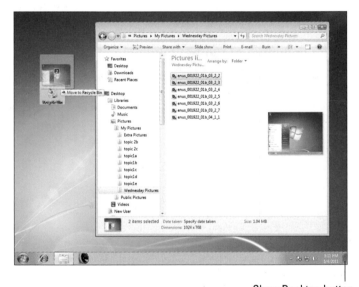

Show Desktop button

Figure 2-18

If you can't see the Recycle Bin on the desktop, drag the files to the
Show Desktop button on the very end of the taskbar (usually the far
right), and hover them there for a moment. All open windows become
minimized so that you can see the Recycle Bin. You are not asked to
confirm the deletion. Windows moves the files to the Recycle Bin immediately. However, at this point the files aren't truly gone.

Purging deleted files from the Recycle Bin

The Recycle Bin icon is a transparent trash can, which means you can actually see trash piling up in it. The icon basically tells you when something is in the Recycle Bin. To get rid of those files for good, right-click the Recycle Bin, and from the drop-down list that appears (see Figure 2-19), choose Empty Recycle Bin.

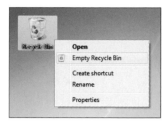

Figure 2-19

Restoring a file from the Recycle Bin

Because you can delete a file accidentally or change your mind, you can restore a file from the Recycle Bin to the location where it was stored before it was deleted.

To restore a file to its old location, follow these steps:

1. **Double-click the Recycle Bin on the desktop.**

   The Recycle Bin opens in its own window.

2. **Right-click the file you want to restore.**

   A context menu opens, which is shown in Figure 2-20. No, this isn't the regular context menu for the file; that's available only when the file is in its restored state.

Figure 2-20

3. **Choose Restore.**

   The file is restored to its rightful place.

Managing Libraries

Libraries are about two things: collecting files over multiple locations that have the same type or purpose (all your pictures, all your documents, all of everyone's music); and sharing those files with other users of your computer and of your network.

Sharing in Windows 7 is a lot easier than it used to be with older versions of Windows.

✔ You have some folders that are shared so others can read their contents, and also save to those folders and perhaps overwrite or delete their existing contents. These are public folders which have read/write access for everyone.

✔ You have other folders that are shared so that others can read what's in them, but only you can add files to them or overwrite or delete their contents. These are also public folders, but they have read-only access for folks other than yourself.

✔ Finally, there are folders that are private that others can see but cannot enter and which might contain other folders that also can't be seen. These are in the private folder.

If you want to share a document, you store it in a folder that's for sharing. If you want it private, then store it in a private folder.

Rearranging a library

Windows provides you with pre-existing media libraries, one each for documents, music, pictures, and videos. With media libraries, you can organize the contents of your media folders however you want (pictures, pictures of family, pictures of a specific kid, summer vacation, and so on). You decide which categories of such things do *not* get shared with others — and for media files, that's probably not going to be a lot of stuff.

The default arrangement of library contents by folder is handy, but it's not always the way you want to display your files. Depending on the library you're in, you can change how library contents display by choosing an option from the Arrange By drop-down list (see Figure 2-21) in the upper-left corner of a library window. (You see the Arrange By drop-down list only if you're in a library.) The options for rearranging a library depend upon the library that you're in. The following examples explain how the Arrange By options work in each of the media libraries:

> **EXTRA INFO**
>
> When your family looks for pictures in a library, Windows checks its registry to see *who that family member is* (not just what PC he's using, but who he is based on how he logged on), and then shares those files he's entitled to see. Libraries take care of the problem of gathering everything you're sharing with others and making them accessible through one place.

✔ **In the Music library,** to see all the albums in your collection (or at least the albums to which all your tracks belong), click the down-arrow next to Arrange By to change the arrangement from Folder to Album. Windows then removes all mention of folders and instead builds a catalog based on the albums that songs throughout your network belong to, as shown in Figure 2-21.

Double-click an album cover to bring up a list of tracks you own from that album. To play a whole album from the first track to the end, right-click the album cover and choose Play with Windows Media Player.

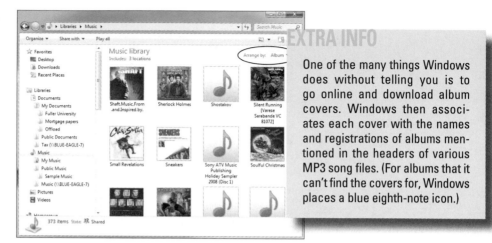

Figure 2-21

✔ **In the Documents library,** you'll find your My Documents folder (which contains the documents produced by you), the Public Documents folder (all the files in your network that are intended to be read or used by everybody), as well as any other documents folders in the network that users wish to share with you. Choose to arrange these by Folder, Author, Date Modified, Tag, Type, and Name.

✔ **In the Pictures library,** you'll find the My Pictures folder (which usually contains all the photos you've imported from your digital camera, all the pictures you've downloaded from the Internet, and images you've created or drawn yourself), the Public Pictures folder (the photos meant for everybody), and any other folder on your computer or network containing pictures meant to be shared with you. To arrange pictures by the date they were taken by camera (if that information is available), click the Arrange By down-arrow and choose Day.

✔ **In the Videos library,** you'll find the My Videos folder (those from your camcorder and those you've downloaded), the Public Videos folder (those meant for everyone), and any other folder containing videos meant to be shared with you. To arrange videos by their type — for instance, to separate .FLV videos you downloaded from the Web from .MP4 videos you shot yourself — click the Arrange By down-arrow and choose Type.

Adding a folder to an existing library

By default, libraries contain both public and shared folders. For example, the Music library contains your personal My Music folder as well as the shared Public Music folder. You may have applicable files in separate folders elsewhere on your system, and there may be shared folders available to you elsewhere on the network. Here's how to include one of them in an existing library:

1. **In a folder window, open the folder whose contents you wish to associate with a library.**

   This may be in the Navigation pane at left, or a folder icon inside the files list. This folder may be on a different PC in the network, which you would access through the Network group of the Navigation pane. You need to open the folder's contents so that its files appear in the files list; you can't just right-click, get the context menu, and go. And try as you might, you can't select multiple folders and enroll them all at once in a library.

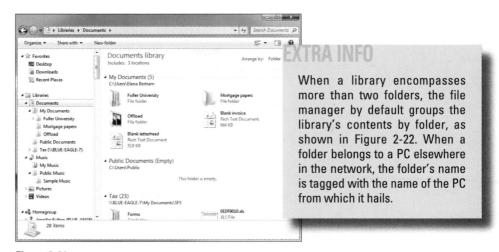

EXTRA INFO

When a library encompasses more than two folders, the file manager by default groups the library's contents by folder, as shown in Figure 2-22. When a folder belongs to a PC elsewhere in the network, the folder's name is tagged with the name of the PC from which it hails.

Figure 2-22

2. **Right-click the folder and choose Include in Library.**

3. **Click the name of the library in the pop-up menu.**

   It may take more than a moment for Windows to incorporate the folder's contents into the library.

Creating a new library

You get to decide which types of documents throughout your network are important enough to list in a library.

TIP

Here is an instance where you can make Windows make your life easier. For example, I like having a Downloads library. All the PCs in my house have Web browsers, and all the browsers are used to download files. When I have one place to review all downloaded files, weeding out the unnecessary files and subjecting the remainder to virus scans is easy.

The creation of a new, empty library is nearly as simple as creating a new, empty folder:

1. **Right-click Libraries in the Navigation pane of the folder window and choose New⇨Library, as shown in Figure 2-23.**

   Windows generates the library and temporarily gives it the name New Library, which is editable.

Figure 2-23

2. **Type a new, unique library name and press Enter.**

   That's all. The library now exists. At this point, you can add folders to it using the method I explain in the preceding section.

Accessing libraries via the Start menu

You know how to launch programs from the left pane of the Start menu. It's time to see what goes on with the right pane of the Start menu. A newly created Windows 7 account will include a Start menu whose right pane, just below your name, contains links for Documents, Pictures, and Music, as shown in Figure 2-24.

COURSEWORK

Do you have a lot of spreadsheets on your PC yet? If you do, try making a Spreadsheets library. First create the empty library, and then find the folders on your PC that have spreadsheets in them using the search tools covered earlier in this lesson, in the section called "Finding a program to start (or a file to open)." Maybe those folders will have other types of files in them too, and for now, that's fine. Enroll those folders in the new library. Now, if you arrange this library by Type, you can separate the spreadsheet files (.XLS and .XLSX) from all the others.

Figure 2-24

EXTRA INFO

With a fresh Windows installation, your personal folder shares the same storage device as the one where Windows itself is installed — where its system files are located. Windows 7 has three main folders: Windows, Program Files, and Users. Inside the Users folder are all the folders associated with the accounts of users of this PC, including yourself. Also inside Users is another personal Public folder, where Windows automatically places files that may be shared with everyone who uses this computer.

At first, each of your libraries has two folders: one that's yours, and the other that belongs to everyone. Windows maintains an account for everyone called Public. All the storage folders in that account are designed to be shared with everyone in the homegroup.

Click the Start button and click Pictures to open the Pictures library window. In this example, you can see the two folders for yourself by clicking the 3 Locations link that appears near the top of the main frame. A dialog box opens, shown in Figure 2-25, listing the names and locations of each member folder in the library. As you can see in the figure, there's one extra way you can add other folders to this library: click the Add button on the right. (Click Cancel to exit this dialog box.)

Click to add more folders to this library.

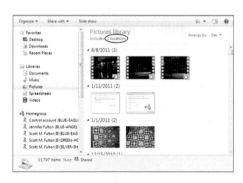
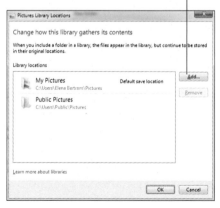

Figure 2-25

As a way to promote and help ensure security, Windows keeps files that belong to you compartmentalized. To access your personal folders, click your Personal folder on the right pane of the Start menu (refer to Figure 2-24). The folder that's automatically associated with you and your files is given the same name as the one you gave your Windows account when you logged on the first time. At the top of the Start menu's right pane is your own name. When you click this link, a window for the folder containing just the files that belong to you and are associated with your account appears.

Probably the most important folder that appears inside your personal folder is My Documents, as shown in Figure 2-26. Most Windows applications are set up to store the files they produce here in My Documents.

To explore other Personal folders, go back to the Start menu and click Computer. This brings up the highest-level directory available for your PC, as shown in Figure 2-27. For Windows, the main storage device is the one that it marks with the four-color Windows flag logo.

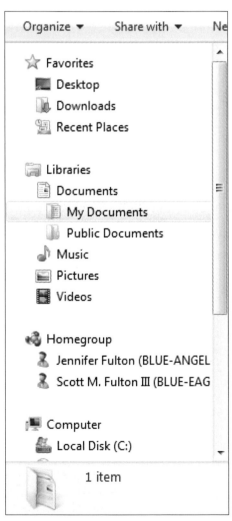

Figure 2-26

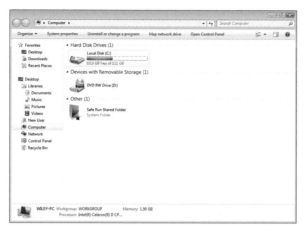

Figure 2-27

Each storage device has its own directory of files, which makes this particular view the directory of directories. Later in this lesson, I show you how to navigate a directory and what each folder window tells you. For now, I tell you that you move into the root directory for a storage device by double-clicking that device's icon. In the root directory of Windows' main device is where you find the Windows, Users, and Program Files folders.

TIP

If you have more than one computer at home, and you sometimes need more than the usual visual cues to remind you *which* computer you're using, you can rename Computer on the front of the Start menu and in the Computer window. From the Start menu, right-click Computer and then choose Rename. Computer becomes a text box where you can type a new name and then press Enter. You can use any name you want here: Frank's PC, Upstairs, whatever. Keep in mind that this will change the name of the PC as it appears in your other family members' accounts and on their Start menus, but it will not change the name of the PC as it appears on your network. The network name is set elsewhere, which you read about in Lesson 4.

LINGO

A **directory** is the list of all files and folders in a storage system. Just a few years ago, it had a second meaning as well: Any partition of a directory was a *subdirectory*. So in MS-DOS (the forerunner of Windows), in a very non-intuitive way, when you entered a program's private storage area, you changed directories (literally *cd*). It's believed to have been Xerox's idea, later Apple's, and finally Windows' to represent subdirectories as folders. However, some got the idea that *all* directories were folders, so you find some literature that refers to the root folder. Windows 7 has straightened this problem out by representing only subdirectories as folders.

Adding links to more libraries

You can add access to more libraries, folders, and lists of devices. For
instance, you can add flyouts to give
you quick access to lists of items or
links that give you full access to these
items in a folder window (Windows
Explorer). Here's how:

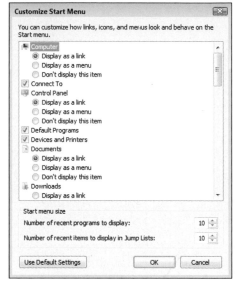

Figure 2-28

1. **Right-click the Start button and choose Properties.**

   The Taskbar and Start Menu
   Properties dialog box appears
   with the Start Menu tab active.

2. **Click the Customize button.**

   The Customize Start Menu dialog
   box appears, as shown in Figure
   2-28. This dialog box mainly gives
   you a choice whether to display
   each of the principal libraries and
   personal folders in Windows.

Here's an explanation of each choice, some of which refer to attaching
libraries to your Start menu, others to making other options visible:

- *Computer:* An index listing all the available storage devices on your
  PC. For example, every hard drive and every optical disc drive
  (DVD-R) on your PC appears here, as an icon with a DOS-style
  letter (such as C:) and perhaps a name.

- *Connect To:* An alternative method of selecting available networks, especially for Wi-Fi connections. (The Network icon in the
  Notifications area performs the same purpose.)

- *Control Panel:* The system for configuring the many myriad settings
  in Windows.

- *Default Programs:* A tool also available through the Control Panel,
  for associating types of documents with the applications best-
  suited to use them. This tool comes in handy with media files, such
  as pictures, that newly installed applications often claim for themselves when another existing tool is more suitable.

- *Devices and Printers:* Shows external devices that may be attached
  to your computer. Printers make up a pretty obvious category, but
  you might also find external disk drives and even smartphones
  that you frequently sync with your PC.

- *Documents:* A library that initially is comprised of your own My
  Documents folder and the Public Documents folder on your PC.

- *Downloads:* A folder inside your My Documents folder that's the default storage location for files downloaded by Internet Explorer.

- *Enable context menus and dragging and dropping:* There's really no reason to turn this option off. Leave it on so you can right-click on files and get menu commands, and so you can move files between folders by dragging them between windows.

- *Favorites Menu:* "Favorites," as the folder is actually called, resides inside My Documents where Internet Explorer stores bookmarks for saved Web pages. You can also use this area for storing shortcuts to other folders you access frequently that you'd rather not hunt down every day when you need them. (From the Start menu, this folder is available only as a flyout menu, not a separate window.)

- *Games:* A central window (technically not a library) where Microsoft advises games manufacturers to not only install links to their games during installation, but also to special functions related to playing those games — for instance, as a member of an online team.

- *Help:* Enables the Help and Support option, which actually brings up the Web browser and dials up Microsoft automatically when you're confused about something.

- *Newly Installed Programs:* Not a library, but an option to let Windows apply a peach-colored highlight to new entries in the Start menu after you install new applications.

- *Homegroup:* The pool of all folders on your network that are enabled to be shared with others. You see how to build and manage a homegroup in Lesson 4.

- *Music:* A library of folders containing downloaded and collected tracks for syncing with MP3 players and playing through Windows Media Player.

- *Network:* A list of the names of all the devices, including the PCs, that are recognized as members of your network. When you turned on your PC for the first time, you may have been asked to give it a name. This name identifies your PC on the network. This Network list may also include your router, if it includes hardware that makes it recognizable as a unique device — which is necessary, for instance, if it can have independent storage units attached to it that are accessible throughout the network. The Network collection may also include so-called *media devices,* which are actually virtual access points through which Windows Media Player and other programs may access media files and nothing else, the exclusion being for security purposes. This way, a PC with a recorded TV show can stream the contents of that show to another PC in the homegroup. So in short, the Network collection lets your PC access media streams from other PCs.

- *Open submenus when I pause on them with the mouse pointer:* This gives you the option of traversing panels on the Start menu by hovering the pointer over its contents, rather than just clicking on them. Some folks find this option weird or unexpected, and for this reason, uncheck the box.

- *Personal Folder:* This option enables to the second link from the top on the right pane. It's the "Documents" link, and it brings up your My Documents folder.

- *Pictures:* A library of folders containing pictures (not video) that you and your family members download and collect.

- *Recent Items:* A folder inside your My Documents folder containing shortcuts to documents you've recently created with applications, such as Microsoft Office. (This one is available only as a flyout menu, not a separate window.)

- *Recorded TV:* A library of all the default folders in your network used by Windows Media Center for storing shows that it records. This is different from the Videos library, which is reserved for videos from your camcorder and downloaded videos.

- *Run command:* Gives you the option of launching an application by typing its name. Some folks from the MS-DOS era (about eleven of them) prefer this option.

- *Search Other Files and Libraries:* When you search for something using the Start menu's search box, you may want Windows to pull up matching results for program names or names of MP3 tracks or files of any type, that may not have actually been installed in the Start menu before. To have Windows do this, leave this option checked. To restrict the Start menu to searching only things inside the Start menu, uncheck this option.

- *Sort All Programs Menu By Name:* Ensures that the list of items that the Start menu shows is sorted in alphabetical order, rather than the order in which items are found or in which they were added to the menu.

- *System Administrative Tools:* A folder containing shortcuts that launch some of the higher-level computer management tools, such as Performance Monitor and System Configuration, that are used more often by admins. These tools are typically found in Windows 7 Professional and Ultimate versions, and not Home Premium or Starter Edition.

- *Use Large Icons:* Just makes the Start menu easier to read, that's all.

- *Videos:* A library of folders containing the files collected from your camcorder and downloads from Web browsers and portable devices.

3. **Choose the way you want the Start menu to display each library or folder.**

Notice in the list from Step 2, not all folders are available as standalone windows. For most items, however, you have these choices:

- *Display as a Link* has the Start menu bring up the library or folder in a separate window.

- *Display as a Menu* installs the item as a flyout menu from the side of the link in the Start menu.

- *Don't Display This Item* simply means you don't need the item to be available from the Start menu. You can still get to it another way.

4. **To finalize your choices, click OK and then click OK to exit the Taskbar and Start Menu Properties dialog box.**

 Summing Up

In Windows 7, the real trick is to get a handle on where everything is. So it's nice to have one-button access so that you can easily find the features and programs you use most often. Here are the key points you learned about in this lesson:

✔ The Start menu is the principal place for launching applications in Windows 7, as well as keeping track of the applications you've installed thus far. You pin a program to the Start menu when you want it to be readily available.

✔ The taskbar's main purpose is to show you which programs are open, and which documents are open in those programs. When you have windows all over the place, use the taskbar to switch among them. Yes, you can pin programs to the taskbar, too, but really, you should pin only a couple or so — the ones you know you'll use daily.

✔ An application's window is really all about the document it creates. Many applications are constructed so that a document has a window all to itself; multiple documents use multiple windows. Here's where the taskbar comes in extremely handy, especially for bouncing between open documents when you're transferring data between them.

✔ When you feel as though you have so many programs that you don't know what to do, use the search box in the Start menu. From this box you can find not only your lost programs but also your lost documents. When you find a document, you can have the document load the program for you rather than you loading the program for it.

✔ In the Windows file manager (or Windows Explorer), three factors affect how you see the contents of a folder or file container: arrangement, such as how the list is laid out, how many columns it uses, whether the tiles are big or small, and whether contents are included; sorting, such as whether the list is sorted by filename, file type, or some other characteristic that may even be specific to a certain file type; and grouping, such as how big lists are subdivided into smaller lists so you can get a better visual clue as to how many more files belong to one grouping than another, or the relative age of documents you've created.

✔ Libraries are cool. With libraries, you can see in one place all the files that share certain characteristics, not only throughout your PC but all over your network.

Know This Tech Talk

application: A program you use to do *your* work, to produce documents and media that are helpful to you in your life, as compared to helping the PC do its thing; often called *app* for short

CPU (Central Processing Unit)**:** The principal processing device of a computer, often termed the "engine"

filename extension: A suffix attached to the end of a filename, and separated by a dot (.), that denotes the file's type and often its program of origin

My Documents: The default folder on your account for storing documents created using applications. Only you will see the name "My Documents" for this folder; other users on your network will see it named personally, as in "John's Documents."

Notepad: A simple text-editing program that has been featured with Windows since version 3.0

notification: A small icon that acts as a signal from a program running "in the background" (so that it doesn't bother you), letting you know there may be information you need to see

partition: A division of a storage device, especially a hard disk drive, that enables the entire storage space to be accessed as one segment

pin: Placing an item in a list in a secure and certain place so that it will reappear in the same place when you access the list again

shortcut: An item — sometimes one of many — that points to a program and can be used in place of the program's own icon or ID to launch that program

Windows Explorer: The formal name of the program that provides Windows with its folder windows, often confused with "Internet Explorer" although they are not the same

workspace: The area of an application where documents are produced; also, the area of any window where the majority of the work takes place

Lesson 3

Organizing Your Pictures, Movies, and Music

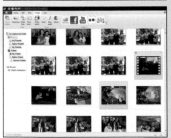

✔ Set up Windows 7 so that you can watch video and listen to music while you work.

✔ Create and edits playlists in your audio library, copy music from a CD, and burn custom music CDs.

✔ Transfer digital photos from your camera to your PC, and then browse and print those images.

✔ Set up a Windows Live Account and install Windows Live Essentials, and then use Live Essentials to create and share an online photo album.

*W*hen folks buy a new PC, they typically have two expectations. They expect their life to get simpler. But first, they're afraid it will get a lot harder. (And when you see their photo collections, you can't blame them.) If you're like most folks, you probably want to be able to organize all your photographs, post some online, and maybe pop in a DVD and watch a movie while you work. Can you really do that?

Absolutely. It will take you some practice because most of today's movies, songs, photos, and books are digitally encoded. And that can potentially be a problem because working with streams of unseen digits isn't as easy as dropping a needle on an LP. Media companies like to paint it like some "immersive media experience," but in the end, we just want to hear the music, please.

However, Windows 7 — and this book — comes armed with plenty of tools and methods for you to organize and share your photos, music, and movies.

Wrangling Windows Media Player

When you slide an audio CD into your optical disc drive, Windows 7 prefers to use Windows Media Player as the tool for playing it, seeing its contents, shuffling through tracks, and possibly for importing those contents to your local storage. When you slide a DVD into the drive, Windows 7 would also like to use WMP to play the movie. However, your PC manufacturer or dealer may have installed other tools for these purposes, but WMP might be the default, so don't be alarmed if the AutoPlay dialog box appears (see Figure 3-1). To see what your default player is, insert a disc and see what happens.

Figure 3-1

And even if your computer's manufacturer installed some other program for playing CDs or audio tracks, you may find that you prefer WMP.

When you slide a Blu-ray Disc into your optical drive, WMP will *not* be able to play it. You will require a different tool because the necessary *codecs* for decoding Blu-ray streams aren't usable by WMP. Read more about this in the section, "Knowing your usage rights." You might be able to play a Blu-ray Disc in Windows Media *Center*, which is a different program entirely. More on that later.

Thanks to modern technology, a video that will play one week might become unplayable the next. Yes, you read that correctly. All is not lost, though. Keep reading to find out why.

Yes, WMP has some shortcomings, but not every user will experience them. So later in this lesson, in case WMP is *not* the default player for video or audio on your PC, I'll show you how to set it up so that it is.

Understanding Digital Media

Windows Media Player wants to be your "one-stop shop." The first time you run it, WMP gives you several setup options for setting up that shop, along with recommendations for which options to choose. The recommended options, naturally, allow WMP do anything and everything, but not to let anyone else come in and try to change things — and there are good reasons for accepting these options. Before I show you the step-by-step process of setting up WMP, though, I want to discuss some of the issues you have to think about when installing this or any other kind of media player on your PC.

Maintaining your privacy

When you use WMP to play any kind of media that you've purchased (you did purchase it, didn't you?), it's designed to communicate quite a bit of information back to servers at Microsoft, like the identity of tracks that WMP is playing. For instance, when your average CD-ripping program stores the contents of a song to your local storage, it typically fails to include information about the song — who sang it, what album it's from, and when was it published.

WMP queries an Internet-based database to retrieve that information. It can also retrieve pictures of album covers, which are then stored in hidden files in your song folders. And it can retrieve pictures of a movie poster or the DVD's original sales cover.

Windows Media Player will help you rip your CDs. If you find a program that helps you rip a DVD so you can play the movie from your hard drive, or even burn a backup copy for yourself, this is legal, too. Blu-ray Discs are expressly designed with a kind of dynamic protection mechanism. There are tools to help you rip a Blu-ray Disc, but they may only work for so long because the dynamic mechanism is designed to change over time.

For a lot of folks, letting other people know what song they're listening to is no big problem. In fact, some social networks such as Facebook and MySpace can communicate with media players so when someone's listening to a song, that fact is posted to the Web.

Hmm. So can this information, even in theory, be used by someone unknown and remote to determine when and where you listen to music?

Here's the truth: Every computer that communicates with the Internet is given an *Internet Protocol address*, or *IP address*. The long and the short of it is that WMP does, by default, share your IP address with Microsoft's servers. Your Internet service provider (ISP) does know who you are and what IP address you've been given. But someone wanting to track you down would need to correlate the data from your ISP with the data from Microsoft, which would presume that person was looking for you specifically. Unless you have a beef with someone in law enforcement (say, the Attorney General), this is extremely unlikely. What's more, no accidental leakage of data from either source separately could ever hurt you directly.

If you're the least bit concerned, know this: WMP isn't a spy tool. The data that Microsoft collects with WMP can't be used (by itself) to deduce any information about you personally. And you have every right not to share *anything* about how your computer uses music or videos.

Shopping where you like

Windows Media Player wants to be the one online "store" from which you purchase music. To be honest, not a lot of people actually use WMP for that purpose. There's plenty of stores in the world, both on the Web and on planet Earth, all of which are probably nicer.

GO ONLINE

There are different ways for you to be an online MP3 music customer.

✔ Apple's iTunes (http://itunes.com): For people with iPods, iPhones, or iPads, although you can create iTunes libraries with an iTunes program for a Windows PC rather than a Mac. Here, you purchase tracks by the song or by the album. You can purchase tracks from iTunes that play using Windows Media Player, although these are typically slightly more expensive than those which play through iTunes only.

✔ Rhapsody (http://rhapsody.com): A subscription service that lets you pay by the month for an unlimited number of tracks. However, these tracks are engineered to run on Rhapsody applications and devices made to support Rhapsody. You can play Rhapsody tracks on an Apple device, but with the Rhapsody app and not through iTunes. You cannot play Rhapsody tracks through WMP although you can use the Rhapsody app made for Windows.

✔ Amazon Music Store (http://amazon.com/music): Purchase tracks by the song or by the album. The tracks are un-tampered-with MP3s, so you can play them using WMP. You don't subscribe to Amazon to be a customer. (You can also purchase CDs from Amazon and have them shipped to you.)

✔ Napster (http://napster.com): A service of Best Buy. Although you can buy some tracks *à la carte*, its principal feature is a subscription service that lets you download unlimited tracks for a variable monthly fee, based on term of service and level of portability. With the lowest-priced subscriptions, you can play your tracks only through Napster software and its approved devices; for more, you can get fully portable, "unmanaged" MP3s.

Or you can rip music from the CDs you already own, and I'll show you how in "Ripping tracks from audio CDs."

Deciphering media file formats

Media comes to you in two ways:

✔ **Streaming:** The player receives and repeats images and sound that the server has decoded.

✔ **Your files:** You already have files that the player decodes behind the scenes so you can watch and hear them.

For example, if you're watching a video on YouTube, you're receiving a stream, like how a digital HDTV receives a stream from the cable or satellite company. The main difference is that the YouTube video uses a different format. With YouTube, you never possess the entire stream, so your rights are different with respect to seeing it. At any one time, your browser (or whatever program you're using to view YouTube) only has a piece of the video's entire contents.

Comparatively, when you put an audio CD into your computer and listen to music, you possess the files. So when you rip a CD and place the files in an accessible folder, you still possess the files — and nothing has changed legally, just technically. And when you play a DVD with WMP, you're in possession of the files on the disc. Whenever you possess the files, it's the player (not a server) that needs to be able to decode them as they're being played. (Note: This is different from decoding a picture file, which is all taken care of before you ever see it.) However, you cannot "rip" a DVD with WMP. Rest assured, though, that chances are good that WMP can play these videos.

With audio and video, this decoding takes place while you're listening and watching. The decoding process is ongoing, using a kind of template that helps it decode the next part of a track based on the contents of the current part. This template is a *codec*, and for every audio and video format in the world, there is at least one codec and, most likely, several.

If WMP encounters a video whose format it doesn't recognize, it uses your Internet connection to try solve this problem. Behind the scenes, it tries to download the proper codec(s) to play the video automatically, without you having to do Thing One. WMP is usually successful although you may wait a few minutes between pressing Play and seeing something.

Video files have formats for storing their formats. In Windows 7, the file type (Introduced in Lesson 2) denotes how WMP can start looking for ways to decode the actual format of the video. However, the likelihood that a video will play in WMP is high. When WMP doesn't know how to decode a file whose format it *can* read, it goes online to look for a codec it doesn't have yet. If it finds one, it downloads it and installs it automatically. If it doesn't find one, Microsoft's server takes note, which helps its administrators to determine which new codecs to make available.

Knowing your usage rights

Today, using a codec to decode media is tied closely to the process of permitting a person to watch a movie. For many lower-resolution video formats, as well as for music files of many types, WMP can be your advocate in negotiations for "usage rights." In a nutshell, for videos and tracks that require authorization, WMP can get that authorization for you through the Internet. Some tracks you purchase can only be played if this authorization can be obtained — and that means *each and every time you play them.* So, if you're not using an Internet connection, even if your tracks are stored locally on your PC, you might not be able to hear them.

Windows Media Player contains a fairly sophisticated digital rights management (DRM) system; in fact, Microsoft markets this system to content providers in hopes that they'll let WMP and Windows 7 process and manage the multitude of files that enable users to access their media.

EXTRA INFO

When the studios first sought to create a standard for multimedia files, they created an organization called the Motion Picture Experts Group. That group is responsible for the standard known as MPEG, as well as the original audio track for digital video that we now call (ironically) MP3. MPEG does *not* specify the video's file format, but rather how the video is to be encoded and decoded.

EXTRA INFO

Every Blu-ray HD movie uses a codec that acquires a kind of digital key (a predetermined sequence of digits) from the device playing it. WMP can't "impersonate" a Blu-ray console because it's not allowed to by the studios. That's why you can't play a Blu-ray movie on WMP, even if you have a Blu-ray drive in your PC. You can play a Blu-ray movie on your PC if you have a Blu-ray Disc drive.

Setting Up Windows Media Player

The setup routine for WMP begins the first time you launch WMP. Each user of your PC with an account will see this routine. (Read about user accounts in Lesson 1.)

Windows Media Player's setup routine may start itself again in the future, even if you've already set it up once, or twice, or 60 times. Usually, clicking Close (upper-right corner; see Figure 3-2) aborts a redundant setup process, and takes you to the actual player where you want to be anyway.

This procedure assumes that you're online and working from home. If you're out someplace, you'll want to connect to a Wi-Fi network — and if you're not comfortable doing that yet, wait until you get home to connect to your own network). Here's how to set up WMP the first time:

1. **Launch Windows Media Player.**

   On a fresh Windows 7 installation, you'll find WMP pinned to your taskbar. If for some reason it's not, click the Start button, select All Programs, and scroll down to Windows Media Player. If this is the first time you've launched WMP, you'll see the screen in Figure 3-2.

Figure 3-2

2. **Select the Custom Settings radio button.**

Avoid selecting the Recommended Settings radio button. You want to be able to restrict the amount of information that's "shared" over the Internet, you want WMP *not* to behave like it's an online store, and you want to have the right to allow other programs (for example, Apple QuickTime for online MP4 videos) to display certain video formats if those other programs perform better on your PC.

3. **Click Next.**

4. On the Privacy Statement tab, click the top View Statement button.

Take the time to peruse this little privacy statement, which appears in your Web browser (Internet Explorer). The main thing to note is that quite a bit of information can be exchanged between WMP and Microsoft, especially about what you're listening to.

None of this information can be used by anyone or anything to identify you, or to match who and where you are with what you're listening to.

5. Return to WMP and click the Privacy Options tab.

You see the settings panel shown in Figure 3-3.

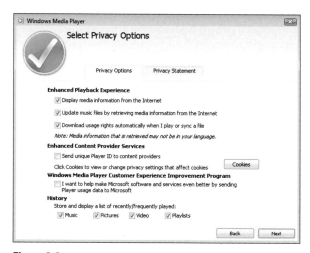

Figure 3-3

6. Choose how much extra data WMP collects from the Internet.

"Media information" in this dialog box pertains to what you're listening to or watching: for example, album covers and track titles.

- *Display Media Information . . .:* WMP shows album covers, track titles, and other identifying information for what you're listening to or watching. This assumes that you will generally be online when you're using WMP; if you typically disconnect from the Internet, you may want to clear this check box to avoid delays.

- *Update Music Files . . .:* This allows WMP to store the "media information" along with your files so it doesn't have to retrieve it again.

When you use WMP to listen to CDs, this actually doesn't matter because WMP cannot update a CD.

- *Download Usage Rights . . .:* This allows WMP to authorize you as a listener/viewer online before showing protected files — the kinds of files that require authorization or proof of purchase.

7. Don't select the Send Unique Player ID to Content Providers check box.

This option was designed to enable streaming content services to associate specific instances of WMP with their subscribers. No major services do. What's worse, security companies report that malicious Web sites pretending to be video servers exploit this Player ID to obtain information about users' PCs. May as well leave it turned off.

The Cookies button in this section deals with pieces of data that servers leave on your system, but you're better off setting this option in the context of Internet Explorer (part of Lesson 5).

8. Decide whether to Select the I Want to Help Make Microsoft Software and Services . . . check box.

Many Windows 7 programs can report *telemetry* back to its home servers. For example, when WMP misbehaves or crashes, a signal is sent saying that a copy of WMP somewhere misbehaved or crashed, along with a statistical snapshot of what the program was doing at the time. This way, developers can be informed when there's a serious problem with the program. However, some folks may not want a record of what they were listening to or watching when WMP crashed.

> **EXTRA INFO**
>
> None of the Customer Experience Improvement information sent to Microsoft is the least bit personal; it doesn't say what you were doing, just what a copy of WMP was doing. Still, you don't have to allow this.

9. Leave the check boxes marked for Music, Pictures, Video, and Playlists and then click Next.

This enables WMP to keep track of the files you play and their locations. Having this history means being able to go back and review something you watched yesterday.

10. Select Choose the File Types That Windows Media Player Will Play radio button and then click Next.

The Set Program Associations window appears, as shown in Figure 3-4. This is the complete list of file types that WMP recognizes, and whose media formats it will attempt to play.

11. **Choose the file types to be associated with WMP and then click Save.**

Table 3-1 shows you the formats you should pay attention to. The rest are mostly archaic, and somewhat rare. You may never encounter them, but if you do, you can enable them from the list in Figure 3-4.

Your safest bet is to click the Select All button, and then selectively clear the check boxes for those formats you specifically intend for a different media player to use.

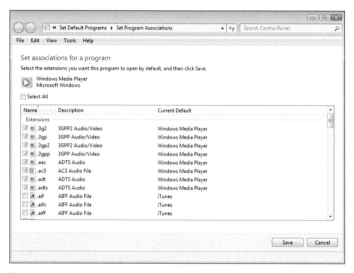

Figure 3-4

12. **In the Choose an Online Store window, select the Don't Set Up a Store Now radio button.**

13. **Click Finish.**

WMP begins compiling its internal media libraries.

Table 3-1	File Types to Enable in WMP
File Type	*What It's Used For*
3G2, 3GP, 3GP2, and 3GPP	Designed as a standard for digital cameras, cell phones, and smartphones that capture video. When you import video from your device, it may use one of these file types.
ASF, AVI, and the entire WM* suite	Designed to be interpretable by Windows Media Player. You should select these file types at least.
MP4, M4V, and MP4V	The most commonly used video formats today. Collectively, they're called MPEG-4. Some MPEG-4 files won't play in WMP although they may play in Apple QuickTime.
MPG, MPEG, MPE, and others in the vicinity	Older MPEG video encoding standards. Whether they play in WMP depends on the availability of their codecs. The oldest videos may not play in WMP.
MP3	The most common audio file type today. This type alone doesn't denote whether the file is protected (has usage rights attached) or unprotected (free for anyone to hear). Most MP3 files play in WMP without difficulty.
WMA	Microsoft's Windows Media Audio format; some files from Microsoft may still use this format although it's going out of style (fast). By default, when WMP rips a CD, it stores the tracks in WMA format, which will play in WMP, but not many other places. You can change this default when you rip your first CD.
WAV	A "raw" form of encoded audio without compression, usually reserved for things like sound effects or system noises. The only reason a WAV file wouldn't play in WMP is if the file were defective.
MID, MIDI, and RMI	Not encoded tracks at all, but sequences of notes to be played by electronic musical instruments.
MMS	A protocol for streaming audio and video directly to WMP through the Internet. This is very safe to select unless you prefer to use another media player.

Watching and Listening to Files in WMP

When WMP plays, it has two "modes," which look and feel almost like two distinct programs.

✔ **Now Playing:** Comes up whenever you double-click an audio track or a video from a regular folder window.

✔ **Library:** Where you can mix playlists, organize files, rip audio CDs, and sync with MP3 players and mobile devices. Read more about this in the upcoming section, "Assembling playlists."

I'll look at the WMP Library later. For now, assume that you want play something, starting with an everyday DVD.

Watching DVDs

Windows 7 no longer does anything automatically when you pop in any kind of disc into your optical disc drive until you give it permission to do so. This is true whether you use WMP or not. When you insert a DVD (as opposed to an audio CD, a Blu-ray Disc, or a disc with data on it), Windows takes a moment to recognize it as a DVD. After that, Windows presents you with a list of options, such as the one depicted in Figure 3-5.

If you just finished setting up WMP, you might see `Play DVD Movie` at the top of the list, under Current Default. However, it might not appear at the top, depending on how your PC's manufacturer or dealer set up Windows for you. Nonetheless, it should appear on this list somewhere. If it doesn't, and you want to use WMP to watch DVDs, eject your DVD and start the WMP setup process again.

After WMP launches the DVD, you're in Now Playing mode, and the movie plays exactly like it would if you plugged it into the DVD console on your TV. If you usually see credits or previews of coming attractions, or FBI warnings about illegal copying, you'll see them here, too. And the remote control menu shows up plain and unadorned.

Use your mouse to click Play. Or, to jump to a particular chapter, click Scene Selections. Easy. In just a bit, I show you how the Play controls work.

Figure 3-5

WMP doesn't change how a DVD was designed to work. However, how well WMP plays your DVD depends on a mind-numbing array of factors. In the case of this widescreen movie in Figure 3-6, the DVD manufacturer encoded a widescreen picture into a standard 4:3 TV aspect ratio. The result is letterboxing. Because WMP doesn't change how DVDs play, you can't do much about this.

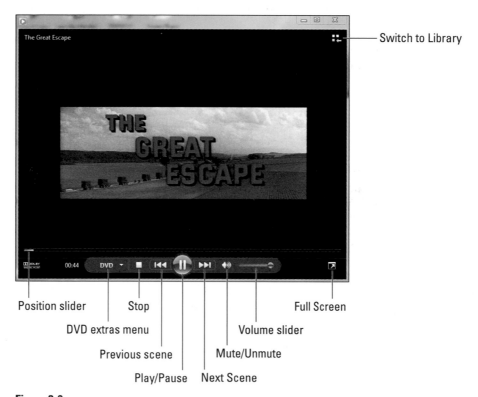

Figure 3-6

When you move your mouse to the WMP playback window, and for a few seconds after, its onscreen gadgets appear at the bottom of the window. They fade out afterwards to let you watch your movie in peace, but just point your mouse toward the bottom of the window to make them reappear.

The WMP video playback window has a Maximize button, but if you want to blow up your movie to full screen, look for the View Full Screen button in the lower-right corner. This button effectively converts your monitor (or whichever monitor the window is on) into a complete playback system, free of any window gadgets or evidence of other running applications.

Now back to the Play controls:

✔ **Play and Pause:** The blue button in the middle of the gadgets is a toggle to start and stop the movie. This is a little counterintuitive, but it shows the Pause sign (two vertical bars) when the movie is playing (as in Figure 3-6) and the Play sign (a right arrow) when it's paused.

✔ **Slider button:** The long horizontal slider indicates the position of the playback relative to the rest of the movie. The brightest spot on the slider is the button itself. Slide it left or right to move to a new location, indicated by the timestamp at the lower left.

✔ **FF and Rewind:** What appear to be the fast-forward and rewind buttons (in the case of a DVD) let you jump forward or back up one chapter at a time.

✔ **Stop:** Click the big square button to stop the movie.

✔ **Volume:** Drag this slider to turn the sound up or down. This doesn't affect the volume level of your PC.

✔ **Mute:** Click the speaker button to switch the sound off completely (especially when you're talking to someone else), and click again to switch it back on.

✔ **DVD menu:** The commands that appear here depend on what the DVD makes available. When you play a DVD on a regular console, you might find yourself accessing its own "home menu" to set up features like foreign language tracks, subtitles, or enhanced sound. If WMP can facilitate any of those features, they appear here.

Playing video files

The contents of a DVD aren't designed to be accessible from a Windows folder window. When you're watching a video file that you can access from a folder window — like one you downloaded — the onscreen gadgets may not be the same, as indicated in Figure 3-7. The buttons to the left and right of Play/Pause will try to behave as standard FF/rewind buttons, but whether they actually can behave that way depends on whether the active codec for decoding the video permits them.

Figure 3-7

Playing audio CDs

When you insert an audio CD for the first time into WMP, you should see an options panel similar to the one that comes up for DVDs. Windows is asking what you want it to do when it encounters audio CDs. For now, you want them to play in WMP.

If you're online, WMP may take a moment to try to download information relevant to what you're hearing, such as the album cover. Then the player comes up with the cover and the first song, like in Figure 3-8. The onscreen gadgets work much like those for playing a DVD; for instance, Forward and Back move up and down one song in the album. However, the slider represents the player's position in the song (not the whole album); and the volume slider changes to a pop-up that appears when you click the down arrow.

Rip CD

Stop Rewind Fast Forward Volume slider (hidden)

Position slider

Play/Pause Mute/Unmute

Figure 3-8

Assembling playlists

As I mention earlier, a *playlist* in Windows Media Player is any list of accessible media files (songs, videos, and even pictures) to be played in sequence or random order. You assemble a playlist in WMP to go through what it calls the *Library*, with a capital "L." An example of the Library on one system appears in Figure 3-9.

LINGO

The **Library** (capital L) is made up of individual **libraries** (lowercase L), like Music, Videos, and Pictures.

You've already been through the process of setting up media libraries in Windows; a big chunk of the previous lesson was devoted to that. The good news is that the WMP media Library comprises the contents of Windows 7's media libraries. The bad news is that if you've subdivided your own library into folders — perhaps by type or genre or artist — those subdivisions won't appear here. Instead, when you add folders to the Music, Videos, and Pictures libraries, their contents become available to the collective WMP Library pool, for use in making playlists.

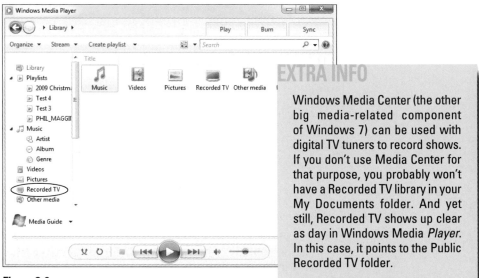

EXTRA INFO

Windows Media Center (the other big media-related component of Windows 7) can be used with digital TV tuners to record shows. If you don't use Media Center for that purpose, you probably won't have a Recorded TV library in your My Documents folder. And yet still, Recorded TV shows up clear as day in Windows Media *Player*. In this case, it points to the Public Recorded TV folder.

Figure 3-9

Here's how to make a playlist:

1. **Launch WMP.**

   When you launch it from the Start menu (as opposed to double-clicking a media file), it should bring up the Library. If not, click the Switch to Library button in the upper right (three boxes with a left-pointing arrow). The area where you compile playlists may appear along the right side, and may read Unsaved List.

2. **If the playlist area on the right isn't visible, click the Play tab in the upper-right corner; see Figure 3-10.**

3. **Click Clear List, in the right pane.**

   Any number of earlier actions could have been interpreted by WMP as a "default add to playlist." If not, the Clear List option will be grayed out and inactive. At this point, the Play tab's list area should be marked as an Unsaved List.

Figure 3-10

4. Click Save List.

The Unsaved List line, which now reads Untitled Playlist, should immediately become editable. You'll want to replace this with a title more suitable than Untitled Playlist, of course.

You can create an Unnamed List first and save it after it's full of tracks. It's easier, though, to start with an empty but named list, fill it, and save it as you go along.

5. Type a unique name (see Figure 3-11) and press Enter.

6. Click a library name in the navigation pane.

The contents of the library appear in the center. For the Music library, the list is grouped by artist's name, with first names first, so "Barbra Streisand" appears under "B," not "S," with albums as subgroupings. The names of individual tracks appear in the Title column.

Figure 3-11

7. To sample a song, hover over its title. Then, from the pop-up that appears, click Preview. See Figure 3-12.

You can move further into the selection by clicking Skip. Moving the pointer away from the tooltip stops the playback.

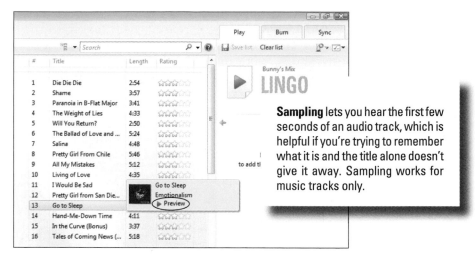

LINGO

Sampling lets you hear the first few seconds of an audio track, which is helpful if you're trying to remember what it is and the title alone doesn't give it away. Sampling works for music tracks only.

Figure 3-12

8. **Drag the titles you want into the Playlist pane.**

   You can select multiple titles and drag them all at once. If sequence is important, drag each one individually into the list area on the right, and release it in the position you wish to hear/see it. Figure 3-13 shows a complete round of selections in the Playlist pane.

9. **Rearrange titles to find the sequence you want.**

   Just like rearranging shortcuts in the Start menu, you drag a title to its new location and release. As you add titles, the approximate time of the playlist is displayed at the bottom. That's important when burning an audio CD, whose play time is typically 80 minutes. However, for playing on your PC, you can make a playlist however long you want.

10. **Click Save List.**

    Yes, again. But this time, at least, you don't have to name it.

When you're ready to play your playlist, you'll find it as a file in the Playlists folder in the left pane. You can get to it either from the top of the left pane of WMP, or from your Music library window. From either place, you double-click to start playback.

Library mode has two extra gadget buttons along the bottom. If you don't want the music to stop, click Turn

Time counter

Figure 3-13

Repeat On (the circle-arrow). If you want WMP to play your sequence each time in random order, click Turn Shuffle On (the flip-flop arrows). In Now Playing mode, you might have to stretch the window wider, like in Figure 3-14.

Turn Shuffle On   Turn Repeat Off   Switch to Now Playing

Figure 3-14

When you launch a playlist from Library mode, WMP stays in Library mode. However, when you launch it from a folder window, WMP comes up in Now Playing mode. There, you'll see just the album cover for the song currently playing, and the gadget controls along the bottom.

When WMP is in Now Playing mode, there's a Switch to Library button in the upper right that takes you back to Library mode. If you just want to see the playlist but not fiddle with its contents, right-click the WMP window, and from the pop-up menu that appears, choose Show List. The contents of the right pane appear, as shown in Figure 3-15.

Figure 3-15

Editing an existing playlist

If you're the official DJ of your household, time to get accustomed to WMP's unusual system for editing multiple playlists. You have the contents list in the center of the window and the Play tab in the right pane.

Figure 3-16

To look at the contents of your saved playlist, under the Playlists folder in the left pane, click its title once. That brings up the playlist in the center. To edit those contents (add songs, take out others, change the sequence), double-click the playlist's title, which brings it up in the right pane.

You can have multiple playlists open in this tab, which is handy if you're borrowing items from one to put in another. Imagine your playlists on a kind of rotating carousel, like the suit rack at a dry cleaners. As pointed out in Figure 3-16, arrows to the left and right of the playlist name in the Play tab turn blue when there's a list preceding or following it.

Although the Library (big "L") in the center of WMP isn't officially a playlist, it acts like one in one respect: When you double-click any song title in the list in the center, WMP plays that song. Then when it's done, it plays the next song in that list unless you click Pause or Stop.

On the Play tab, select the items you want to relocate and then right-click one of them. From the pop-up that appears, choose Add To followed by the name of the other open playlist. You can delete items from a playlist using this menu by choosing Remove from List (not deleting the song, just its entry).

Burning your own mixes

To play your music on your home stereo and in your car, you don't need a CD-R that contains data for your computer — you want an *audio CD*. There's a very big difference. Conceivably, you could store several hundred MP3 tracks on a CD-ROM (CD-R, CD-RW), but you probably won't be able to burn more than a dozen tracks onto an audio CD.

Today, you probably have an optical disc player in your PC that can at least write to CD-R (read-only) and CD-RW (read/write) discs. Most PCs sold with Windows 7 likely can write to DVD-R or DVD+R and/or -RW/+RW as well, but that's only if you're burning to the same type of disc used for video. For audio CDs, though, you just need CD-Rs. And if you don't have a writable disc drive, WMP puts a little message in the Burn tab asking you to go attach one.

There are two ways you can use WMP to burn an audio CD, but here's the one that doesn't force you to repeat the same steps.

1. **Insert a blank CD into your optical drive.**

   This disc has to be fresh and never used because an audio CD burn always consumes the entire disc even if it's not full of music. WMP shows a disc icon in the upper-right corner to let you know if you've inserted the right type, and whether it has enough space for your playlist, as depicted in Figure 3-17. Make sure your total elapsed time stays under about 80 minutes.

Available time

2. **Create a new saved playlist for your CD.**

   Follow the steps outlined earlier.

3. **Click the Burn tab.**

   The list in the Play tab will be replaced with a blank Burn list.

Figure 3-17

4. **Drag the saved playlist from the navigation pane to the Burn tab.**

   At the top of the Burn tab is an indicator of how much time your playlist consumes. If that's more than 80 minutes, WMP automatically divides the Burn list into volumes, meaning that you'd have to burn as many CDs as needed to hold all the tracks you chose. Or, pare down your list.

5. **Click Audio CD from the Burn Options menu on the command bar.**

   Find the icon at the upper right with a check mark; see Figure 3-18.

Figure 3-18

6. **Click Name Disc from the same menu.**

7. **Enter a title for the disc (see Figure 3-19) and then press Enter.**

   If you have a CD player console on your stereo set or in your car that tells you the name of what it's playing, this is the title it will use.

8. **Click the Start Burn button.**

   Burning the contents of a full audio CD takes about four minutes. You can watch the burning progress; see Figure 3-20.

Don't do a lot of time-intensive stuff with your PC while the disc is burning, like playing a 3-D game or watching a video.

Figure 3-19   Add title here.

Figure 3-20

Burning progress

Ripping tracks from audio CDs

"Ripping" sounds violent, but it's actually the harmless process of copying song tracks from a legitimately purchased audio CD onto your PC. Before you see how to rip a CD, though, I want to show you one thing that you need to do to ensure you'll be able to move ripped tracks to other devices, such as MP3 players. All portable music players (at least, all that count) do play WMA (Windows) format also play MP3, but not all MP3 players play WMA.

1. **Click Organize on the command bar.**

2. **Click Options.**

3. **Click the Rip Music tab in the Options dialog box.**

4. **Choose MP3 from the Format list.**

5. **Set Audio Quality to at least 256 Kbps.**

   This refers to the bit rate of the audio file. Higher bit rates do make for bigger files, and you can store fewer of them on your player, but you may be able to hear the difference. Just like how lower-resolution pictures tend to be fuzzier, lower bit rate audio files can often have slight echoes, both before and after the notes.

6. **Click OK.**

LINGO

Bit rate is the bandwidth of a media file's encoding, usually measured in kilobits per second (Kbps). A higher bit rate usually enables a broader spectrum of audio and/or video.

Now you can get on to actually ripping the CD:

1. **Insert the blank CD.**

2. **If asked, click Play in Windows Media Player.**

   In a moment, you should see Now Playing mode, with the disc's tracks in the list.

3. **Click the Switch to Library button.**

   The disc's complete contents are in the list in the center of the screen. By default, all the tracks have been check-marked, meaning they've been selected for ripping, just like in the list in Figure 3-21. Yes, you use the center list to select files for ripping. Go figure.

Display Additional Commands

Figure 3-21

4. **Remove the check marks for any tracks you don't want.**

5. **Click Rip CD on the command bar.**

   It might be hidden behind a >> button with the tooltip, Display Additional Commands.

   The process begins soon, and for each song being transferred, you see a progress bar in the Rip status column.

Playing with Your Photos

Windows 7 makes it easy to manage and share digital photos. Start by downloading them from your camera to your PC. From there, printing is a snap.

Adding pictures to the Pictures library

Windows 7 camera-to-PC transfer process is pretty general purpose. You can also create tags that can help you sort out and identify pictures later. You tag photos without affecting their location; for example, you don't have to create an "Uncle Fred" folder just to identify pictures with Uncle Fred in them. That way, if Aunt Marilyn also appears in the photo, you can tag it with both names.

LINGO

A **tag** is a word or symbol that's representative of multiple items in a database or a file list.

1. **Connect your camera to your PC, or insert the memory card from your camera.**

To prevent power spikes, insert the little end of the cable into the camera first and then the big end into the PC. If you're inserting a memory card, turn the camera off first, then eject the card from the camera.

Windows 7 should respond with the dialog box in Figure 3-22. If you've inserted an SD card, Windows should be able to recognize that fact and identify the card as such. If you always want Windows to start this process when you insert your cable or memory card, select the Always Do This for Pictures check box.

LINGO

SD cards are plastic-coated tabs of flash memory about the size of the first joint of your thumb. Some smaller devices use MicroSD cards, which are more the size of a corn flake. **Flash memory** is a category of circuit that can retain data even when it's not powered.

Windows may not respond with the dialog box shown in Figure 3-22, for reasons so numerous that merely listing them would require another volume. If you don't see this dialog box, choose Start⇨Devices and Printers. A window will appear, and here you'll want to look for a device you don't recognize, such as Mass Storage Device. Right-click this device's icon, and from the pop-up menu, select AutoPlay, followed by whatever entry Windows shows you (probably something that includes the words Removable Disk). At that point, you should see the dialog box in Figure 3-22.

2. **Click Import Pictures and Videos Using Windows.**

Many digital cameras and smartphones can shoot short videos, using common formats such as MPEG-4.

You can now set a prefix for the filenames of all the pictures in each folder in the camera's memory, using a dialog box similar to Figure 3-23. This allows you to replace the not-helpful default names that your camera gives your pictures. Windows then uses this prefix in each filename, followed by a three-digit sequence, as in 001, 002, 003, and so on.

3. **Type a unique prefix name and then click the Import button.**

Windows may ask you again for a new prefix name if it encounters more folders with photos in your camera's memory. When the file transfer process is done, Windows

Figure 3-22

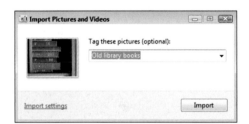

Figure 3-23

brings up a folder window like the one in Figure 3-24, showing just the photos that it has imported. Note that Windows has created a folder for them inside the Pictures folder, and has named this new folder using the current date and the prefix name you just created. Although the folder window is headed Imported Pictures and Videos, that's not the name of the folder; you'll find the real name at the group heading along the top of the batch of new thumbnails.

The one type of tag you don't need to apply to a set of photos is the timestamp.

Group heading

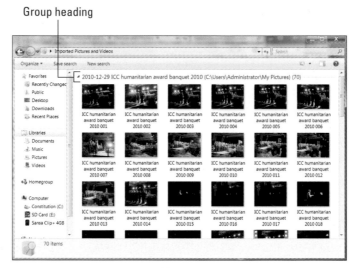

Figure 3-24

Browsing your photos

When you're looking through your imported photos, Windows shows you something that resembles a contact sheet, from the days when photos captured on film. Here, your photos are represented by *thumbnails* (small images; see Figure 3-25) although you may need to increase their size a bit beyond just a "thumb" so you can see what they actually contain.

Windows 7 includes a little Photo Viewer utility that runs almost like a slide projector. You don't launch it from the Start menu or the taskbar, though. Instead, in your Pictures library, double-click any image. This brings up the Photo Viewer shown in Figure 3-26.

The controls along the bottom are similar to what you've already seen in WMP. However, not everything you can do in Photo Viewer is represented by a gadget along the bottom.

- ✔ **Zoom:** Click the magnifying glass, and then when the slider pops up, slide it up. You'll always zoom toward the center, so use your pointer like a hand: Click and grab the image at any point and then slide it so that the point you want to see comes into view.

- ✔ **Fit to Window:** When you're zoomed in, the button next to the magnifying glass becomes Fit to Window, a box with arrows pointing *away* from it. Click this to restore the photo like it was. When you're fully zoomed out, this button becomes Actual Size, a box with arrows pointing *toward* it. Click this to see the photo at its native resolution and size, without any shortening or magnification.

✔ **Previous and Next:** On either side of the round blue button in the center are Previous and Next, just like in a Web browser (see Lesson 5). If you're looking at the first photo in the folder, the Previous button is dimmed and unavailable; likewise, for the last photo, the Next button is dimmed.

✔ **Rotate Counterclockwise** and **Rotate Clockwise:** Change the rotation of the photo in the viewer. This repositions and resaves the file supposedly without losing content or adjusting the timestamp.

✔ **Delete:** To delete the photo (which typically means moving it to the Recycle Bin), click the Delete button (the red slashed X). You'll be asked to confirm.

✔ **Play Slide Show:** To view the contents of this folder in sequence as a full-screen slide show, click the big blue Play Slide Show button in the center. The lights will be dimmed, as it were, and each photo shows for about five seconds of screen time by default. Your projector controls are on your right button. Use it to bring up a menu that speeds up or slows down playback, or that pauses and lets you step through each slide.

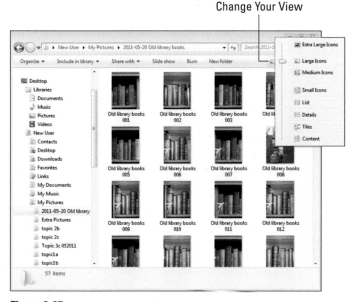

Change Your View

Figure 3-25

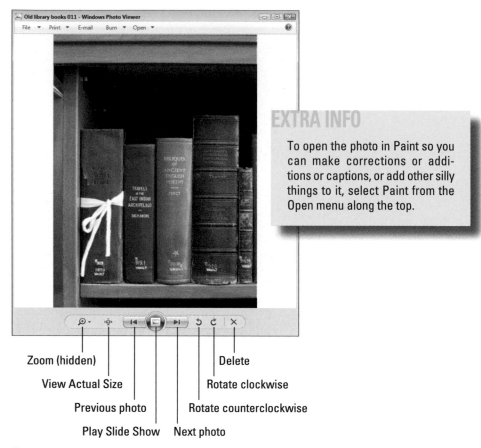

EXTRA INFO

To open the photo in Paint so you can make corrections or additions or captions, or add other silly things to it, select Paint from the Open menu along the top.

Zoom (hidden)

View Actual Size

Previous photo

Play Slide Show

Next photo

Delete

Rotate clockwise

Rotate counterclockwise

Figure 3-26

Printing a photo

As simplistic as Photo Viewer is, it's actually a fairly sophisticated photo printing utility. Photo printers use many different types and qualities of paper, and Photo Viewer gives you a multitude of options for adjusting the quality, quantity, and size of your prints. Here's how to print a photo for the right size and paper quality:

1. **Open the photo in Photo Viewer.**

2. **Click Print from the Print menu.**

   The Print Pictures dialog box appears, as shown in Figure 3-27.

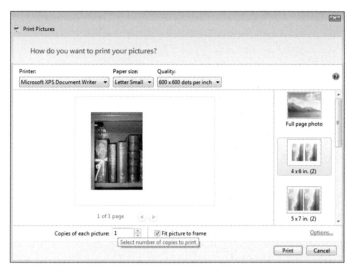

Figure 3-27

3. Choose your printer from the Printer list.

If you have a black-and-white laser printer you use for everyday documents and a separate color photo printer, switch to your photo printer.

4. Choose your paper size.

Photo paper comes in many different sizes, especially so you can make multiple prints on a single sheet. Choose your precise paper size, or your printer may print to one side or off the margins.

5. Choose Photo or Advanced Photo quality.

The Text quality option isn't good enough for a photograph. Go for Advanced Photo if your printer supports it.

6. Choose a paper type.

Your printer will use a different intensity of ink for photo paper, which is both highly reflective and not nearly as porous as everyday paper.

7. Choose a layout from the right pane.

Your layout choices in this pane are all compatible with the paper size you already chose. Here you can see how many photos appear on each print; for example, the 4 x 6 in. option (shown in Figure 3-27) for an 8" x 10" sheet will give you two prints.

8. **Choose the number of runoffs under Copies of Each Picture.**

   This is a little confusing; what it should say is the number of print runs the program will make. For example, if you choose 4 x 6 in., and ask for two copies, you'll get four pictures on two sheets.

 Load your paper correct side up. Your printer should tell you what side.

9. **Click the Print button.**

   A progress bar will show you how long it's taking for your PC to communicate with the printer. That could be a little misleading too, because your printer will take at least another minute to run off a single sheet.

Using a Windows Live Account to Share Photos

The free Windows Live online service is part of Windows 7. It extends Windows so you can do more things, including sharing photos. Microsoft also publishes software called Windows Live Essentials. It would have been much less confusing had these two entities been given separate names because they're not really the same thing at all. You can share photos with other online users through the Windows Live service. For editing photos, and for a handful of other tasks such as e-mail, instant messaging, and policing your kids' online use, you install Windows Live Essentials.

To edit the photos that you want to share with others, you'll use both. First, I want to show you how to share the photos you just imported. After that, I show you how to install Live Essentials to do a few more things.

EXTRA INFO

Much software that Microsoft used to ship with earlier versions of Windows (like Vista and XP) was installed with the operating system. Now you'll find much of that software online. There isn't a Windows Mail or Outlook Express program anymore. Now, Windows relies on Microsoft's two mail services, Hotmail.com and Live.com. Windows Live Essentials includes more software that replaces what used to be called Movie Maker and Photo Editor.

Getting a Windows Live account

To use Windows Live, you need to enroll yourself with Microsoft services. Registering with Windows Live is not the same as registering or activating your Windows operating system. Windows Live registration generates a kind of electronic key that Microsoft sometimes calls a *passport*. It identifies and authenticates you so you can use services that require communicating with Microsoft's servers over the Internet. You can also get (if you want) a free e-mail address.

You do *not* have to sign up for the Microsoft Hotmail service to get a Windows Live account, but you do need a valid and working e-mail address with which Microsoft can communicate with you.

Also, you don't need a Windows Live account to use the Microsoft search engine Bing, or to read articles on the Microsoft MSN Web site. But if you intend to use your Web browser to download files from Microsoft's servers (a technical white paper about Windows, or a Windows Service Pack), you do need a Windows Live account. This is different from the Windows Action Center (Lesson 6) to download updates and security patches for Windows; you do *not* need a Windows Live account to use Action Center. But if you plan to use Live Messenger for instant messaging, or SkyDrive to store and share photos, or to use Office Web Apps to read business documents while you're on the road, you do need a Windows Live account.

True, you do supply your personal information when you create this account: your address and phone number, perhaps another e-mail address besides the one that will identify you. This information is used only by Microsoft (as of this writing), and it's the same level of personal detail you'd give out when signing up for a magazine subscription.

After you sign up, Windows Live uses the limited information you gave it to create a new personal profile for you. This profile is designed to be shared with some people to some extent, but you choose the information, and you choose the extent. Typically, folks use their Windows Live accounts to share with somebody, and the profile is necessary for that somebody to make contact with them.

To get Windows Live started — getting an account and downloading the software you'll need to install — follow these steps.

1. **Launch your Web browser.**

   For Internet Explorer, this is the blue "e" icon that's probably on your taskbar.

2. **Type** windowslive.com **into the address bar.**

   At the time of this writing, the sign-up page for Windows Live looks like Figure 3-28.

3. **Click the Sign Up button.**

   Windows Live shows the sign-up form in Figure 3-29. This is a little tricky because if you just nonchalantly fill in the blanks, you'll find yourself with a new Hotmail address even if you don't want one.

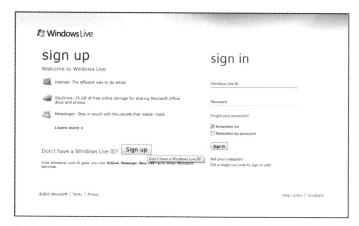

Figure 3-28

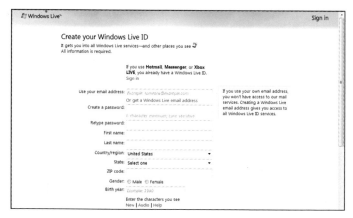

Figure 3-29

4. **To use an existing e-mail address, click the line that reads,** Or use your own email address.

   By default, Windows Live asks you to enter a unique name for a new Hotmail address. You can use the list box to change this to a Live.com address if you prefer. Either way, you would be getting a new e-mail address from Microsoft, which lets you use your browser to manage mail. This might not be a bad thing if you actually need a new address; trouble is, many folks find themselves having signed up for e-mail addresses they never knew they had.

5. **Type a complex but memorable password in the Create a Password and the Retype Password fields.**

   You won't be able to see what you're typing; the text boxes will show dots in order not to give away your password to anyone looking over your shoulder. You're limited to 16 characters here, and it's a good idea to include digits and non-alphanumeric characters. I typically suggest that folks pick a character's name they'll remember from fiction and misspell that name if they can, and also substitute digits and symbols for letters with similar shapes, like this: Harry^ngstr0m or Sc8ut%FInch. Windows Live will let you know how difficult or obscure your chosen password is, as shown in Figure 3-30.

WARNING!

Don't type something easy to guess, like *password* or *1234* or your birthday, or anything that could easily be guessed.

Create your Windows Live ID

It gets you into all Windows Live services—and other places you see 🌐
All information is required.

If you use **Hotmail**, **Messenger**, or **Xbox LIVE**, you already have a Windows Live ID.
Sign in

✉ After you sign up, we'll send you a message with a link to verify this ID.

Use your email address: annettedavid22@yahoo.com
Or get a Windows Live email address

Create a password: ••••••••••   Strong

6-character minimum; case sensitive

Retype password:

First name:

Last name:

Strong passwords contain 7-16 characters, do not include common words or names, and combine uppercase letters, lowercase letters, numbers, and symbols.

Figure 3-30

6. **Complete the remainder of the form.**

   Windows Live will ask for your birth year for legal reasons; Microsoft can't sign you up if you're younger than 18.

At the bottom is a puzzle for you to solve (see Figure 3-31), which Microsoft uses to make sure you're a human being and not some automated Web bot. Just type what you see as best you can, or click New to have Windows Live generate a set of characters that may be easier to read.

Figure 3-31

7. **Click Submit.**

Windows Live takes you to your new home page for services available to you, which may look something like Figure 3-32. You don't need to bookmark this

particular page (see how in Lesson 5), but you should bookmark windowslive.com, which will take you to the sign-in screen that leads you to your home page.

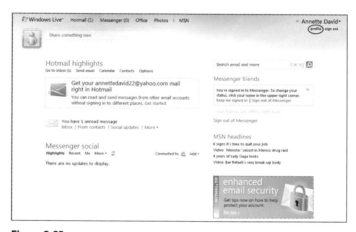

Figure 3-32

Establishing your Windows Live profile

For folks to see the photos you're sharing, they need to be Windows Live users, too. You both need a Windows Live profile. How much you share depends on how much information you allow Windows Live to share about yourself and to whom you grant sharing permission. To protect your files and personal information from being shared with everyone, you create a list of friends who are your (relatively) close contacts. This is a two-way process: You invite someone else to be your friend, and that person may accept or decline. Of course, inviting someone to be your friend makes your profile visible to that person.

Depending on how much you allow Windows Live to share about yourself, your new friend may have access to your list of other friends. You might not want that. To prevent some not-so-close friends (say, business colleagues) from seeing details of folks in your inner circle (your own family), you can limit the amount of access a new friend has to your personal data. However, you have to do this on a case-by-case basis. On a social network such as Facebook, you want to make yourself searchable so new folks can find you. Windows Live isn't a typical social network, though. You can use it not only to share files with specific people only and no one else, but unlike with typical social networks, you can decide not to make yourself searchable or visible to anyone else outside the list of people you designate.

You can get very specific about the level of detail that Windows Live is permitted to share with people you may know only vaguely, as well as with people you don't know at all. To keep things simple, Windows Live divides its privacy settings into three basic tiers. You can see a very explicit explanation of each tier by clicking the Profile link in the upper right of Windows Live (just beneath your name; refer to Figure 3-32), followed by the Privacy Settings tab. You should see something similar to Figure 3-33.

Add friends.

Figure 3-33

Public

This option lets you publish your entire profile and shared files with everyone without restriction.

- ✓ **Personal profile:** Visible to everyone.

- ✓ **Personal contact information, such as your e-mail address:** This remains visible only to designated friends. This way, Windows Live doesn't become an open phone book for the world.

- ✓ **Windows Live Messenger:** People may see when you're online, including when they're using Outlook. This doesn't mean that your ID shows up in everyone's contact list. However, it does mean that if another Windows Live user finds your profile, he can determine whether you're online with Live Messenger even if you've never communicated with him before.

- ✓ **Office Web Apps documents saved to SkyDrive:** Designated friends may see the documents you save to your online space (not the ones you save to your own local storage).

- ✓ **Photo albums:** Everyone may see these unless you specify otherwise for a specific album.

Limited

A limited profile enables you to share certain files with a limited number of people, but not just anyone and everyone.

- ✓ **Personal profile:** All other Windows Live users can see this, so they can still search for and find you.

- ✓ **Personal contact information:** Limited to designated friends only.

- ✓ **Windows Live Messenger:** Only your friends will be able to see when you're online.

- ✓ **Office Web Apps documents saved to SkyDrive:** These documents, and any other files you upload to SkyDrive, are private to you and you alone. You may change this policy and share individual documents on a per-item basis; in fact, you can designate the privacy level the moment you create the document.

- ✓ **Photo albums:** Only designated friends can see these.

Private

The Private setting is for when you want to be visible only to certain, designated people.

- ✓ **Personal profile:** This is hidden from all other Windows Live users except your designated friends.

✔ **Personal contact information:** Limited to designated friends only.

✔ **Windows Live Messenger:** Only your friends will be able to see when you're online.

✔ **Office Web Apps documents saved to SkyDrive:** These documents, and any other files you upload to SkyDrive, are private to you and you alone by default.

✔ **Photo albums:** You can choose which friends on your list are not privy to your shared photos.

After you set your privacy level, follow these steps:

1. **Click Profile below your name at the top-right corner of the Windows Live home page.**

   A page appears with the heading, `Welcome to your new profile`.

2. **Click the privacy option you prefer: Public, Limited, or Private. See the preceding sections.**

   To make adjustments to your privacy settings, click Advanced.

   Say, for example, that your basic privacy setting is Limited, but you'd like for the friends of your friends to know when you're online with Live Messenger. (Perhaps someone a friend of yours knows would like to get to know you. This is how people get jobs nowadays.) Move the Status Messages slider from Friends (meaning just your friends and no one else) to My Friends and Their Friends. This may enable some folks you don't know to see your photos, although they'd be people who are friends of folks you *do* know. It's a little more open than just Friends, but a little more private than Public. There's a plethora of other sliders for other features of the service, and their meanings are well explained on this page.

3. **Click Save.**

4. **Click Add Friends to Your Profile (refer to Figure 3-33).**

   This is especially important if you choose a privacy level other than Public.

5. **Type the e-mail address your friend uses on Windows Live.**

6. **Click Next.**

   You should see that friend's Windows Live ID name and (if he has one) his icon.

7. Click Invite.

That person will need to accept your invitation, which will appear in his inbox, before the two of you are officially "friended." Then, your new friend has privileges that you set with respect to your protected shared files.

When you accept an invitation to become a person's friend on Windows Live, you have the option at that time to limit that person's access to your shared files, which is useful if you've set your privacy level to Private.

Creating and sharing photo albums

Sharing photos online is different from sharing the contents of your photo library with other PCs and other accounts in a Windows 7 network. To share photos online, you create an album in Windows Live and then upload photos to that album. From there, other Windows Live members can see those photos.

An album can contain multiple photos with a common theme, and you can have multiple albums simultaneously.

As is common online, the way that Windows Live works and looks changes now and again. These steps reflect how to share albums at Windows Live as the book went to print.

Here's how to make an album, fill it, and share it:

1. Go to your Windows Live home page (windowslive.com**).**

You can always get here by pointing to the Windows Live logo in the upper-left corner, and clicking Home from the pop-up menu.

2. Click Share Photos, in the SkyDrive menu.

If this is your first album, the Photos page that pops up will say so.

3. Click New Album.

4. In the Create a Photo Album page that appears, type a new album name in the Name text box.

5. (Optional) To adjust privacy and sharing settings, click Change next to Share With: Friends.

You'll see the settings that appear in Figure 3-34. The Share With slider is set to whatever your privacy setting currently allows. In this example, this user has a privacy setting of Private, with the default album setting of Some Friends, which enables two not-so-obvious things: restrict what friends can do to the photos in albums (including deleting them), and restrict which friends can even see your photos.

LINGO

SkyDrive is Microsoft's brand name for the online storage area where your albums are kept.

Figure 3-34

The drop-down list to the right of Some Friends is set by default to Can View Photos. Except for specific friends that you denote, friends can only see your photos, but not add captions to them or change them or delete them. You can change this to Can Add, Edit Details, and Delete Photos, and then friends can make any changes they want to — including deletion — except for specific friends you denote who cannot.

6. **(Optional) Click Select from Your Contact List to change certain friends' privileges.**

TIP

This is perhaps the least intuitive setting in all of Windows Live, so do read carefully: The intent of this section is to enable you to make *exceptions* to the rule you choose in Step 5.

To create exceptions for an individual friend

a. *Click the People tab.*

b. *Select the check box beside that friend's name.*

That name will be repeated in a new list below this one.

c. *Click the drop-down list to change that person's sharing setting to something else.*

For example, if you want someone in particular to also be able to edit your photos, click that person's name in the first list.

d. *In the second list, change that person's setting to Can Add, Edit Details, and Delete Photos.*

Yes, I know that's the long way around, but it eventually works.

7. Click Next.

The next page shows five unmarked text boxes with buttons next to them marked Browse. These boxes are for the filenames of pictures you're adding to the album.

8. For each picture being added, click Browse.

A folder window pops up pointing to your Pictures library. From here, you select a *single* photo (not multiple ones) and click OK. An additional box will appear after you fill the last entry.

9. Click Upload.

The photo(s) you selected are uploaded, which may take a few minutes.

Installing Windows Live Essentials

There are two ways to create a photo album. I just explained one way, which uses only Windows Live. The second way is done offline, may be easier for you, and involves something called Windows Live Photo Gallery. This is one of the family of so-called Windows Live Essentials applications that also includes the Messenger app for texting your friends online, and the missing Mail utility that's no longer directly included in Windows.

Although there's a single installation process for *all* of these Essentials programs collectively, you can indeed choose which ones you want to install and which you don't. Here's the process:

1. Point to Windows Live (windowslive.com**) and click Downloads.**

This is the main menu in the upper-left corner of your Windows Live home page. The Live Essentials page appears.

2. Click Download Now.

If you're using Internet Explorer 9, a dialog box should appear at the bottom of the window, asking whether you want to run or save something called wlsetup-web.exe.

3. Click Run.

Running an executable (EXE) file you've just downloaded from the Web requires administrator permissions, so you'll probably see a User Account Control dialog box asking for permission to continue. See Lesson 1 for more about User Account Control.

4. Click Yes.

You see a progress box that reads Preparing to install. In a minute or so, you'll see a new dialog box where you choose which Live Essentials programs to install.

5. **In the page that opens, click the option to Choose the Programs You Want to Install.**

6. **In the Select Programs to Install page (see Figure 3-35), clear the check box for any Live Essentials programs you don't want.**

- *Messenger:* Refers to Live Messenger, the text communication utility.

- *Photo Gallery:* Make alterations and improvements to photographs, as well as create albums to upload and share with others (which you'll see a bit later).

- *Movie Maker:* Import video from your camcorder or smartphone and edit scenes linearly to make movies, which you can then upload and share.

- *Windows Live Mesh:* A utility for synchronizing folders and files between PCs on two different networks.

- *Bing Bar:* A toolbar for your Web browser that adds search features.

- *Mail:* The "missing" e-mail manager that Windows no longer supplies by itself. Manage your e-mail accounts without using the Web browser.

- *Writer:* An editing system for posting an online blog (not a word processor, like WordPad).

- *Family Safety:* Includes more tools for filtering Web content you may not want certain family members to stumble onto. I'll show you Family Safety in greater detail in Lesson 6.

- *Messenger Companion:* Make Live Messenger work more like a social network, with shared likes and dislikes.

- *Outlook Connector Pack:* Useful for accessing your Hotmail or Live.com e-mail account through the Outlook component of Microsoft Office.

- *Silverlight:* Not really a Windows Live Essentials component, but Microsoft really wants you to have it, anyway. It's a system for enabling Web applications, either through Web browsers or as stand-alone programs.

 You can always come back and install or reinstall some programs.

Figure 3-35

7. **Click the Install button.**

The installation process begins, will probably take a few minutes, and alerts you when it's finished.

8. **Click Close.**

Windows Live Essentials asks you to log in; see Figure 3-36. This happens even if you're already logged into Windows Live.

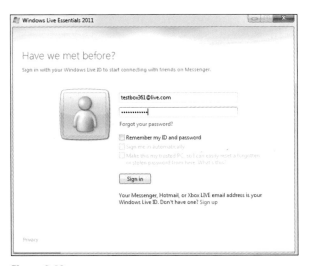

Figure 3-36

9. **Type your Windows Live ID and password.**

10. **(Optional) Select the Remember My ID and Password and the Sign Me in Automatically check boxes.**

11. **Click the Sign In button.**

Because you've already signed onto your Windows account locally (using a different password, I hope), there's a low chance that anyone will be impersonating you on this account. In a moment, you'll see a dialog box that reads, `Connect your services`, which gives you the opportunity to link your Windows Live profile with profiles you may have on other social networks.

12. **Click a social service you'd like to import settings from, or click Skip.**

If you're a member of Facebook, MySpace, or LinkedIn, Live Essentials has some features for integrating your activities with those services. This way, for example, you can invite a friend from Facebook to share your photos and photo albums on Windows Live although doing so will give that person an invitation to join Windows Live first.

13. **When the next panel asks you for your mobile phone number, click Skip.**

    Microsoft wants to send your mobile phone number an SMS link that lets you download Windows Live services for your mobile phone, or at least bring up Windows Live in your phone's browser. You can do this from your phone, anyway, without giving Microsoft your mobile phone number.

Sharing Photo Gallery Albums with Windows Live

Okay, you have a library, a gallery, *another* library, and an album. This may bring up the musical question, "Why? "Earlier, I showed you how to create a Windows Live photo album. You upload several photos individually to your SkyDrive, and then you initiate the album and enroll selected photos into it. That's not exactly a "breeze." Now that you've installed Photo Gallery, you can select a group of photos and upload them collectively to the online album you already created. Here's the process:

1. **Select the photos you want to include in the album.**

2. **Click SkyDrive in the Share menu on the Home tab.**

   The dialog box depicted in Figure 3-37 appears.

Figure 3-37

3. **Click the album in the Publish on Windows Live SkyDrive dialog box.**

If you haven't created an album yet or want to create a new one instead, enter its name in the blank text box at the top, next to the blank icon. Then, from the list box below, choose the level of sharing you want to apply: Everyone, My Friends and Their Friends, Friends, Some Friends, or Me.

4. **Click the Publish button.**

The uploading process begins, and a progress dialog box keeps you apprised.

5. **Click View Online to see the results in Windows Live.**

This brings up your photo album in the Web browser (Internet Explorer) as others will see it.

 # *Summing Up*

Here are the key points you learned about in this chapter.

Digital media formats aren't getting any easier to sort out or sort through. These days, downloadable videos come with rights management packages that limit (or attempt to limit) how long you can see a video, how many copies you can make, and how many complaints you can lodge with the producers. Windows Media Player does try to play as many formats as there are, and even learn the formats it's never seen before.

You can watch a DVD in a WMP window; and you can scoot that window into a corner of the screen while you're working on other things, or you can blow it up to full size and watch movies while you're pretending to work.

WMP collects some information about what you're watching or listening to, from an online catalog. For a movie, for example, it collects a movie poster; for a song, its album cover. These visual cues are then used in Windows 7's media libraries to help you identify videos and tracks.

A playlist in WMP is a collection of any kind of media (usually songs) intended to be played in sequence. Sure, libraries can be used to group similar music together; but playlists aren't always about similarity. You can build variety in your playlists, then you can save them and actually share them with others online.

You can burn a new audio CD using tracks ripped from other ones, and downloaded from the Web. There are a few tricks you have to do in WMP to keep the results from looking and feeling a little too. . . well, too Microsoft. When you remember these tricks, you can burn an audio CD that plays in most audio CD players.

Windows 7 does come with some facilities for organizing photos in a collective library. There are far more functions in Windows Live Photo Gallery, which can enable you to organize and group libraries of thousands of pictures without having to create ghastly stacks of folders upon folders.

Photo Gallery is among the programs no longer shipped with Windows directly, but rather downloaded from Windows Live. Every Windows user is entitled to use Windows Live and its various programs, called Live Essentials, for free. You're also entitled to some free online storage for sharing online photo albums with other Windows Live members.

Sharing files is partly what Windows Live is all about although maintaining one's privacy is important. There are very specific privacy restrictions available in Windows Live, capable of limiting what specific people are allowed to see and do with your uploaded files.

Know This Tech Talk

aspect ratio: The width of a playback system or video format relative to its height.

codec: Software used to decode media files so they can be played using a given format as well as to encode media so they can be stored as files and transferred over a network.

firmware: The operating system of a small device embedded in flash memory or other read-only memory (ROM). Essentially, this is software stored on a chip rather than a disk, either permanently or semi-permanently.

flash memory: A storage mechanism designed to retain data contents even in the absence of electrical current, such as on smartphones and MP3 players.

MP3: Short for Motion Picture [Experts Group] layer 3; a published standard for encoding of audio data, originally intended for use in video files.

Paint: The program shipped with Windows for drawing bitmapped images or painting onto digital photos.

playlist: Any list of accessible media files intended to be played in sequence, although may be shuffled in random order.

ripping: Copying media files to a PC from an optical disc whose format is intended for playback via a console, as opposed to data storage using a PC.

streaming: Delivering a media file to a client in segments, such that it can be played on the receiving end while later portions are still being transmitted by the server.

tagging: The process of making data in a database accessible through a distinguishing mark, such as a symbol representing a common characteristic of multiple data items.

USB (Universal Serial Bus): A standard for a small, portable, high-speed external connection between computers and devices.

Windows Live: Resources and applications provided by Microsoft online for registered Windows users.

Windows Media Center: An application that enables Windows 7 to control a home entertainment system and, in conjunction with a TV tuner card, to function as a DV-R.

Windows Media Player: The program used by Windows 7 for playing downloaded movies, and MP3 and CD audio.

Networking Your PCs

✔ Learn the common features of a home broadband router so you can integrate it into a Windows 7 network.

✔ Locate the best spot for a Wi-Fi router for maximum coverage and minimum interference.

✔ Learn how to create a foolproof map of the IP addresses for all the devices in your network, including Windows PCs.

✔ Build connections that Windows 7 can use to recognize your router, distinguish that router from others in the neighborhood, and use it automatically when your laptop comes in range.

✔ Create a homegroup that enables you to easily, and in most cases automatically, share media files and documents among all the PCs in your house as though they were all in one place.

*I*f you can access the Internet through your PC, you have a working Windows network connection. Everything about that connection has to work for you to see a Web page as opposed to some error message. If you cannot see a Web page, your PC is not in a state where it can use any network that may be available to it. This could mean two things: Either the network is set up properly but disabled, or it's not set up yet.

Your Internet service provider (ISP) may have offered to set up your home PC network for you. Hopefully, you said no because after this lesson, you know how your home network is set up and how to maintain it.

Assessing Your Network Connectivity

Here's a quick and painless way to find out whether your PC can connect, or is already connected, to the Internet:

- ✔ **Wired:** Look for a plugged-in cable that's slightly fatter and whose connector is slightly thicker than a telephone cable, such as the example in Figure 4-1. The other end of this cable may be plugged in to the box that the ISP installed for you, or perhaps to a wall outlet that leads to that box.

- ✔ **Wireless:** Look in the notification area of Windows 7 for five little bars (also in Figure 4-1), like a connectivity indicator on a cell phone. If you see five bars, you have a Wi-Fi (wireless) connection to some network in your vicinity, hopefully in the building where you're located and not belonging to some unsuspecting neighbor.

Figure 4-1

If at least one of the five bars — perhaps the smallest one — is white, you're online. If you can't pull up a Web page in your browser, though, something is wrong with the settings that connect your local network to the Internet.

Point to the icon and read the tooltip, like the one in Figure 4-1.

✔ **Internet Access:** If you see `Internet Access` in the tooltip, you should be online with a local network and receiving an Internet signal. This doesn't mean the signal makes sense to your computer (like a radio tuned to the wrong station). If you can't pop up a Web page, something may be wrong with the Wi-Fi router or the broadband modem that receives its signal upstream from the ISP.

✔ **No Internet Access:** If the tooltip says this instead, you *are* connected with the local network (your PCs at home), but most likely the nearby broadband modem is not making a connection with the Internet.

If every connection in this tooltip (typically there's only one, but there could be two or three) reads `No Internet Access`, like in Figure 4-2, you're not online, and you need to establish a new Internet connection. This is an easy process, especially if you're trying to connect with a public Wi-Fi network, like a municipal system or one in an airport, a hotel, or a coffee shop.

Figure 4-2

If the five bars are all dark gray, Windows 7 has been set up to use an Internet connection that either isn't available or that Windows didn't find. A gold star next to the five gray bars indicates that a connection can be made right away, maybe to recognize a network someplace else, away from where you are now. To find out, point to it. You might see

Figure 4-3

a tooltip like in Figure 4-3, reading something like `Not Connected`. If it also reads `Connections Are Available`, the Wi-Fi radio on your PC is obviously working because it can see signals from available Wi-Fi routers being broadcast in its vicinity.

 If you don't see the five bars, look in the notification area for an icon that, for some reason, resembles the trident of Neptune, which is really a little Ethernet network plug. This is the wired connection icon. If that's not there, no network connection has ever been set up on your PC.

If you do see the wired connection icon but it has a red X beside it, Windows is set up for a wired connection that it can't find right now because the PC isn't plugged into the network. Double-check both ends of the cable to make sure they're plugged in firmly. There's not enough electricity running through this cable to shock you.

Connecting to a Wi-Fi router when a connection is available, and when your PC recognizes connections are available, is quite easy:

1. **Click the network icon in the notification area.**

   A list of available wireless networks appears, similar to Figure 4-4. Windows sorts this list by placing the names of the Wi-Fi signals with the strongest signals at the top.

2. **Click the network you want to connect to.**

   If Windows has never connected to this network before, you'll see a check box marked Connect Automatically. Select this if you know this is your home network, and you want your PC to remember this network so that it connects without your help soon after it's turned on next time. See Figure 4-5.

Figure 4-4

Figure 4-5

3. **Click the Connect button.**

   If this is the first time Windows has seen this network, and the Wi-Fi router has secured this connection, you'll see the Connect to a Network dialog box, as shown in Figure 4-6.

4. **If asked, enter the security pass-phrase and then click OK.**

   For security, you can select the Hide Characters check box.

Figure 4-6

You know that you made a successful connection cleanly when the five bars change from dusky gray to ivory. You may see a yellow "!" warning right beside these bars telling you that you don't have an Internet connection. Sometimes Windows takes a minute to resolve this problem, but it usually gets resolved automatically, after which the warning disappears.

Setting Up a Home Network

If you own any kind of device that connects to the Internet, such as your PC, smartphone, game console, Blue-ray Disc player, and so on, you run a communications network. (Congratulations.) You're the *de facto* system administrator of a system vastly more complex than most businesses could afford at the turn of the century. For you to feel more comfortable with this role, it might help if you knew for certain your network security weren't as perforated as a slice of baby Swiss.

Securing your file sharing first

When you set up your home network for the first time, you could expose your PC's files to the outside world, at least during the few minutes that you're setting up your network. So before you get started, make absolutely certain that you're secure with the network you're using now.

If you don't see Network on the right side of your Start menu, put a handy link to it there. Right-click the Start menu and choose Properties. In the Task Bar and Start Menu Properties dialog box that opens, click the Start Menu tab and then click the Customize button. From the long alphabetical list in Customize Start Menu, select the Network check box. Click OK and then click OK again to finalize.

First, here's how to secure your file sharing settings, with respect to all the different networks you may connect with during the day. You can do this without being connected to a network.

1. **Click the network icon in the notification area.**

   The network status list appears, which should show at least one available network's name if you're connected.

2. **At the bottom of this list window, click the Open Network and Sharing Center link (refer to Figure 4-5).**

   The Network and Sharing Center (see Figure 4-7) is where all the various settings and controls may be accessed. The "map" at the top very simply depicts that between your PC and the Internet is (or should be) a network. It doesn't matter whether you're the only PC within a hundred miles: If your "local network" isn't working, you're disconnected from the Internet.

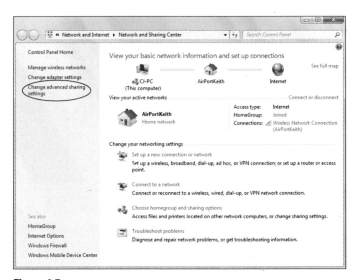

Figure 4-7

3. **Click Change Advanced Sharing Settings, in the left pane.**

   The Advanced Sharing Settings panel (see Figure 4-8) contains two sets of options, each of which pertains to a network profile class: Home or Work, and Public.

4. **If the Home or Work settings aren't visible, click the down arrow next to Home or Work.**

Figure 4-8

LINGO

In this context, a **profile** is the image your PC presents of itself to other users in two types of networks, which Windows clearly distinguishes from one another: your home and business networks; and "public" networks, such as an airport, the library, a coffee shop, or a hotel. In a private network (such as the one in your home), your PC uses protocols to introduce itself to other PCs. You don't want it using those same protocols in public. Windows knows you're at home when it spots your homegroup. Here, the Home or Work settings apply to two profiles: Home and Work. When you use homegroups (more on those in a bit) on your laptop, Windows 7 knows when you take it to work and when you're home.

Here's what these settings mean:

- *Network Discovery:* If your computer is discoverable, your files may be shared with the computer that discovered it unless you put restrictions on those files and/or on sharing in general. You turn off network discovery when you don't want your PC to be seen, and you don't want to share files or resources.

- *File and Printer Sharing:* What your PC can share when it's discoverable. (If it's not discoverable, there's no point to this setting.) When this setting is turned off, your PC is essentially a lurker — it can take from the network but can't give back. When it's on, files and folders that you set to be visible are visible.

EXTRA INFO

I'm not talking about visibility of your computer to the Internet; your files and file system are not visible to the Internet. These settings have to do with the local network, which on the map links your PC to the Internet.

- *Public Folder Sharing:* An easier way to share a file than explicitly declaring it "shared" is to save it in a public folder that Windows already shares throughout the network. There are public folders on your PC, but if you turn off this setting, others in the network don't see them.

- *Media Streaming:* Denotes whether your PC may send media files to other PCs in the network via streaming, which can affect the timing of other programs you may run.

- *File Sharing Connections:* The degree of encryption Windows uses when sending files over a local network. If every computer in the network has Windows 7 or at least Windows Vista, you're safe with 128-bit encryption; for older systems, you may want lower unless you know for sure that Windows XP has the proper updates to handle 128-bit.

- *Password Protected Sharing:* The PC's ability to use accounts to designate who gets access to shared files. If you turn off this feature, file sharing on your PC is a binary status: Either every other PC has access to it, or it's hidden. With it on, your PC is happy to share files you designate as shared with legitimate users — who also, by definition, are authenticated users.

- *HomeGroup Connections:* A Windows 7 homegroup, a PC, and the files on it accessible by everyone or no one. If none of the other PCs on your network use Vista or XP, and you want to keep your home network simple, Allow Windows to Manage Homegroup Connections is the way to go. However, if you know there will be files that you're fine sharing with another specific PC but not with everyone else, you'll want more control over your permissions, so set the option Use User Accounts and Passwords to Connect to Other Computers. This way, Windows knows specifically whom to grant access to, and whom to deny.

LINGO

A **homegroup** is what Windows 7 uses to simplify access permissions. It breaks down sharing into these simple rules: If you want to share files from your PC, you either store those files in shared folders (such as Public Documents) or designate the folders where they're located as shared. Files and resources (such as printers) are either shared with everyone in the homegroup or not.

5. **After you set the access options for the Home or Work profile class, set the access options for the Public profile class.**

   This refers to the separate file-sharing settings for when you take your PC to the coffee shop or the library, where you don't want to share or stream with anyone else.

6. **Click the Save Changes button.**

   Windows returns to the Network and Sharing Center.

With these settings in place, Windows knows how to deny unrestricted access to your files while you're setting up the rest of your network.

Introducing your router

Don't be embarrassed if you have a router and don't know it. A router used to be a device separate from the cable modem, which is generally leased to you by your ISP. Normally, the cable modem is supposed to be the part that marks the end of the ISP's side of the Internet, and the beginning of your home ("on-premises") network equipment.

In recent years, ISPs have been leasing combination cable modem/router boxes that perform both jobs: receiving the broadband connection and serving the devices in your home.

Routers transmit their data at specific frequencies: *channels*. TV channel frequencies used to be measured in megahertz (MHz); Wi-Fi frequencies are measured in gigahertz (GHz, billions of cycles per second).

When transmitting data on a channel, a router can consume more *bandwidth* — more space on the spectrum — than the actual distance between channels. So some interference is almost endemic to the system.

LINGO

Here's what a **router** does. **Digital signals** break down into their simplest form: **bits.** Transmit eight of these bits, and you can send a single digit or letter over the wire. A million of these bits is a **megabit** (Mb), which is one-eighth of a megabyte (MB); and the speed of a router's data throughput is measured in **megabits per second** (Mbps).

EXTRA INFO

Digital signal interference is different than analog radio interference in one key respect: If you degrade the signal to any small degree, it's like cancelling it out altogether. Data doesn't come through faintly because degraded signals are discarded by their receivers. A small amount of interference can effectively turn your Wi-Fi reception off, even if only for a few seconds at a time.

Two classes of routers are sold today, both of which have various models and features. The main difference is *throughput speed*, or how fast they transmit data. Your PC needs the same class of Wi-Fi receiver or card as the router.

✔ **Wireless-G**, or 802.11g, transmits as high as 54 Mbps over any of 14 20-GHz channels, the first 13 of which are stationed 5 GHz apart. That's right: The channel distance is only one-fourth the bandwidth, so you can imagine two routers (say, one on channel 3 and the other on channel 5) encroaching into one another's signal. The typical sustained data rate for G is said to be 25 Mbps; in practice, it's more like 12.

EXTRA INFO

The router you use at home is like your postal carrier, the one who receives these envelopes at the tail end of the process and forwards them to you. Because cable modems and routers these days may or may not be separate devices, you'll see some references to the more collective term "access point" (AP) to refer to the bridge between your local network and the Internet.

✔ **Wireless-N**, or 802.11n, has a theoretical peak data rate of 150 Mbps although most folks experience an average of more like 32. The system is designed to split its bandwidth between multiple channels in the 2.4 GHz and 5 GHz bands yet the distance between channels is so narrow that router manufacturers typically divide the channels . . . into channels. You might be able to select from only about eight of those channels.

The important difference between Wireless-N and Wireless-G is that the data rate of N is just fast enough to enable streaming high-definition video, albeit compressed. If you're looking to stream video across your network, G will be too slow.

Many Wireless-N routers also contain Wireless-G capability, which is an absolute must-have if you're going to include non-PC devices in your network, such as smartphones.

Planning for better wireless accessibility

The typical router sold for the home may be called "wireless," but it isn't — at least, not completely. It has a dedicated Ethernet cable connection to the cable modem. From there, it offers an average of four sockets for direct Ethernet cable connections to other computers, and has a wireless antenna that may transmit signals throughout a 100-meter radius when set up indoors — about 37,500 square yards of coverage.

So when deciding the best place to locate your wireless router in your home, take into account factors that might seem contradictory. Your signals could travel between a tenth and a fourth of a kilometer in any direction. However, you might encounter signal impedance because of thick walls as well as signal interference from devices in your house that emit radio signals. A possible result is that Wi-Fi signals from your router fail to reach your PC in the same room. Not good.

To maximize coverage inside your house, place your router as close to the highest point in the center of your house as you can, like the top story of your house. Of course, that's a problem if the cable guy installed your broadband modem on the ground floor. If you have a router separate from the broadband modem, you need a relatively short span of Ethernet cable to connect your modem to your router, so you can't easily run that cable upstairs. In that situation, pick an out-of-the-way, tall location, such as the top of a china cabinet or bookshelf.

However, that location needs to be as far away as possible from any other electronic devices that emit radio waves, or can cause interference that disrupt the integrity of the signal:

- A *cordless landline phone* can knock out a nearby Wi-Fi router's signal entirely. Such phones typically transmit on the 2.4 GHz band (the band used by Wireless-G, and for the fallback mode of Wireless-N) or the 5.8 GHz band (not far away from N's home territory).

- Some *wireless stereo speakers* can have the same effect, especially if they connect to their base unit on the 2.4 GHz band.

- Other *wireless routers* within your router's transmission radius most likely will interfere because they may use the same channels as yours. This is why getting Wi-Fi to work in an apartment building or a condo can be so difficult. Despite the fact that routers are designed

EXTRA INFO

Here's one way to imagine Wi-Fi signals: Think of your router as a very bright spotlight whose beams radiate but, unlike ordinary light, get heavy and bend down toward the Earth like water from a fountain. And imagine your house as being made not of sturdy house-building stuff, but entirely of stained glass. All the walls in this glass house are translucent, letting some light through to varying degrees, but never completely. This is what your house "looks" like to a Wi-Fi router.

LINGO

There is no standard technical definition of broadband — at least, not one that's the same for any two parts of the world. Although European countries officially consider "broadband" in megabits per second, in the US, the FCC has defined it as low as 384 kilobits per second (Kbps). In all cases throughout the world, however, **broadband** refers to the bandwidth of the carrier bringing service to your access point, not the speed of your router transferring data to your PC. You can have a really fast router but slow Internet connection.

to use multiple channels, they have defaults. Home users tend to leave them set to those defaults, so everyone ends up bunched together on the same channel anyway.

✔ A *microwave oven* (which, after all, uses radio waves) can knock you offline.

✔ A *wireless video camera* trained on the front door probably sends a signal to the security system in your closet. That's a big problem for folks who live in security-monitored apartments.

✔ Some *baby monitors* broadcast in the same 2.4 GHz band as cordless phones.

✔ One *Bluetooth headset* probably isn't much of a distraction for your Wi-Fi, but two within the same vicinity can be enough to cause disturbances.

In many of these cases, the best you can do is mitigate the damage; you can't exactly declare your microwave oven off-limits while the router is on. A Wireless-N router that splits its bandwidth over multiple channels in the 5 GHz band is less susceptible to interference than a Wireless-G router . . . for now. As more radio-transmitting devices seek refuge from the chaos, they too will inevitably creep into the 5 GHz band. And as soon as you get an N router, so will your neighbors.

If your plan is to connect your PC directly to your router using Ethernet cable, the question of location for your router is merely one of convenience. Your cable modem may have been installed close to your cable TV outlet, a choice made mostly for the cable installer's convenience rather than yours. You could place your wired router close to your cable modem or closer to your PC. One factor playing into your decision is the length of Ethernet cable separating the router from the furthest PC in your wired network; after about 50 feet, many routers' signals begin to degrade, a condition that's more noticeable for faster routers.

The most communication-intensive room in many houses is the living room. These days, media center PCs, game consoles, and Blu-ray Disc players either have Wi-Fi or Ethernet sockets. Routing a handful of Ethernet cables from your router to all these devices could make your living room wall look like the famous spaghetti scene in *The Odd Couple*. The solution is a device called a *switch*. You connect one end of it to your router with *one* cable, and from the opposite end, you attach shorter (and thus less visible) Ethernet cables to each device.

REMEMBER

Don't put your router in the closet, like many hotels do just to hide them. Closets are the places with the nearest walls, so even if you have one in the center of your house, the walls usurp all the benefit.

Managing your router from any PC

To connect your PCs and other devices in a local network and make certain they have Internet access, make sure your router is

✔ Receiving an IP address from your ISP

✔ Recognizing your PCs and other devices as connected

✔ Delegating a local IP address to each device

In addition, there are some functions that it would be nice for your router to perform, if it's equipped to do so. Most of these fall under the category of a firewall. When network firewalls were first created, their purpose was to create that separate map of local loop addresses, so that IP hosts on the outside cannot directly address local PCs on the inside. This process, called Network Address Translation (NAT), is now considered a critical function of any home router. So the other principal purpose of a firewall is to make it impossible for clients such as your PC to nonchalantly hand over information that malicious users can use to break into your system.

Not only do all routers not work alike, but they don't do their business through Windows — intentionally. They are designed to be managed independently of any operating system, and this is for the benefit of every operating system that they could otherwise render more vulnerable to outside attack. For that reason, I can't show you exactly, step by step, how to set up your router, but I can show you what to look for using a top-of-the-line router as an example.

You access your router's settings through your Web browser. Literally, your browser has a Web page so that when you give the browser the router's gateway IP address — which is probably 192.168.1.1, or possibly 192.168.0.1 — its "control panel" opens up right there. There's no software for you to have to install because all the functionality is in the router's firmware. (Some brands would have you install software

LINGO

One of a **firewall's** key jobs is to restrict the flow of traffic between the Internet and the local loop to certain types, sometimes based on specific rules. Data travels through the Internet in equally sized **packets**, each of which contains a **header** that acts as a kind of manifest. In that manifest is information about the data's eventual destination: its **port**. On the Internet, port numbers are assigned to specific applications, so when a firewall sees a port number, it knows what application it's referring to, and therefore what type of data it is. A firewall can restrict ports to specific applications, so malicious programs can't impersonate them and siphon their traffic.

LINGO

With a small device, usually a portable one, **firmware** refers to the operating system and other resources that are stored in its permanent, or semi-permanent, memory. It really is the device's software. Your router and your broadband modem both use firmware, and when you communicate with your router using your Web browser, it's the firmware that provides a Web page.

anyway, but often 100% of that software is actually promotional junk, and you're just as well off leaving it alone.) And you can access your router's Web page even when you can't access the Internet yet because your router comes between your PC and your cable modem.

Unlike Control Panel in Windows 7, you get to your router's controls by logging on. If you've never logged on to your own router before, you need its temporary password. Your logon name will almost certainly be admin. The most often used temporary passwords by router manufacturers are, in order of prominence, password, 1234, and admin. Not many routers use anything different.

Because your router's temporary password is a matter of public record, change it right away.

If you can't find your router's manual to retrieve the temporary password, most router manufacturers post their manuals online. That's no help to you if you can't get your router going. Some routers' Web Control Panels actually contain links to their manuals, which you can download from the router (they're embedded in the firmware).

Here's the typical procedure for using a Web browser to log on to your browser settings:

1. **Open your Web browser.**

   For Internet Explorer 9, launch the blue "e" icon.

2. **In the address bar at the top, type the router's IP address.**

   Most often, this is 192.168.1.1. It may instead be 192.168.0.1. After you press Enter, you should see a credentials screen like in Figure 4-9.

Figure 4-9

3. **Type** admin **(all lowercase) for User Name and then press Enter.**

4. **Type the password for Password and then press Enter.**

Use the temporary password if this is your first time logging on, or if you've recently reset the router back to factory specifications. (Many routers offer that feature as an "all-else-fails" measure.) In a moment, you should see whatever welcome screen your browser maker produces, as shown in Figure 4-10.

Figure 4-10

Comprehending how routers map addresses

Regardless of whether it shares a box with the cable modem, the router is the switchboard between all the devices in your home that need to connect to one another and the Internet. To do this, it maps your devices using a kind of virtual geography.

What the IP address is

The Internet has an address system. For the foreseeable future, all accessible points on the Internet are addressable by four numbers. These numbers are like street addresses but in an alien number system, which replaces our 10-digit, or *base-10,* code with a 256-digit system. In this system, each digit is an *octet.* Because we don't have 256 symbols to represent each one, use numerals from 0 to 255, separated by periods. For example, the service known to your Web browser as dummies.com has this address: 208.215.179.139. Here, each of the four numerals between the digits are octets. With a four-digit, base-10 number, there are 10,000 possible combinations of digits; with a four-octet IPv4 address, there are 4,294,967,296 possible combinations (256 to the fourth power).

In the Internet Protocol address system called IPv4, each point of access is given an address from these 4.3 billion possibilities. You'd think that would be enough. As it turns out, more devices need access points than do people, so the theoretical population of potential access points could easily exceed the estimated 6.8 billion world (human) population.

It's an impossible job, from one perspective: Your router has to assign all the addressable points on your network — including your PCs, smartphones, game consoles, Blu-ray consoles — an address from a system that has already run out. How it ends up doing this is a stroke of genius: literally by disconnecting your devices from the Internet.

Because there are more devices in the world than IPv4 addresses, certain segments of the IP address system have been sacrificed and reserved for local networks only, or what are called *local loops*. The theory is this: Because devices on such things as local and home networks only share resources with one another anyway, and not the outside world, it wouldn't matter if the local devices all borrowed from the same small set of IPv4 addresses.

So one big "global loop" makes up the Internet at large, and which uses most of the world's available IP addresses. Your service provider leases one of these addresses to you. One. That address is assigned to your broadband modem, which is the endpoint of the ISP's equipment and the starting point for yours.

Then there are a countless multitude of local loops, all of which borrow from the same small, reserved set of IP addresses. In fact, devices with those addresses can't "call out" because the reserved nature of those addresses prevents them from doing so. Between each local loop and the global loop is a router, which is the gateway for traffic exiting one loop to enter another.

The basics of local loop networking

Internet Protocol reserves a patch of addresses for exclusive use by local devices. When a router that handles Internet traffic more toward the backbone of the network receives a packet of data intended for an address like 192.168.1.105, it doesn't forward that packet. It can't. The 192.168 prefix is reserved for local networks only.

Your router has a gateway IP address used by the devices on your local network as an intermediate destination for outgoing packets. Figure 4-11 shows the basic address settings for one router.

Most routers use this address as their gateway: 192.168.1.1. Some use 192.168.0.1. There are only a few minor exceptions, but either of these addresses make a perfect gateway address for any router.

LAN Setup				
Device Name		WNDR3700		
LAN TCP/IP Setup				
IP Address	192	168	1	1
IP Subnet Mask	255	255	255	0
RIP Direction			Both	
RIP Version			Disabled	
☑ Use Router as DHCP Server				
Starting IP Address	192	168	1	2
Ending IP Address	192	168	1	254

Figure 4-11

When a device like your PC wants to make a connection with the network, it negotiates for that privilege with your router. It's up to the router to decide whether to grant that request, and usually the answer is yes. When that request is granted, the router assigns the device an IP address from the local loop.

Now, exactly what address that is, is important. If the router's gateway address is 192.168.1.1, most likely, the address that it assigns will be in the range from 192.168.1.2–192.168.1.254.

You can discover this address by looking for a setting called the *subnet mask*. This digital mask that designates which bits of an IP address belong to the broader network (the "1" bits) and which remaining bits can be apportioned for the subnet (the "0" bits). In a common setting like 255.255.255.0, every digit in the first three octets is reserved, but the entire fourth octet is open for use by the subnet (except for the gateway address 1, and the address at the other end 255). Thus, you have room for exactly 253 simultaneous device connections.

LINGO

A **subnet**, in the lexicon of Internet architects, is the portion of the IP address map that's available to be assigned to local devices.

Just what address the router ends up giving out depends on the protocol used in the negotiation. All home routers today can use Dynamic Host Configuration Protocol (DHCP), and Windows 7 is very adept with DHCP. A device asks for the first available address in the subnet, and using its DHCP server, the router responds with that number.

If you're using two or three devices in your network, DHCP usually creates no problems. If you have many different classes of devices (PCs, smartphones, game consoles, video consoles) all requesting simultaneous access, conflicts can and do arise. Occasionally, a router assigns an address that another device thinks belongs to it. The result is an *address conflict,* and at least one conflicting device (perhaps both) will be kicked off the network.

The solution is to assign a fixed IP address to those devices that give you trouble. This can be done from Windows, or from Windows and your router. I show you how to do this in this lesson. In the meantime, trust DHCP to get your devices and router to cooperate with one another . . . until it fails, and *then* react.

Setting up your router

You want to check whether your router can send a wireless connection right out of the box. If not, you need to use a short length of Ethernet cable (usually supplied with the router) to directly connect your router to your PC, or a PC in what will become your home network, even if just for an hour or so. This will get you through the setup phase. If your PC is a desktop model, chances are that it's connected to your router by cable already, in which case, you don't need to do anything to it.

Even if your router can work wirelessly out of the box, you might not want to go that route because a default wireless setup is typically unsecured. Avoid exposing your PC to outside intrusion if you can.

I can't tell you exactly where to find each of your router's settings because each router is different and its controls are different as well, but keep reading to see the basic settings you need to evaluate and perhaps change.

You might see another login panel from your router if you leave it idle for three minutes or so. Nothing's ruined; your router just wants to verify that you're you and not some man-in-the-middle intruder.

Your IP address from the ISP

When you lease broadband service from your ISP, you're given an IP address that represents your endpoint, your spot on the bigger Internet. It's up to the ISP to determine how it leases that address to you.

- **Static:** A permanent address that lasts as long as your contract

- **Dynamic:** A temporary lease on an address in its vast collection, that lasts as short as a day, after which your lease is re-negotiated for you and your ISP gives you another address (or maybe the same one again)

By default, routers are set to negotiate upstream for an IP address dynamically, just as Windows negotiates with your router for a local loop address dynamically. This may be what you want, but some broadband providers may give you instructions to use a fixed address instead. In that case, you'll need to enter that address manually into your router. Figure 4-12 shows an example of how your upstream IP settings tend to look.

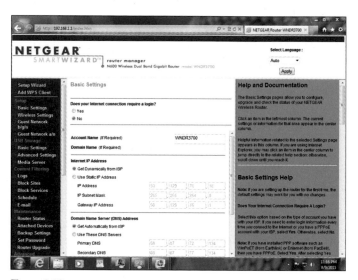

Figure 4-12

Subnet mask

Just like setting up your PC's local loop address, your router needs to know the gateway address of the ISP's router (which usually ends with ".1"). Your ISP will tell you what this should be. In addition, your router needs the subnet mask. Again, that's not an address in itself, but rather a quartet of octets whose individual "1" bits mask out the part of the *actual* address that belongs to the ISP.

Your ISP may be able to send this setting to your router automatically as part of DHCP. If it doesn't (many ISPs in rural areas do not), then you'll need to know what it means because you'll be the one entering it into your router. A subnet mask of 255.255.255.0 informs the router that the first 24 bits of the address are fixed by the ISP and cannot change. In the example in Figure 4-12, 255.255.254.0, the ISP needs all the binary digits from the fourth octet and one extra binary digits from the third octet, to set up the ISP's own local loop. The IP address that's leased to you uses a local loop that's masked by the "0" bits at the tail end; it's the bits denoted by "0" that pertain to your address.

SSID (network name)

After your PC scouts for an available wireless network, it shows you a list of networks' names. Technically, such a name is a Service Set Identifier (SSID). Figure 4-13 shows the SSID settings for a Wireless-G router. If you're using a dual-band (G/N) router, you'll need to set names and channel settings for both networks.

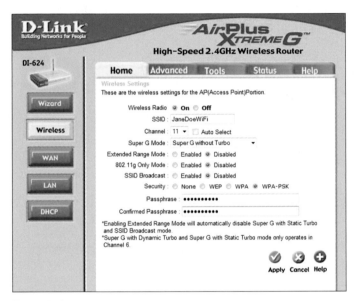

Figure 4-13

Manufacturers typically give their routers default network names although almost invariably, those defaults are the manufacturers' names themselves: for example, linksys. Folks tend to leave the default settings as they are, and then when three or four Wi-Fi signals named linksys show up in a 50-meter region, they wonder why they can't get a signal.

Give your network a unique name — something you'll recognize when you see it in the list of available signals — but don't identify yourself.

Channel and bandwidth mode

When SSID broadcasting is engaged, your Wi-Fi router uses a radio to announce its presence to the world. When you give your network a name, everyone within the transmission radius of your router (which could be 100 meters) will see this name. They won't see where the signal is coming from, so unless you choose some self-evident name like "Bob Morley's Wi-Fi," no one has to know it's yours.

There's no hard-and-fast rule about choosing channels, or any one necessarily being faster than another. Folks who leave their routers at default settings tend to use lower-numbered channels, so lower numbers could be subject to greater interference than others. Just pick one to start. Then if your network isn't as fast as you believe it could be, pick a different number several digits off from the current channel.

A Wireless-G signal has 20 MHz of bandwidth, but a G channel is only 5 MHz wide. Signals on channel 5 will bleed into channel, so if 5 appears to be problematic, try 10.

Enabling SSID broadcasting

Setting up a Wi-Fi connection is somewhat simpler for Windows 7 if you let your router announce its SSID (its "name," along with its public key) for Windows to discover. However, if Windows can discover this data, so can any other Wi-Fi adapter within range.

If you work in close quarters with other routers, you may elect to take a more secure, if less automatic, course of action: Turn SSID completely off. Windows won't be able to locate your router for itself, but you can go through a process where you fill in that data manually. You can then keep SSID off because after you tell Windows where it can locate the router, it will record that information and won't need to rely on SSID again.

Another equally secure alternative is to set up your router connection using a wired session. Windows can discover your router through the wire, and then you can still opt to turn off SSID broadcasting.

Session encryption

The common perception of encryption is that it encodes a signal so that someone trying to listen in won't understand what it says. Actually, it has other benefits as well, not the least of which is

LINGO

A **session** is an exchange of data between two components, from beginning to end.

its ability to restrict a wireless session to the parties that created it: namely, your PC and your router.

When a session is encrypted, both components assert their identities to one another using digital certificates — keys. Using those keys, one of the two parties creates a third key, called the *session key*. Both parties then use that key to encrypt and decrypt data sent to one another. If some other party were to try to decrypt a data packet not belonging to it, the result would be garbage data.

PCs and other clients use a number of different protocols to generate this session key and enable encrypted communication:

- ✔ **WEP (Wired Equivalent Privacy):** Avoid it.

- ✔ **WPA-PSK (Wi-Fi Protected Access with Pre-Shared Key):** The first reasonable attempt to plug the security hole actually created by WEP. First, it doesn't share it in the open and highlight it with the network equivalent of neon lights that spell out, "Hey, hackers, here's the key!" Second, it rotates the key from time to time so it doesn't use the same key for the entire session.

- ✔ **WPA2-PSK:** Notice that "2" in the middle. Improves upon the first edition of WPA by enabling unpredictable options for how the key is shared. Some router makers figure it can't hurt to layer WPA2 on top of WPA, using different encryption methods (TKIP and AES) for each layer.

- ✔ **WPA2 Enterprise:** A version of WPA2 that follows a precise and certified method used in businesses to ensure that session security meets government standards.

So why not choose the toughest method to crack? The answer involves the devices you plan to use as Wi-Fi clients. If you're using only PCs in your home network, using a setting like WPA-PSK [TKIP] + WPA2-PSK [AES] may be excellent. However, video game consoles and handheld game units are among the devices that can't wrap one security method over the other. Maybe you don't need to use the Internet on your Wii or Xbox, but you'd be missing out not only on features but on system updates.

You could set up your G network for WPA2-PSK [AES] — which consoles and handheld devices do support — and your N network because small devices don't yet support N. However, you may notice that this double method slows down communication at the highest 300 Mbps transfer mode, and some routers have even begun disallowing the wrapped security option at high speeds.

Security passphrase

WPA and WPA2 both require the use of a passphrase (not just a PIN) to begin the session key generation process. And routers now actually disallow weak passwords of eight characters or less.

Create a phrase that you'll remember but at the same time complex enough to help generate a very unique session key: Consider a line of song lyrics that you can easily remember, where you use letters or symbols instead of some of the characters and punctuation in particular places. For instance:

☑ **Ain't no mountain h1gh enough!** (notice the "1" in "h1gh")

☑ **That train keeps a-rollin'|On down to San Ant0n** (with a hyphen after the "a" and a strange "|" character, called a *pipe*, between the apostrophe and "On" and, oh yeah, the intentionally misspelled "San Ant0n").

DHCP server setup

It's your ISP's job to give your router an IP address for its access point, but it's your router's job to give your PC an IP address as well. Essentially, there's a sequence of numbered tickets, and DHCP gives a PC a ticket to enter the network.

LINGO

Anything (including software) whose job it is to deliver data over a network is, in networking parlance, a **server**. The thing being served that data — or more accurately, the thing (including software) that requests that data and receives it — is the **client**.

Figure 4-14 shows the most common router settings for enabling DHCP. Here, the router's own IP address serves as the gateway for your devices. More often than not, this address will be 192.168.1.1.

The router maintains a starting address that begins after the gateway, and an ending address just before the "cliff" at 255. When DHCP is turned on, the router picks an available address in that sequence — usually an early one — and assigns it to a new client requesting to enter the network. When DHCP is off, the new entrant must request a specific address, which you provide to Windows.

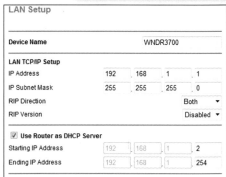

Figure 4-14

Consider disengaging DHCP if you find folks mooching off your Wi-Fi signal. The alternative isn't pretty, but it's feasible: Assign a fixed IP address to every PC on your network; and after you disengage DHCP on the router, you make this assignment through Windows.

However, not every smartphone with Wi-Fi is smart enough to let you designate a fixed IP address. And newer game consoles, such as Nintendo Wii, don't offer a fixed IP address option, either. So even if you do set your PCs to use fixed addresses (and there are legitimate reasons you might have to), you're probably better off leaving DHCP turned on.

Managing Your Windows Connections

If you installed Windows 7 yourself on your PC, it created a "network connection" at that time. With Windows, a *connection* isn't the act of being connected — it's what you use to connect. This is why Windows maintains a list of network connections but manages only one active session at a time.

After you successfully connect to the Internet, Windows remembers how that was done, and the result is a remembered connection that it can use again to connect to the same network. If you use a wired connection to access a network, and later you use a Wi-Fi connection to access the same network, those are two connections because one uses your Ethernet adapter and the other your wireless adapter.

> **LINGO**
>
> A **connection** is a method that Windows uses to access a network.

> **LINGO**
>
> An **adapter** is the device that a PC uses to communicate with a network. Modern notebook and many netbook PCs have two adapters: one for wired connections and the other for wireless. As a result, Windows 7 often maintains two connections, even if to the same network.

Setting the network connection profile

Just after Windows makes a connection to a new network for the first time, you'll see a dialog box asking you what type of network this is, similar to Figure 4-15. It sounds like an easy enough question to answer: Are you at home, are you at work, or are you in a restaurant someplace?

Figure 4-15

The response you give at this point (the first time you use this network) determines which network profile Windows will use whenever you use this network now and later. Earlier, you chose your file sharing settings for the Home or Work profile class and the Public profile class (refer to Figure 4-8). At home or at work, you want to share files with someone and let them share with you; at a coffee shop or the library, you'd rather that no one see what's on your computer. So here is where you tell Windows whether it's safe to share over this network — or not.

✓ **Home Network** enables Windows 7 to use a homegroup if the other PCs are using Windows 7. Even if they're not, though, it creates an expectation for Windows that the other PCs that will try to connect to it are (probably) Windows-based peers.

✓ **Work Network** is quite different because you can't build the same expectations. Network policies are more restrictive at work because it's assumed that different PCs belong to different people, probably unrelated to one another. So, Windows prepares to use a kind of policy-based management system better suited to be administered by a professional being paid for the job.

✓ **Public Network** is a profile that assumes at the outset you're not here to share files; you just want to connect with the Internet.

Now you can see that it becomes perfectly feasible for you to create an open file sharing policy for the Public network profile. There are perfectly legitimate scenarios where you need an open profile at work: Say you're a school-teacher. You're setting up a PC at your desk to share certain files with students; this may be a PC designed to be shared. As long as it doesn't also contain sensitive information, like your students' grade reports, that's fine. Nevertheless, you should consider your school settings a Work profile, not a Public profile; in all circumstances, you can and should maintain a very restrictive Public profile.

Manually establishing a Wi-Fi connection

Earlier, I said you had the option of turning SSID off on your home router, and then manually entering the router's identity, avoiding the chance of spilling any clandestine information into the neighborhood. Different routers give different locations for the SSID broadcast off-switch, but after you've gone that route, the next step involves Windows.

EXTRA INFO

If you have a Mac in your home network, even though the Home Network profile is geared toward Windows PCs, you can still choose Home Network for your profile because later versions of Mac OS X (at least since version 10.2) are equipped with the tools necessary to introduce themselves to Windows peers, including the workgroup protocol Windows Internet Name Service (WINS). You won't be able to enroll a Mac into a homegroup, but it can be recognized as a network peer in a Windows workgroup, and you can instigate file sharing. The secret, users have discovered, is to create accounts on both Windows PCs and Macs with identical usernames and passwords, to the letter, and to ensure strong passwords rather than blanks.

Although SSID normally helps steer Windows in the direction of a good connection, in the absence of SSID or in the event that Windows can't find your router on its own, you can steer Windows the right way if you know the following:

- ✔ The network's name (which the router would normally be broadcasting)
- ✔ The session encryption method it's using
- ✔ Its security passphrase

The first thing you have to do — and this seems counterintuitive — is to turn off your PC's wireless radio. Your PC will always try to connect with a Wi-Fi network whose SSID is turned on, and if you turn yours off for security purposes but your neighbor hasn't done the same, your PC will try to connect with your neighbor's router. With a notebook or netbook PC, there's usually some obvious way to turn off the radio, but there's no standard way to do it yet. Try one of the following:

✔ **Desktop PC:** You'll be able to see where the wireless adapter card is located by looking for its obvious black antenna (sometimes there are two) on the back of the system. There may also be a switch located along the same metal strip on the back of the adapter card, and if there's one there, it's probably the manual radio control.

✔ **Notebook or netbook PC**

- *Switch:* Look for a switch on the PC itself, perhaps marked with some kind of "radio beacon" icon, maybe with an on/off light. If it's there, this is the manual radio control.

- *Function keys:* Look on the function keys of the keyboard of your notebook or netbook PC for a radio beacon icon. This could be in any of several places, most often the F2 or F8 key. Look also for a special function key, usually marked FN or Fn, located near the Ctrl and Shift keys. Use Fn like a shift key and press the function key with the beacon icon. Your PC should respond with some message (it won't be from Windows, but rather a superimposed message from the PC's hardware) telling you whether you've just turned the radio on or off.

- *Mobility Center:* Some portable PCs are equipped to use Windows Mobility Center feature. Search for it from the Start menu, or you can try pressing the Windows key on the keyboard and the X key (Windows+X). Figure 4-16 shows you the Mobility Center, which is a central panel for managing all the characteristics of your notebook PC's hardware. Note: Because not all PCs are alike, the contents of Mobility Center will vary.

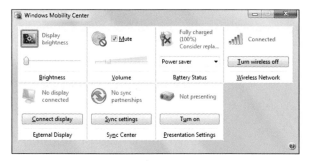

Figure 4-16

In this panel someplace, perhaps not in the same location as in this figure, is an entry for Wireless Network. Here's where you can either make certain the wireless radio is already turned off, or turn it off by clicking the Turn Wireless Off button. This setting should override any hard switch on your PC.

With that bit of fun out of the way, here's how you manually plug in the data to get the connection started:

1. **Choose Start⇨Network.**

2. **Click Network and Sharing Center on the command bar.**

3. **Click Set Up a New Connection or Network.**

   A range of options appears, as depicted in Figure 4-17. For most users, the Manually Connect to a Wireless Network option will appear only if Windows can't find a wireless network at the moment; if it can, you won't see this option. That's a problem if you intentionally turned off SSID on your router but someone else in the neighborhood has SSID turned on; Windows will try to automatically connect with it instead. Go back and turn your wireless radio off if this option doesn't appear.

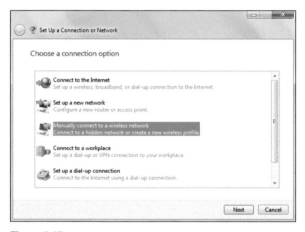

Figure 4-17

4. **Click Manually Connect to a Wireless Network and then click Next.**

   The manual entry panel appears, as shown in Figure 4-18.

5. **Enter your network name in the Network Name field.**

   You should already have given your router a unique network name.

Routers use case-sensitive names, so if you named your network DC-24, then don't use dc-24 here.

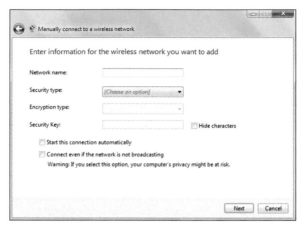

Figure 4-18

6. **Choose the network session security scheme.**

As you'll recall, this is the way your PC and router "handshake" with one another. Yes, WEP is still a choice, but avoid it like the Plague. WPA2-Personal in this list equates with what some routers list as just WPA2, which is separate from WPA2-Enterprise.

7. **Choose the network encryption type.**

On your router, the security scheme and encryption type are usually one choice. There, you'll see the encryption type written off to the side, as in [AES] or [TKIP]. Choose the encryption that matches the one you chose for the router.

8. **Enter the network security passphrase (Security Key).**

For added privacy, first select the Hide Characters check box.

9. **Select the Start This Connection Automatically check box.**

You don't want to go through this rigmarole each time.

10. **Select the Connect Even If the Network Is Not Broadcasting check box.**

This is if you intend to leave SSID turned off on your router, and you don't intend to ever open your network to smartphone, first-generation wireless game console, or Blu-ray player traffic.

Yes, Microsoft put an obvious security warning below this choice (refer to Figure 4-18), which seems odd for a setting you'd only be considering to be *more* secure. This means that your PC will scan for the network you just entered even in the absence of evidence that this network exists. Therefore, if you take your laptop PC somewhere else, it may broadcast this data to the outside world, and a maliciously crafted router might accept that data, effectively saying, "Sure, I'm the network you're looking for." From there, the other router may attempt to establish a network with your PC and read your files.

However, this danger exists just as much at home as in a coffee shop. So if you believe it is or will be a problem for you, do not select this option, and be sure to go back into your router and turn SSID back on.

11. **Click Next.**

In a moment, you should see a panel that reads Successfully added... along with the network name. *This does not mean you are connected.* It simply means that Windows has created a connection based on the data you supplied.

12. **Click Close.**

If you switched off your network radio earlier, switch it back on now. Windows should try to launch a session with your router without further input from you.

Manually setting Windows' IP address

As I mention earlier, if you end up with a half-dozen or more Wi-Fi devices in your household, you inevitably increase the likelihood of an IP address conflict, where two devices appear to have been assigned the same address, and one or both can't access the network. For example, say that your son is playing on the family Xbox. After you check your e-mail on your PC, you both take a dinner break, and you put your PC to sleep while your son puts the Xbox on pause. After dinner, your son goes back and finishes his game while you reawaken your PC. Hmm, there's a message about an IP address conflict. Apparently your router decided your PC was off the network and leased the IP address your PC was using earlier to the Xbox when it was unpaused.

Earlier, I informed you that your router can assign static IP addresses to specific devices. I couldn't show you how to do that specifically because every router works differently. Alternatively, you can leave DHCP turned on for your router but assign a specific IP address in Windows for your PC to request. The router will give only your device that address.

Here's one potential problem: The address number you pick in Windows doesn't reserve that same number in the router. You could go ahead and reserve that number in the router as well. Or, because the router is likely to give new devices with dynamic IP addresses a low number anyway (like 192.168.1.4 or .5 or .6), you could assign Windows a higher number (like .101 or .202) that DHCP is unlikely to choose unless and until a hundred or so devices log onto your network.

Here's how to assign an IP address:

1. **Open the Network and Sharing Center.**

2. **Click Change Adapter Settings (left pane).**

   The Network Connections window opens, where Windows keeps track of the methods it uses to reach a network. This isn't a list of networks (despite entries having default names like Local Area Connection) but a list of schemes Windows may use to access a network.

   Windows uses paired monitors as its symbol for a network, but there's a little mini-icon in the lower-right corner that denotes the type of connection. An Ethernet plug denotes a wired connection, five bars symbolizes Wi-Fi, and a telephone (looks like a cash register) denotes either a dial-up connection (from the Dark Ages) or an Internet connection that requires tethering to your smartphone.

3. **Click the connection you wish to change.**

4. **Click Change Settings of This Connection, on the command bar.**

This command is usually tucked so far to the right that there isn't room for it. You may have to click the >> arrow first and then choose the command from the menu; see Figure 4-19.

Figure 4-19

The Local Area Connection Properties dialog box opens.

5. **Because you're changing the IPv4 address that Windows has on file for this PC, select the Internet Protocol Version 4 (TCP/IPv4) check box.**

Clearing this check box turns it off.

6. **Click the Properties button.**

The empty Properties dialog box shown on the left of Figure 4-20 deals only with setting the IP addresses this connection will use. When Windows sets up a connection automatically, it assumes it will use DHCP to obtain addresses dynamically, so it sets the automatic options for IP address and DNS server (for looking up the IP addresses of domain names, such as dummies.com).

Figure 4-20

7. Enter a fixed IP address, subnet mask, and default gateway address.

When you enter these values, Windows sets the Use the Following IP Address option. The examples in the right side of Figure 4-20 are valid entries for a router whose gateway address is set for 192.168.1.1. This is the same gateway address you set earlier for your router (refer to Figure 4-11).

- The first three octets of the IP address here should match the octets of the IP address you set earlier for your router. These are usually 192.168.0 or 192.168.1.

- The fourth octet of the IP address should be a unique number that no other PC on your network will use. You won't find this in your router settings; in fact, your router will look to your PC for this number. You can't use 0, 1, or 255 because they're taken. I like to start with 101 myself. Then when I'm setting up the next PC in the network, 102, then 103 for the next one and so forth.

- Enter **255.255.255.0** as the subnet mask for your network. Windows might fill this in for you automatically because on most home networks, it's typically the same.

- The default gateway for your network should be all four octets of the IP address of your router. That's the address you do find on the router, and that's the one that ends in 0 or 1.

8. (Optional) Enter a primary and alternate DNS server address.

Your ISP should have its own separate IP address for your Web browser and other Internet tools to use when trying to acquire the IP address for a given domain name. This is its DNS server address.

EXTRA INFO

You're not obligated to use the same DNS address that your ISP gives you. In fact, many free services are advertised to be faster, such as Google Public DNS (8.8.8.8, 8.8.4.4), and subscription or registered services such as OpenDNS. You can opt for a DNS server that filters content you might find objectionable. The examples here are for a DNS server (4.2.2.1, 4.2.2.2) maintained by Verizon, which doesn't use filters.

LINGO

DNS refers to the **Domain Name System** that gives every IP address a name that sounds better in TV commercials. Even though you may know Web sites by their domain names, your browser eventually has to dial each one up by number; so it uses a DNS server to find out what the number is.

9. **Click OK.**

10. **Click Close to finalize your settings.**

   If you changed the IP address, then in a moment, you'll notice you're disconnected from the network. As the changes cycle through the system, your connection should be re-established with the changes you made.

Verifying the connection status

If you appear to have lost your upstream connection to your ISP, probably the first thing you should do is restart your broadband modem and router. Unplug both from their power sources, and then plug in the modem and wait for it to (appear to) regain a connection. Then plug in the router and wait for its cheery holiday lights to start blinking majestically.

If there's still no joy from the Web browser, check for an address conflict, or a lack of a definitive Internet connection. Here's how:

1. **Open the Network and Sharing Center.**

2. **Click Change Adapter Settings (left pane).**

3. **Double-click the connection in question.**

   A status dialog box appears like the one in Figure 4-21.

   This is the status box for a wireless connection. Few home routers support IPv6, so don't be alarmed by seeing `No Internet Access` appearing beside IPv6 Connectivity. It's the IPv4 Connectivity you should be worried about:

   • *Not Connected* means that your PC isn't connected with your router.

   • *No Internet Access* means that your PC is connected with the router, but the router doesn't have a gateway for the ISP.

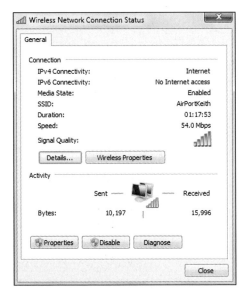

Figure 4-21

• *Local* means that your connection doesn't appear to be set up for your router to obtain an IP address from the ISP although the router is making connections between the devices in your local loop.

• *Internet* means all your network connectivity is active, so if things appear to be offline, it's not because the ISP cut you off.

4. **Click the Details button for more data.**

The Network Connection Details dialog box shows up, as depicted in Figure 4-22. Here's where you'll see the IP address your PC is currently using, and whether it's a fixed address (DHCP Enabled: Yes) or one assigned by you (No). Take note of this data and compare it with the other PCs, consoles, and phones on your network to ensure there's no conflict.

5. **Click Close.**

6. **Click Close (again) to exit.**

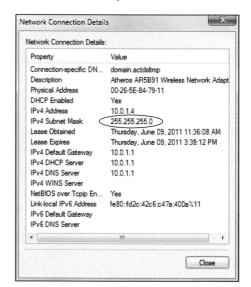

Figure 4-22

Restarting the network from Windows

If you've checked out the context menu for a network connection, you may have noticed a command called Diagnose. If you feel comfortable with the knowledge of everything discussed to this point in the lesson, including what to look for with respect to your router settings, you will never need to use this command. To be honest, all it does is either tell you things seem okay (when they're not), or lead you through a series of steps where you do the diagnosis ("Is everything plugged in?") rather than Windows. If you know how to do that anyway, you don't need Windows leading you by the pinkie finger.

So I'm going to surprise you and ignore this command. Instead, most of the time when you get an IP address conflict or you can't seem to access the Internet even when you appear to be online, the solution involves less panic and more action. Rebooting your broadband modem and router often resolves such issues unless the cause is an upstream outage that only your ISP can fix. With Windows, another way you can "reboot" is by disabling and then re-enabling the connection, which is far easier than treading through Windows' monotonous and ineffective diagnosis wizard:

1. **Open the Network and Sharing Center.**
2. **Click Change Adapter Settings (left pane).**
3. **Right-click the faulty connection.**
4. **Choose Disable from the pop-up menu.**

   Wait for the network icon in the notification area to show a red "X" or dull gray bars. This may be superstitious, but I usually count to five.

5. **Right-click again and choose Enable.**

   Windows goes through the same network initiation sequence as when you're starting the computer, so you don't have to reboot the computer to reboot the network. If rebooting your router and modem don't resolve the issue, and the cause is local, usually this does the trick.

COURSEWORK

Here's an assignment that comes with a bonus: When you're done, you'll have a network connection you can keep as my free gift to you, no questions asked. Get your broadband modem set up, and attach your router to it using Ethernet cable. Turn off the wireless radio on your PC. Attach your PC to your router, again using Ethernet cable. Log onto your router using your Web browser. First thing, turn off SSID on your router. Reboot the router. Log on again, and then change your admin password on your router. Set it up so that its gateway is 192.168.0.1. (You may have to log on again in your Web browser using this new address.) Set up its DHCP server so that it administers addresses from 192.168.0.2–0.254. Change the network name to that of your favorite 18th Century German composer. Use WPA2-PSK handshaking if you can, WPA if not. Don't use WEP. Go into Windows and set its IP address to 192.168.0.91. Unplug your PC from the router and let the connection be dropped. Turn SSID back on in your router, and then on your PC, turn the wireless radio back on. Let Windows create the connection, and set its profile to Home Network. When you're done, you should have a very safe wireless connection without ever having transmitted your router data to your neighbors.

Building a Homegroup

If you work in a large office complex, you're familiar with the complexities of networked file storage: folders with permissions granted to you, resources with privileges extended to you, groups of users, and privileges and permissions extended to some groups but denied to others.

Folks at home tend to think of their files as private or not private. If the printer isn't there for everyone to use, it's usually because the kids don't use it responsibly. So at home, files and resources are usually either "shared" or "not shared."

Homegroup networking in Windows 7 embraces this basic principle. There are probably very few instances, if any, of situations where you want to share certain files with "everyone in your family *except* your 12-year-old," or "except your husband." You can still make such exceptions if you truly need to, but the tools for doing that don't make it difficult for you to simply share or not share as warranted.

On a properly established Windows 7 PC, each user has her own account. If every account on every PC is going to have the same name and password anyway, a homegroup enables folks with accounts to access the files they're entitled to, regardless of which PC they're using at the time.

In Windows 7, all file sharing follows the same rules, whether you're networked or not, and this improves security immensely while giving you a simpler way of sharing files.

When you take your computer to work and it joins your employer's network domain, all sorts of sharing and usage policies are maintained by the system administrator. These policies will all pertain to your computer only during the time that it's connected to that domain. Of course, when you take your PC home, you don't want those policies applied there, so homegroup networking applies only to *home*.

Just one small bump: Every computer in a homegroup has to run Windows 7. No Vista, no XP, no Xbox. An older Windows-based systems can network with one another under the earlier Windows concept of the *workgroup*, and the same folder- and resource-based permissions that applied before can still apply now. But if you want to get every PC on the same, simpler homegroup plan, they all need to run Windows 7.

Getting the homegroup started

When a Windows 7 computer belongs to a network, the system automatically generates its own homegroup passcode and hands it off to the installer. A lot of good that does you if the installer is far away.

An exceedingly common problem that new PC users discover is when they try to create a homegroup and being told that one already exists. What they're not told is that it exists in a factory in Round Rock, Texas. What factory installers tend to do is turn on everything they expect their customers to want as defaults or presets. But when homegroups are turned on, Windows 7 creates a passcode and shows it to the installer right then, thinking the installer is the user. Maybe the installer jotted it down on a sticky note someplace, but right now it's in his wallet along with a five and some pizza coupons. Meanwhile, you turn on your PC for the first time and are given the option to "Join a homegroup" because the passcode already exists. You click the button, the network can't find the homegroup, and you're stuck in a rut.

There is a solution to this rut, but it's not self-evident. You need to leave the non-existent homegroup. You do this the same way you would leave an existing one:

1. **Choose Start⇨Control Panel⇨HomeGroup.**

2. **In the Change Homegroup Settings window that appears, click Leave the Homegroup; see Figure 4-23.**

3. **In the Leave the Homegroup window that opens, click Leave the Homegroup.**

   Windows should erase the existing homegroup passcode, and tell you when it's finished doing so.

4. **Click Finish.**

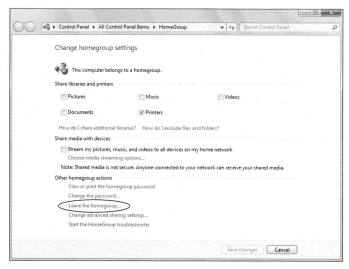

Figure 4-23

Now that you know for certain that no homegroup exists on your system, create a real one:

1. **Choose Start⇨Control Panel ⇨HomeGroup.**

   In the Share with Other Home Computers Running Windows 7 window, you'll see the Create a Homegroup button at the bottom if no home-group exists and no data for it was ever created during installation. If a homegroup appears to exist, the button reads Join a Homegroup.

2. **Click the Create a Homegroup button.**

   You'll see a list of libraries (see Figure 4-24) that you can share from your computer on the homegroup you're creating: Pictures, Music, Videos, Documents (unchecked by default), and Printers.

3. **Mark the libraries you wish to share and then click Next.**

4. **Make note of the passcode that appears in the following screen.**

Write down this passcode now although you can also have this PC recall it for you later when necessary.

5. **Click Finish.**

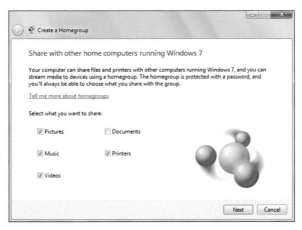

Figure 4-24

Sharing files and printers with a homegroup

Windows 7 initializes the file and resource sharing system for your home-group with a very basic logic:

- ✔ Media libraries are probably to be shared.
- ✔ Printers are probably to be accessible to everyone.
- ✔ Your documents are probably *not* to be shared.

So if you want to share a file, you place it in a folder in a shared library, or in a public folder. Simple enough. You can make some exceptions:

- ✔ For a series of media files that you do want included in your library as it appears on your PC but you don't want to appear on other PCs in the homegroup, create a folder for them in your library, and specifically share that folder, literally, with Nobody.
- ✔ For files amid your private documents that it would be convenient for you to make available elsewhere in your network (for example, down-loaded user manuals), create a folder for them within My Documents and share that folder with Everybody in the Homegroup.
- ✔ If you and your spouse have separate accounts on one PC, create exceptions that permit files or folders stored in an otherwise restricted folder to be shared between the two of you.

✔ If the two of you have files to be shared with perhaps one member of your family elsewhere in your network but not the little ones, create an account for that other member on your PC as though that member were a user of your PC. Then the files that you share with that other account member will also be accessible to that person on her remote PC in the homegroup.

Everyone or no one

Start with simple exceptions, the kind that apply to everyone or no one. Specifying exceptions to Windows involves bringing up a folder window, selecting the files you want to make exclusive to everyone or no one, and selecting the exception from the command bar.

1. **Open the folder window to the files or folders you want to share/not share.**

2. **Select the files or folders.**

3. **On the command bar, click Share With.**

   From the menu that drops down (see Figure 4-25), your choices are

   - *Nobody* places a firm restriction on these items, so that they're only accessible to you from your account.

   - *Homegroup (Read)* makes the items accessible to everyone in the homegroup, but to a limited extent. No one can use an application (such as Word or Excel) to change them; no one can overwrite them with another file; and no one can delete them or move them to a new location, thereby removing them from the old location. The file can be copied by anyone in the homegroup, however, and the resulting new file can be changed unless someone puts restrictions on it as well.

   - *Homegroup (Read/Write)* makes the items accessible to everyone in the homegroup without limits. This means the file can be changed, moved, and deleted.

Placing a Nobody restriction on a file in a shared folder doesn't make that file's existence invisible to other users. Folks who browse that folder will see its name, but they'll be denied access to it when they try to open it. If you don't want anyone seeing the file or knowing it exists, place it in a folder with a nondescript name, and then place a Nobody restriction on that folder.

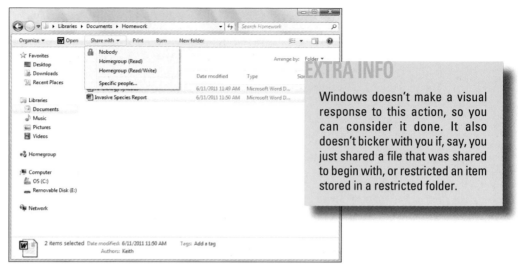

Figure 4-25

Restrictions to individual accounts

Essentially, when you give special access to a person or place an exclusive restriction on a person's use of a file or resource, you make a *rule*. As you'll see, rules created within homegroups apply only to users within the homegroup, which doesn't include folks with older versions of Windows or with Mac OS.

This is an extremely important rule: The only personal accounts to which a homegroup file sharing exception may apply are those on the PC on which the file resides. These are the only "people" whom Windows 7 "knows." If you grant access to a folder to someone else on your PC, and that person uses the same username and password for her PC in the homegroup as for her account on your PC, she can access that folder from her PC just as she can from yours. If you grant access to another account on your PC, but that account's username and password don't match anyone else in the homegroup, those permissions don't extend to anyone else in the homegroup.

EXTRA INFO

Windows doesn't make a visual response to this action, so you can consider it done. It also doesn't bicker with you if, say, you just shared a file that was shared to begin with, or restricted an item stored in a restricted folder.

EXTRA INFO

One of the more important libraries that the homegroup setup process overlooks entirely is Recorded TV, where Windows Media Center stores the recordings it's acquired from your PC's TV tuner card. The library may contain the Public Recorded TV folder, which is already shared with everyone, but that doesn't make it appear under Homegroup in a folder window. To solve this problem, on the PC with the tuner, create a library named Recorded TV and then share it with Homegroup just as you would for a folder.

It follows that the only way to create a rule that applies to another person in your homegroup is to ensure that person also has an account on your PC. This could be a tricky business because that person's password must match on both your PC and her own, so you may have to allow that person to create her account with a private password on your PC. You don't need other users' passwords to create rules that apply to those other users, just their usernames.

With all that out of the way, here's how the exclusive rule-making process works:

1. **Open the folder window to the files or folders you want to share/not share.**

2. **Select the files or folders.**

3. **On the command bar, click Share With.**

4. **Choose Specific People from the pop-up menu.**

5. **In The File Sharing dialog box that appears (see Figure 4-26), click the down arrow (left of the Add button) and choose an account.**

   • *Everyone:* Includes the Guest account on your PC, if there is a Guest account.

   • *Homegroup:* Includes only individual account users with passwords.

   However, the reason you chose this command was to specify one account in particular.

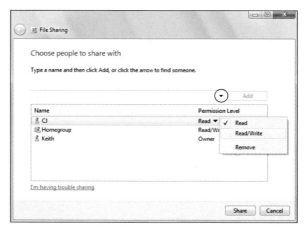

Figure 4-26

6. **Click the Add button.**

   The account's name is added to the list below. By default, Windows gives that account a permission level of Read, which means that account cannot be used to change, overwrite, move, or delete these items.

7. **To change the account's permission level, click the down-arrow beside the account's current level; refer to Figure 4-26.**

   • *Read/Write:* Grant full access rights, including deletion.

   • *Read:* Disallow changes or deletions.

   • *Remove:* Change your mind and clear this account from the list.

8. **Click the Share button.**

   Depending on the number of items you chose, Windows could take a minute or so to change permissions. After that time, Windows will report success.

9. **Click Next.**

When you share a library with another user in your homegroup, that user will find that library located in the Homegroup category of her Windows 7 folder window, sorted in alphabetical order by library name. However, when you share a *folder* with that user, she'll find it in a different place. It'll be under the Network category, beneath the name of the computer (not your name personally, but the PC's name) where the folder is stored. It's confusing, but after a while, you do get used to it.

Sharing (or unsharing) a printer

When you create your new homegroup, you're given the option then to share any printers you have connected to your PC. (Network printers appear in the Devices and Printers window.) If you left everything set the way it was, you're sharing your printer with everyone now. The reason you would want to make a change is if the kids are taking too much advantage of your seemingly endless supply of paper and ink, and printing out hundreds of funny-captioned cat posters for their walls. (You might also want to restrict their rights to masking tape.)

Changing the sharing status of a printer works the same way as changing the sharing status of a media library:

1. **Choose Start⇨Control Panel⇨HomeGroup.**

2. **To remove your printer(s) from the homegroup, clear the Printers check box, as shown in Figure 4-27; or to resume sharing printer(s), select the Printers check box.**

3. **Click the Save Changes button.**

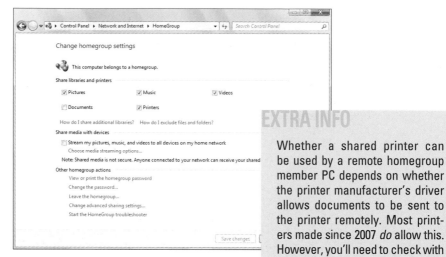

Figure 4-27

 Summing Up

Your broadband router is responsible for managing traffic over your local network. It does this by mapping the various points of access on your network using special IP address numbers that intentionally cannot correspond to any access points on the broader Internet. A router has a handful of these reserved addresses it can dole out, and using a request/response protocol called DHCP, your PC can request an address and your router will fulfill the request with the first available number. This seems all well and good until you add other devices to the network, such as a smartphone, an e-book, a handheld game, an HD game console, a Blu-ray Disc player, and a network-capable HDTV. All of these want network access, too, so you may end up assigning as many of these devices as possible (including your Windows PCs) fixed IP addresses, usually in the range 192.168.1.2 to 192.168.1.254.

Wireless-G (802.11g) routers transmit their signals using radio waves in the 2.4 GHz frequency band. Newer and faster Wireless-N (802.11n) routers use multiple channels in the 2.4 GHz and 5 GHz bands simultaneously. Both are susceptible to interference from everyday household devices, such as cordless phones, baby monitors, microwave ovens, and other neighbors' routers.

Wi-Fi routers acquire connections from PCs and other devices by broadcasting data about themselves within the widest possible radius. This data, called SSID, certainly helps your PC connect to the Internet quickly enough; the problem is, if not set up properly, it could help everyone else's PC connect within a 100-meter radius. Your router also shares access to your personal files, though, especially the folders you haven't secured. So if you live in a concentrated neighborhood (such as an apartment complex), you may want to take steps to secure your installation process, such as using a wired connection to your PC instead of Wi-Fi during the initial setup, and turning off SSID for the duration of the setup process.

In Windows parlance, a *connection* is a method that Windows uses to establish what human beings call a "connection" with a network. After either you or Windows establish a reliable method that apparently works, Windows remembers that method and stores it in its list of connections. If you connect to the same network using Wi-Fi one day and wired Ethernet the next, those are two connections, which Windows will manage separately.

A homegroup makes it vastly simpler for computers you bring together at home to connect with one another over your broadband router, share files and documents, and even play music together. After you established a network, you build a homegroup atop that foundation. Then you can automatically share your libraries, while counting on the fact that stuff you put in your private My Documents folder, or stuff stored in new folders that you create, won't be shared. And after you get a homegroup working properly, you can trade playlists via Windows Media Player, and even stream music from your PC to your family's PCs.

Know This Tech Talk

access point (AP): A device on a network given an IP address, usually leading to a broader range of connections

adapter: A device whose purpose is to enable a computer to receive data that its built-in components were not designed to receive, such as a network adapter

Bluetooth: A form of near-field communication (NFC) used by smartphones, notebook PCs, and accessories for pairing over short distances without the use of wires

DHCP (Dynamic Host Configuration Protocol): A method for an adapter and address point to establish a connection by negotiating for an available address

dynamic IP address: An address leased to a client by a service provider for a definite time limit, after which a new address may be leased

Ethernet: The most common interface used today for wired digital networks

gateway: The IP address of an access point, intended to represent the transfer point between devices

IEEE 802.11: The designation for the international standard for wireless networking, as produced by the Institute for Electrical and Electronic Engineers (IEEE)

ISP (Internet service provider): A service that leases connections to the Internet to homes and businesses

local loop: The group of mapped devices that constitutes a subnet

mapping: The translation of a system of access to an address scheme; for instance, the assignment of IP addresses to a local loop, or the assignment of a network share to a storage device identifier

Mobility Center: A tool in Windows that gathers resources applicable to using your portable computer, usually from a remote location

modem: A device which encodes and decodes (modulates and demodulates) digital signals over a wire

Network Address Translation (NAT): A method used by firewalls to translate the recipient of data into an IP address used by the local loop, and to send addresses from that local loop to IP addresses on the broader Internet

Network and Sharing Center: The panel within the Windows 7 Control Panel for managing a home or work network setup

octet: In IPv4 addressing, a number between 0 and 255 that easily translates to a base-16 (hexadecimal) number between 00 and FF

passphrase: A code for validating identity or authority that is intended to be relatively long

permissions: Settings that enable a network account to use designated resources

server: Any component in a digital network that receives a request for data and may respond with data

session key: Data used to encrypt communication between two parties in a network, usually shared exclusively between those parties

share: *(n.)* A container for data to be shared over a network, which includes permissions and restrictions on certain accounts, and which may be applied to a folder or a storage device

shared folder: A storage location for files whose accessibility is immediately presumed to be public by virtue of their being located there

SSID (Service Set Identifier): The data broadcast by a wireless router to advertise its availability to prospective clients

static IP address: An address leased to a client by a service provider for an indefinite length of time

terabyte: 1,099,511,627,776 bytes of storage

WEP (Wired Equivalent Privacy): One of the earliest protocols used for securing wireless networks, largely disused for its lack of efficacy

Windows XP: The version of the Windows client operating system marketed by Microsoft from August, 2001 to November, 2006

Wireless-G: A marketing term for wireless networking standard 802.11g, which achieves 54 megabit per second transmission on the 2.4 GHz band

Wireless-N: A marketing term for wireless networking standard 802.11n, which achieves high speeds by dividing traffic among multiple simultaneous channels in both the 2.4 GHz and 5 GHz bands

WPA-PSK (Wi-Fi Protected Access with Pre-Shared Key): A handshaking scheme for server and client in a network to establish a secure, encrypted session; superseded in some routers by WPA2-PSK

Lesson 5
Playing on the Internet

✔ Learn how to use the Internet Explorer 9 address bar to identify the resources you use on the Web.

✔ Keep track of the Web sites you use most, and build a library of the best and most useful addresses.

✔ See how to use your browsing history.

✔ Manage open Web pages with tabs.

✔ Set up Windows Live Mail to handle multiple e-mail accounts.

✔ Receive, send, and read e-mail and attachments.

✔ Keep your mail inbox tidy by clearing it of junk mail and using folders to store messages.

The phrase "surfing the Web" was coined at the dawn of its popularity, during a time of wonder and discovery — specifically, when you were more busy discovering it than it discovering you. Today, the term is about as applicable to the online World Wide Web as "thrifty" is to "gasoline," or "music" is to "MTV." Using the Web is work. This lesson is about making sense of the most confusing part of modern computing. Hopefully, I'll alleviate some headaches along the way.

Navigating the Web with Internet Explorer 9

The first time you start Internet Explorer 9 (click the blue "e" icon on the toolbar), it presents the dialog box in Figure 5-1.

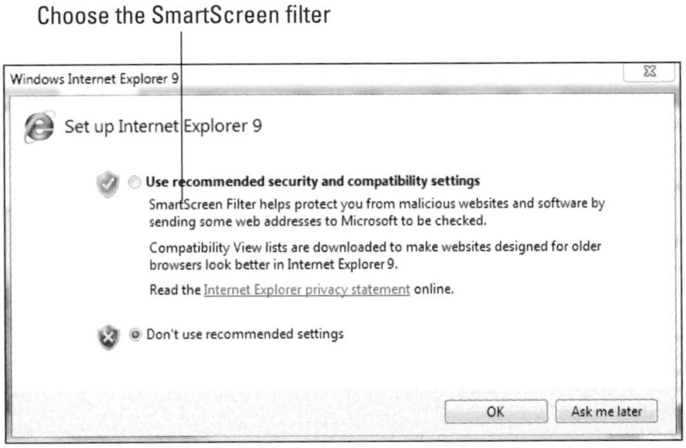

Choose the SmartScreen filter

Figure 5-1

Internet Explorer 9 (IE9) is the browser that comes with the latest Windows 7 installations, and that's what I use in the examples in this lesson.

The recommended choice is the SmartScreen filter, which Microsoft uses to send "telemetry" back to its servers regarding sites that cause IE9 to misbehave or crash. It then uses that database to check against the Web sites or pages you're about to visit, and can stop your browser from proceeding if there's a history of crashing or suspected malicious use. This is a good feature, and Microsoft doesn't share the data that it collects.

Making sense of the address bar

IE9 begins its life by showing you MSN, the Microsoft news and feature service, as well as portal to the company's search engine, Bing. See Figure 5-2.

At the top of the browser window is the address bar, where you can

- ✔ See the Web address of the page you're looking at.
- ✔ Enter the Web address (URL) of a page or site you want to look at.

You also find a Refresh button and a Stop button, and maybe a Back and Forward button. More on Back and Forward later.

A Web page begins with a URL, a kind of "page one" that appears in the address bar of the browser. A Web page can have dozens, even hundreds, of other components, all of which have their own URLs. You don't see them, though, because you don't need to. They're all referenced by the main page whose URL is in the address bar. That's the only URL you need to be concerned with.

Back

Forward   Address bar

Refresh

Search | Stop

Help

Figure 5-2

If you know the Web address or URL of the page you want to visit, you can browse to it by simply typing it into the address bar and then pressing Enter. If you don't know the URL of the Web page you want, enter a search term into the address bar and then press Enter. You read right: the *address bar*. When IE9 doesn't recognize what you typed as a URL, it does a double-take and bypasses it through a search engine — by default, Bing. Bing responds with a list of hyperlinks to pages that appear to have the most content that closely matches your query (search term). Figure 5-3 shows an everyday example. Just click the link to go to the Web page you want.

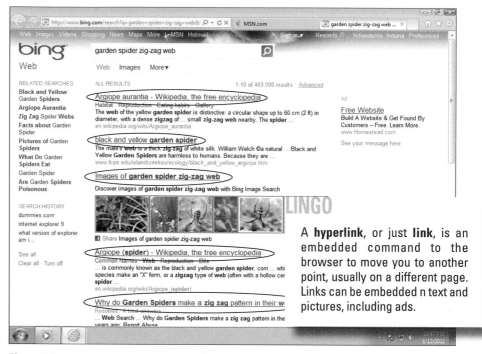

A **hyperlink**, or just **link**, is an embedded command to the browser to move you to another point, usually on a different page. Links can be embedded n text and pictures, including ads.

Figure 5-3

Here's how to decipher a URL behind a link, or the URL in a search result page:

```
http://www.dummies.com/about-for-
            dummies.html
```

- ✔ The **protocol** used for sending the data back to the client. HTTP is the common transport protocol of the Web.

  You can spot whether a site uses encryption by looking for http**s**://. The "s" stands for "secure," which is reassuring if you're entering sensitive information or making a purchase online. Look for a green address bar, too.

- ✔ The **domain name** of the server (also called the DNS name) responding to the request, commonly known as the *Web site*. This is the part of the URL that's easy for you to remember, like www.dummies.com or www.wikipedia.org.

EXTRA INFO

A lot of URLs you see on TV use "www" and a dot in front of them. That's actually an old, outdated protocol — a little like dialing "0" as a prefix for a person-to-person call. If you simply omit the "www" and the dot after it but type the rest, nearly all Web servers today will take you to the same place. The concluding .com or .org or .net part is still very important. Each of those letter codes at the end is called a "top-level domain," referring the server to the directory it needs to look up the name in the middle. So for facebook.com, the server places a call to the Domain Name System (DNS) to access the registrar for .com and ask it for the Internet address (IP address) for Facebook.

✔ When you type a basic domain name — say, dummies.com — IE9 fills in the rest: for instance, *resolving* it to http://www.dummies.com.

✔ (Optional) The **location on the server** where the data resides, which looks a lot like a folder address (except on the Web, the slash marks look like / instead of \). This is tacked on to the end of the domain name, and if it's left blank, it means the "root folder" on the server, or what's more commonly called the *home page*.

✔ Especially in the case of search engines like Google and Bing, a **query** is often tacked to the end of the URL, designed to be used by a database to recover specific information you asked for. In the search engine example shown in Figure 5-4, you see the parts of the actual query — `garden+spider+zig-zag+web` — tucked inside the URL of the search results.

LINGO

A **Web server** is the software that the publisher uses, either on computers it owns or housed elsewhere that it leases, that sends the data over the Internet to your browser client. A **Web site** is a service at a given address. A publisher may have more than one Web site, in which case, they use separate addresses. A **Web page** is the culmination of data from the Web site plus other sources, collected by your browser and assembled in place to produce something you can read and interact with.

Figure 5-4

Back and Forward

Because the Web isn't structured like a book or encyclopedia, with a fixed sequence of numbered pages, there's no absolute way for your browser or any Web server to know what page comes "next." You can click any link on a page, and that one becomes the "next" page. However, your browser does remember where you were and retains the content you already downloaded when you were there, so it gives you a way to move back.

The big blue button in the upper left with the left-pointing arrow is the Back button (refer to Figure 5-2). Here's how it works:

- When you click the Back button, it reloads the previous page from memory.

- When you click *and hold* the Back button, it brings up a menu of the last ten pages you visited, in order from most recent to least, as shown in Figure 5-5.

- At the bottom of this menu is History, which brings up a much more detailed list of every Web address that IE9 currently remembers, organized (at first) by date; see Figure 5-6.

Figure 5-5

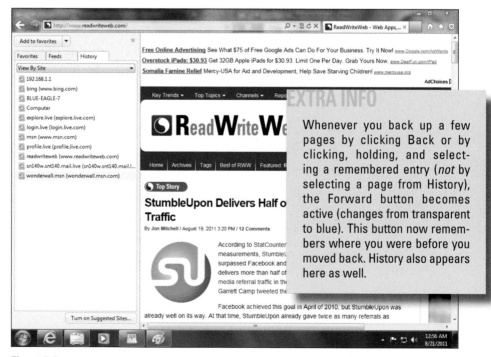

Figure 5-6

EXTRA INFO

Whenever you back up a few pages by clicking Back or by clicking, holding, and selecting a remembered entry (*not* by selecting a page from History), the Forward button becomes active (changes from transparent to blue). This button now remembers where you were before you moved back. History also appears here as well.

Setting your starting point

The *home page* is the first Web page you see in IE9 after you launch the browser, like in Figure 5-2. Think of a home page as the jumping off point for all your Internet browsing. If you want a different Web site to be your home page — say, your favorite search engine or a news site — you can change this page.

Here's how to designate a new home page:

1. **Navigate to the page you want to use as your home page.**

2. **Click the gear icon (Tools) in the upper-right corner.**

3. **From the drop-down menu that appears, choose Internet Options, as shown here.**

4. **In the Internet Options dialog box that appears (see Figure 5-7), under the General tab, click the Use Current button.**

5. **Click OK.**

   Now when you open Internet Explorer by clicking its icon on your desktop, it opens to the home page you selected.

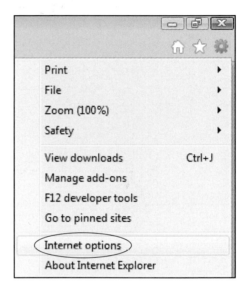

Managing your browsing history

To help you return to pages you've been to, use the History feature in IE9. You can track your online travels via the address bar or the History pane.

On the right side of the address bar is a down arrow. Hover your mouse there to bring up an AutoComplete tooltip. Click that down-arrow to open a list of the last 20 pages you visited, as you can see in Figure 5-8. The list that pops up is divided into three groups. The top group contains URLs

Figure 5-7

that are somewhat similar in content (not subject) to what appears in the address bar now, followed by History and Favorites.

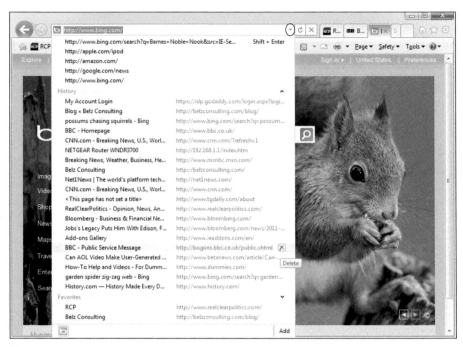

Figure 5-8

When you want a deeper search of your travels, use the History pane. IE9 stores the URLs of pages you've visited, up until its history buffer was last purged. The searchable criteria for IE9's history are Web page URLs, contents of visited pages' titles, and when (what day) you visited.

1. **Click the white star icon in the upper-right corner.**

   This is also known as Favorites, and the star becomes yellow when you hover your mouse over it. The Favorites Center appears with lists of URLs, one of which is History.

2. **Click History.**

   On the History tab of the pane that opens is a grouping at the top of the list, set to View by Date.

3. **Choose a timeframe.**

   Every URL you visited during that timeframe is grouped by root domain name. For example, if you visited several pages on apple.com, they appear together under one heading.

4. **Click a domain name.**

   As Figure 5-9 shows, the titles of pages you visited appear below the domain name.

5. **Click a Web page.**

   IE9 reloads the contents of the URL that was recorded in History.

You're seeing the present state of the page, not a snapshot of how the page used to appear.

You can also search recorded pages by their site location rather than by time (click the top heading, and then click View by Site) or by specific criteria (click the top heading and then click Search History).

Favorites	Feeds	History

View By Date ▼

▦ 2 Weeks Ago
▦ Last Week
▦ Monday
▦ Tuesday
▦ Wednesday
▦ Thursday
▦ Friday
▦ Saturday

🔁 amazon (www.amazon.com)
🔁 apple (www.apple.com)
    🖼 Apple - iPod touch - Video calls, HD v...
    🖼 Apple - Play music and more on iPod.
🔁 barnesandnoble (www.barnesandnoble.c...

Figure 5-9

From time to time, to keep your machine running at top speed, you need to purge your History buffer.

With IE9 running, press Ctrl+Shift+Delete to bring up the Delete Browsing History dialog box shown in Figure 5-10.

The main category of remembered things that consume the most space on your local storage are Temporary Internet Files (the logos, photos, text citations, and graphical embellishments that fill every page you visit). The other entries here don't take up much space, but may be purged nonetheless to help reset your browser, especially if you notice behavior trouble.

LINGO

IE9 stores the contents of certain components of Web pages that it would otherwise have to reload from the Web so that it can recall those parts from storage when it needs to. One example of this is a Web site's bannerhead or logo, which often appears on multiple pages. The (unseen) storage area for these components is called the **history buffer**.

Leave the Preserve Favorites Website Data check box enabled to tell IE9 not to touch the records or contents of Web sites you record in your Favorites.

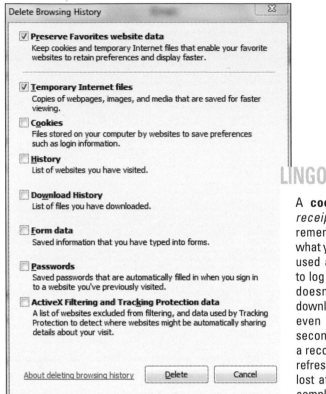

Figure 5-10

LINGO

A **cookie** is a kind of digital *receipt:* a Web site's way of remembering who you are and what you did last, especially if you used a username and password to log on. You see, a Web server doesn't "remember" that you downloaded pages from it before, even if it happened just a few seconds ago. It needs to look at a record of the last transaction to refresh its memory, which will be lost after the next transaction is completed, so hopefully it's stored another cookie on your system.

Marking, recalling, and managing Favorites

If you know how to use the Favorites sidebar in IE9, you won't get stuck using the History sidebar so often. The basic principle of Favorites is simple enough: If you're on a page you want to be revisit, make it a Favorite so that IE9 can remember its URL.

Because pages change, you can't always be assured what you see during your present visit is what you'll see during your next visit. History doesn't recall a Web page from memory or from IE9's cache; it just recalls the URL. So if you record a page for a news story and that story has been corrected, you'll see the correction when you click that recorded URL. Or if you record a page for an item that's on sale from an online retailer and the price changed since you recorded it as a Favorite, you'll see the changed price, not the original one.

Here's one way to mark a page as a Favorite:

1. **Click the star (the symbol for Favorites, upper-right).**

2. **In the pane that opens, click the Favorites tab (if necessary), and then click Add to Favorites. See Figure 5-11.**

   This brings up the Add a Favorite dialog box shown in Figure 5-12.

Figure 5-11

IE9 has already entered the title of the page as it appears in the title bar (actually, the tab) for the page. Depending on what the title reads, this may not be descriptive enough or too long, so you might want to change this.

Figure 5-12

Use folders to keep your Favorites organized:

- ✔ **Place the entry in a folder so it can be sorted by subject.** Choose the folder from the Create In list and then click the Add button.

- ✔ **Create a new folder to place the entry.** Click the New Folder button, and in the dialog box that appears, enter the Folder Name. Choose a folder in which the new folder will appear, if necessary, from the Create In list. Click the Create button to create the new folder and then click Add.

If you don't choose a folder but leave the list set at Favorites, the entry you create will appear next time in the Favorites list below all the folders, sorted in alphabetical order by Name

COURSEWORK

For more organizational help, use the Favorites editor. Click the star icon, click the down-arrow beside Add to Favorites, and choose Organize Favorites. From this dialog box, you can rename and delete an entry or a folder, or relocate an entry. If you delete a Favorites entry by right-clicking it in the Favorites list, it's moved to the Recycle Bin. When you delete it from the Organize Favorites dialog box, it is *not* moved to the Recycle Bin.

Calling up the page at one of your favorite URLs works like this:

1. **Click the Favorites star icon and then click the Favorites tab (if necessary) in the pane that opens.**

2. **If the name you're looking for is in a folder, click the folder's name.**

3. **Click the name of the page you want to load.**

   The Favorites pane disappears, and the most recent contents of the page at the URL will appear in the window.

You can also recall Favorites from a toolbar. Start by making sure you have the Favorites bar showing. Right-click any of the three icons along the top right. From the pop-up menu shown in Figure 5-13, choose Favorites Bar, which should put a check mark beside that command and turn on the feature.

Figure 5-13

In Figure 5-14, you can see what IE looks like with the Favorites and the Command bars showing (also available from the same menu).

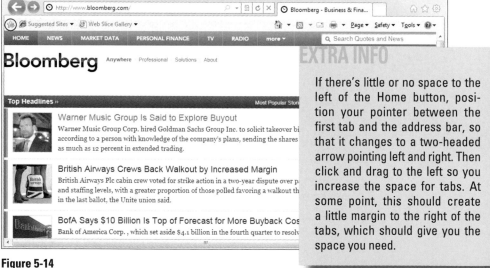

Figure 5-14

EXTRA INFO

If there's little or no space to the left of the Home button, position your pointer between the first tab and the address bar, so that it changes to a two-headed arrow pointing left and right. Then click and drag to the left so you increase the space for tabs. At some point, this should create a little margin to the right of the tabs, which should give you the space you need.

To add an address to the Favorites bar, save it in a Favorites bar folder, using the process just described. Even simpler, click the star + arrow button on the far left, as pointed out in Figure 5-14.

Working with multiple tabs

Tabs give you the option of having multiple Web pages open at once, without having to open multiple windows on your desktop.

Up to this point, you've been browsing within a single tab. When you click a hyperlink, the new page or new location opens up within that tab. You can open a new tab, though, to have more than one Web page open at once.

1. **Click the New Tab button (the empty document icon, on the far right of the set of tabs at the top of the window). See Figure 5-15.**

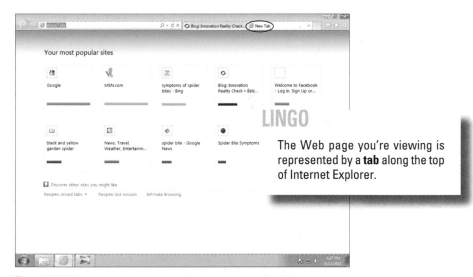

Figure 5-15

IE9 doesn't bring up your home page in each new tab, but a blank page instead.

2. **In the new tab that appears, type a Web address in the address bar and then press Enter.**

Your Web page opens in its own tab.

You move tabs around in the browser like you'd move tabbed folders in a filing cabinet:

✔ **To switch tabs:** Click the tab that you want to view, and it comes to the foreground.

✔ **To close a tab/Web page:** Click the Close button on its tab.

✓ **To rearrange your tabs:** Click and drag a tab to its new location. Then drop your tab in the place you want it and the other tabs make room for it.

✓ **To navigate tabs:** If you have more tabs than space, IE9 creates scroll tabs you can use to navigate left and right through your tabs. Or, as shown in Figure 5-16, hover over the IE9 "blue e" icon on the taskbar to see thumbnails of all your open tabs, or the title of each open tab in a vertical menu.

EXTRA INFO

When you have quite a few tabs open at once, IE9 tries to help you sort them out by tinting those with different Web site addresses using different shades. So when you have a few pages open from the same site, their tabs will be tinted with the same shade.

Figure 5-16

Clicking a tab brings up its contents in the IE9 window. The other tabs don't close, and their contents are undisturbed until you close them. Like tabs elsewhere in Windows, the active tab is the one to the front, with an "X" Close button.

COURSEWORK

Most regular Web users have a handful of sites they visit every day to check current events, do research, shop online, read mail, comment on the issues that affect them, and maybe play a game. Here's something to try: In IE9, create a Favorites folder for your "daily rounds": those places you go every day. Make a list of 12 places you're likely to frequent. If you need help finding out their URLs, use Google. Place seven of these items in your list in this Daily Rounds folder and five on IE9's Favorites toolbar. Then while you're purging IE9's memory buffer, set it up so that the components of your Daily Rounds Web sites are excluded from the purge.

E-Mailing Friends, Relatives, and Everyone on the Planet

The e-mail manager program that's a "part of Windows" now is actually two programs, with somewhat different profiles: Windows Live Hotmail is offered to you through your Web browser. You can use any Web browser, anyplace to access the e-mail accounts you set up to be accessed through Hotmail. To use Hotmail, you need the e-mail address you used to set up Windows Live Essentials (see Lesson 3), which may belong to the live.com domain or the hotmail.com domain (either of which Microsoft considers a "Windows Live e-mail address"), or actually to any e-mail server at all.

By contrast, Windows Live Mail is downloaded to you as part of Windows Live Essentials. It doesn't require you to use your Web browser, however. Live Mail is a Windows 7 program that works on its own. Although Live Mail prompts you to get a Windows Live e-mail address if you don't already have one, you don't have to. In fact, you can use a Gmail address or any e-mail server that recognizes either the widespread, global standard called Post Office Protocol (POP) or the somewhat prominent Internet Message Access Protocol (IMAP) used by Gmail.

Launch Live Mail from the Start menu. The first time you do this, you see a setup panel like the one in Figure 5-17.

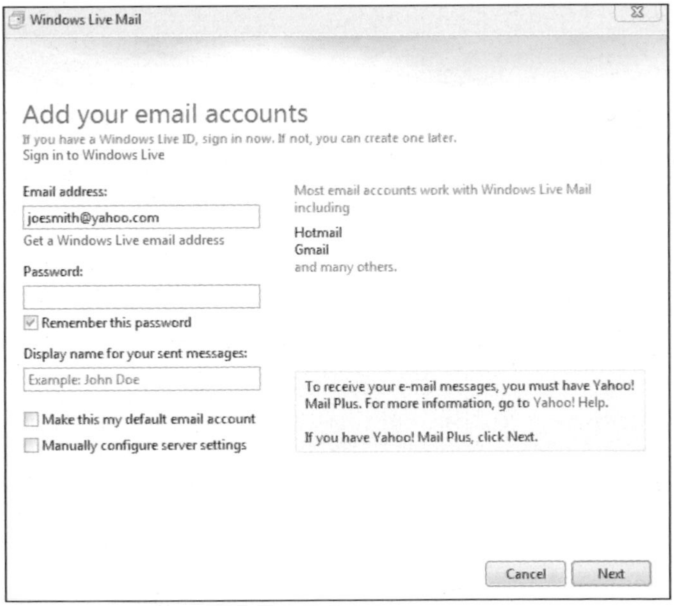

Figure 5-17

To configure Live Mail to use a live.com or hotmail.com account, enter your e-mail address, your password to log on to that account, and the name you want to use at the top of your messages sent to others. You don't need to select the Manually Configure Server Settings check box.

After Live Mail starts and you're officially welcomed, you see an application window that looks something like the one in Figure 5-18. Yes, the welcome message refers to Windows Live Hotmail.

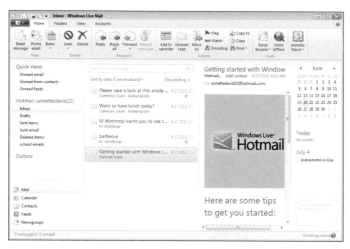

Figure 5-18

Adding one or more accounts

You might find it useful to set up several accounts: say, one for friends and family, one for co-workers, and one for newsletters.

The first e-mail account you entered when you launched Live Mail for the first time was automatically registered as your default account: that is, the account Live Mail uses to send messages in your name, unless you direct otherwise. When adding a new account to Live Mail, you can designate it as the default account instead. Here's how to add another account:

1. **In Live Mail, on the Accounts tab, click Email (in the New Account group).**

   You see the same setup panel shown in Figure 5-17.

2. **Type the account's complete e-mail address in the Email Address field.**

   Include your username, the @ character, and the domain name.

3. **Type the account's password in the Password field.**

4. **(Optional) To have Live Mail log on automatically using your password, select the Remember This Password check box.**

   As long as you're safely logging onto Windows 7 using your exclusive password, this should be a safe choice.

5. **Type how you want your name to display at the top of messages.**

6. **Select the Manually Configure Server Settings check box, and then click Next.**

In the Configure Server Settings dialog box that appears (see Figure 5-19), enter the following, from your e-mail provider:

✔ **Incoming mail protocol:** This is POP or IMAP.

✔ **Separate domain name addresses for the incoming and outgoing mail from your e-mail server:** These may be different. Outgoing mail uses only one protocol, Simple Mail Transfer Protocol (SMTP). Your incoming mail server address might be something like `pop.whatever.com`, and your outgoing server address might be something like `smtp.whatever.com`. On the other hand, both might be accessible through an address like `mail.whatever.com`.

> **EXTRA INFO**
>
> Google's Gmail uses IMAP protocol. Its incoming server address is `imap.gmail.com`, and its outgoing address is `smtp.gmail.com`. You log on using your full e-mail address, including the @ `gmail.com` part. IMAP for Gmail uses port 993, while SMTP uses port 587. Both directions require encrypted connection, and SMTP authentication is required.

✔ **Separate port numbers for incoming and outgoing servers:** Such servers reserve these numbers so that routers can identify messages in transit as e-mail, and give them certain priorities.

✔ **The separate encryption states for incoming and outgoing servers:** Some e-mail servers use encrypted sessions for added security, using the same Secure Sockets Layer (SSL) protocol employed by browsers like IE9. If you're using a secure server for either or both incoming or outgoing mail, select check the corresponding check boxes.

✔ **The authentication method for both servers, if they require one:** Usually if they don't use SSL, they're not going to use authentication either.

✔ **The username used to log on to your incoming e-mail server:** This is typically (not necessarily) the username portion of your e-mail address. Sometimes the server uses the entire address, complete with @ and domain name, as your logon name.

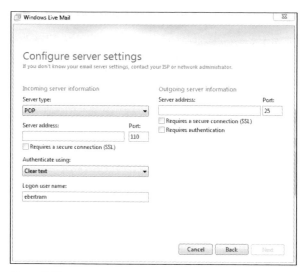

Figure 5-19

After you enter this info, click Next. And then when you see the message `Your email account was added.`, click Finish.

Reading messages

The main Windows Live Mail window (see Figure 5-20) holds four partitions: from left to right, mail categories, the message list, the contents pane for reading what's in the selected message, and a calendar.

To have Live Mail download messages from all your accounts, click the Send/ Receive button (of the Tools group of the Home tab). If you have multiple accounts, click the down-arrow on that button and then choose the account you want to download messages from.

Live Mail maintains separate inboxes for each e-mail account but one collective view of all unread e-mail in all accounts. When you click an e-mail message in the list, it becomes highlighted, and its contents are previewed in the pane to the right. To read a message in its own window, double-click that message, which then opens like in Figure 5-21.

Mail   Message list   Contents pane   Calendar

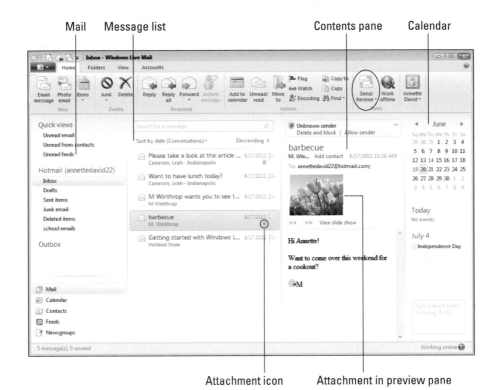

Attachment icon   Attachment in preview pane

Figure 5-20

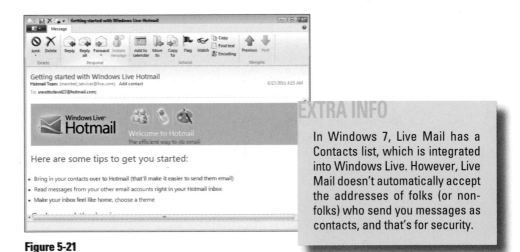

Figure 5-21

Lesson 5

Replying to and sending messages

When you're reading an open e-mail message, at the top of the window is the Ribbon, where you'll find the commands for doing things. Replying is one of them, so here's what you do:

✔ **Reply:** Click the Reply button, enter your response, and click Send. See Figure 5-22.

✔ **Reply All:** If that message was addressed to more folks than just yourself and you want to send your reply to them all, click Reply All, enter your response, and click Send.

✔ **Forward:** To just send along an existing message, click Forward, fill in the recipient's name(s) in the To field, and click Send.

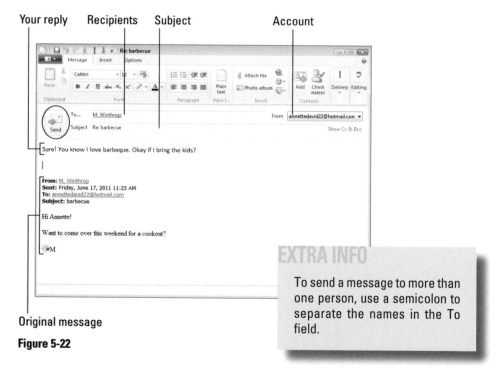

Figure 5-22

EXTRA INFO

To send a message to more than one person, use a semicolon to separate the names in the To field.

To create and send your own (new) message, start by clicking the Email Message button (Home tab, in the New group). In the new message window (shown in Figure 5-23), do the following:

1. **Enter the names and/or e-mail addresses of your recipients in the To field.**

2. **Type a description for your message in the Subject field.**

WARNING!

Some e-mail clients tend to filter out messages without a subject line.

3. **If you have more than one account, choose the account you want, in the From list.**

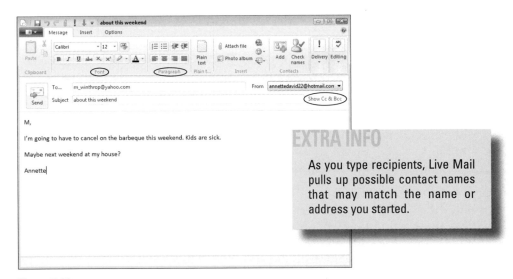

Figure 5-23

EXTRA INFO

As you type recipients, Live Mail pulls up possible contact names that may match the name or address you started.

4. **Enter your message.**

   Formatting tools (like bold, italic, and colors) are available on the Message tab in the Font and the Paragraph groups.

5. **Click Send.**

To bring up two more addressing fields, click the Show Cc & Bcc link:

- ✔ **Cc:** Carbon copy. Use this to include someone on your e-mail, but that person isn't a direct recipient.

- ✔ **Bcc:** Blind carbon copy. Use this when you don't want other recipients to know you're including this person.

Sending and receiving messages with attachments

When you receive an e-mail with an attachment, it shows up in your inbox with a paperclip icon; refer to Figure 5-20. When you open a message with an attachment, the attachment is clearly marked, as in the example in Figure 5-24, which shows a document attached.

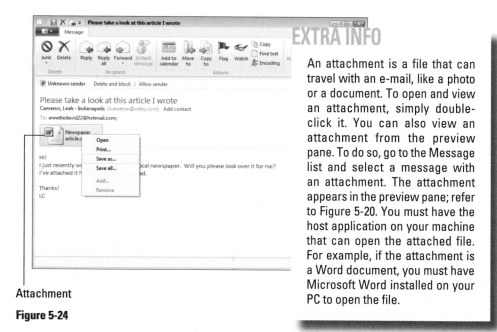

Attachment

Figure 5-24

EXTRA INFO

An attachment is a file that can travel with an e-mail, like a photo or a document. To open and view an attachment, simply double-click it. You can also view an attachment from the preview pane. To do so, go to the Message list and select a message with an attachment. The attachment appears in the preview pane; refer to Figure 5-20. You must have the host application on your machine that can open the attached file. For example, if the attachment is a Word document, you must have Microsoft Word installed on your PC to open the file.

WARNING!

Whether your recipients can receive attachments depends on the policies of their your-mail servers' administrators. Never send (or open) an executable (.exe) file. Also, some ISPs limit the size of attachments (often, 5 MB or 10 MB), so attaching a lot of photo files to one message isn't a great idea.

Here's how to detach and save the attachment(s) in a message:

1. **Right-click the attachment.**

2. **From the context menu that appears, choose Save As; refer to Figure 5-24.**

3. **In the Save Attachment As dialog box that opens (see Figure 5-25), choose where you want to save your file in the Documents library.**

Figure 5-25

4. **(Optional) Rename the file.**

5. **Click Save.**

Sending an attachment in a message is just as easy. Start with an open message window:

1. **Click the Insert tab and then click the Attach File button (see upcoming Figure 5-27).**

2. **In the Open dialog box that appears (see Figure 5-26), choose the file(s) you want to attach from the Documents library.**

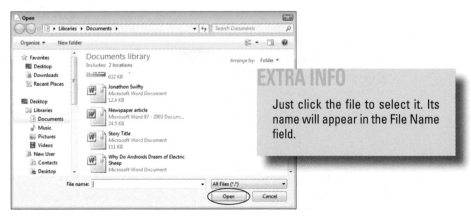

> **EXTRA INFO**
>
> Just click the file to select it. Its name will appear in the File Name field.

Figure 5-26

3. **Click the Open button.**

   The file is now attached, and your new message will show a paperclip icon as well as an icon of the attachment itself, its file name, and the file size. See Figure 5-27.

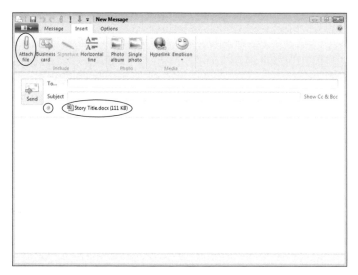

Figure 5-27

Wading through junk (and not junk) e-mail

When you receive a message in your inbox (or one of your inboxes) that you want to mark as junk, you can help "train" Live Mail to help you filter it through. When you get a piece of junk mail, highlight that message in the main window and then just click the Junk button, on the Home tab. The message gets moved to your Junk Email folder, as shown in Figure 5-28.

Now whenever you get an e-mail from the same sender or even an e-mail with the same subject, Windows Live Mail automatically sends that e-mail to the Junk Email folder, completely bypassing your Inbox.

Junk mail isn't automatically deleted. To permanently get rid of a piece of junk mail, select it in your Junk Email folder. Then click the Delete button on the Home tab, and it's gone forever. To empty the whole Junk Email folder, right-click the folder and then choose Empty 'Junk Email' Folder from the context menu. Check the contents of the folder first, though, to ensure good stuff isn't being filtered out before you empty it.

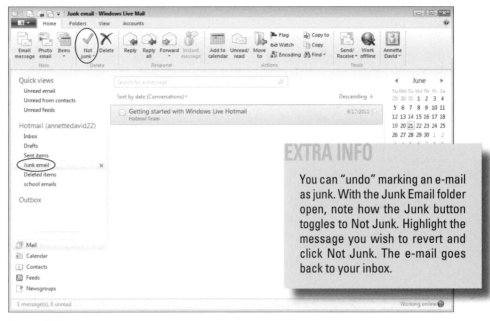

Figure 5-28

Another way to train Windows Live Mail about junk is to tell it what addresses are always — or never — acceptable. These become your Safe Senders and Blocked Senders lists.

1. **Click the down arrow for the Junk button.**

2. **From the drop-down menu that appears (see Figure 5-29), choose the Add Sender to Safe Sender List or Add Sender to Blocked Sender List option.**

To see your Blocked and Safer Senders lists, click the down arrow on the Junk button and choose Safety Options. The Safety Options dialog box opens (see Figure 5-30). To see your Safe Senders list, click the Safe Senders tab; to add an address to this list, click the Add button. Likewise, to see your Blocked Senders list, click the Blocked Senders tab; to add an address to this list, click the Add button.

Figure 5-29

EXTRA INFO

You can "undo" marking an e-mail as junk. With the Junk Email folder open, note how the Junk button toggles to Not Junk. Highlight the message you wish to revert and click Not Junk. The e-mail goes back to your inbox.

Figure 5-30

Sort messages into folders

Another way to keep your inbox tidy is to move older e-mails into folders. You can create as many folders as you need. Before you can move e-mails into folders, though, you have to create them.

1. On the Folders tab, click the New Folder button (see Figure 5-31).

Figure 5-31

2. **In the Create Folder dialog box that appears, type the name you want to give your folder in the Folder Name field.**

3. **Click OK.**

Your newly created folder is now listed in the left column under your Inbox.

 # Summing Up

Internet Explorer 9 is a Web client, which means its entire job is to collect components of data from a Web server. Pages are assembled in an IE9 tab and given a Web address (a URL).

Viewed on another level, a URL is a request for data. A server answers the client's request with an HTML page that happens to contain more URLs, which are more requests for data. Those URLs point to resources that the browser assembles, such as graphics and video, to produce a properly typeset page.

IE9 keeps track of the URLs of the pages you visit. When you recall those URLs from the history buffer, IE9 reloads the latest contents of those pages from the Web. Over time, that buffer can get hefty, so you need to purge it occasionally.

Windows Live Mail is the application that replaces Outlook Express and Windows Mail for Windows 7. This new application now manages the Contacts list, which is now *one* list (hooray!). You don't need an address in the live.com or hotmail.com domains to use Live Mail. In fact, if you want to be able to set up sorting rules for moving messages that meet certain criteria into designated folders, you can't use those rules with live.com or hotmail.com accounts, anyway.

Sending and receiving e-mail is pretty easy, as is creating and receiving attachments. You can even train Live Mail to help you filter junk mail. Another way to keep your inbox uncluttered is to use folders for your messages.

Know This Tech Talk

AutoComplete: A feature of some programs, including Internet Explorer, that can complete the rest of an entry in a form (such as Last Name) after you begin an entry that's recognized

cache: A storehouse, either in memory or on disk, of files and resources that forestalls the request of a more remote resource

executable file: A file whose binary content renders it capable of being executed like a program; an installation package is a common example of an executable file that may be downloaded from the Web

filter: Data used to restrict or exclude information from appearing in a list

HTML (HyperText Markup Language): The system of tagged instructions used to interrupt streams of text to instruct the interpreter of a Web browser as to its proper display and handling

HTTP (HyperText Transport Protocol): The network protocol referred to in most Web addresses that enables the exchange of data requests via hyperlink

HTTPS: The prefix for Web communications that have been encrypted, usually using Secure Sockets Layer(SSL)

InPrivate: A mode of Internet Explorer that intentionally disables recording of Web browsing history, to prevent others from detecting its content or purpose

port: A number attached to an Internet-delivered packet that designates the purpose of that packet, for programs such as e-mail clients and Web browsers

search engine: A Web service, such as Google or Bing, that retrieves hyperlinks for Web resources in response to queries

sidebar: A pane of a Web browser reserved for other functions, such as listing the contents of Favorites or the history buffer

SMTP (Simple Main Transfer Protocol): The most widely used means of communication for a client to send outgoing e-mail to a server

SSL (Secure Sockets Layer): A method for encrypting communication between the Web and e-mail clients and servers, and in so doing, ensuring the authenticity of the parties involved in the communication

Staying Safe and Secure

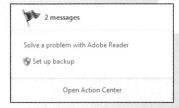

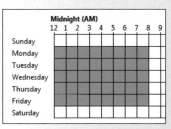

✔ Find out why it's important to set up a special account for something (not necessarily someone) called an "administrator," and why doing so protects everyone else.

✔ Learn to use Task Manager so you can regain control of your PC after some rogue application takes it for a ride.

✔ Take charge of your Windows System Updates so you know what's going into your system and when.

✔ Prevent programs you thought you trusted from having access to the Internet they don't need.

✔ Run a complete virus scan on your PC using an antivirus program that's orders of magnitude better than the one you got with Windows 7.

✔ Manage programs your kids and guests can use on your computer with their accounts and see what they're running and when.

This is the part of the course where you would expect to see the usual nonsense about how important security is in today's expanding technology-dependent world, blah-blah-blah. I know the truth. I know you well enough to know that you don't feel secure on your PC until it stops bugging you. So guess what? I'm going to talk about the thing that's been bugging everyone who uses Windows, right off the bat.

What Is User Account Control?

By now, there's a good chance that Windows 7 has interrupted you, dimmed the screen, and asked you for permission to do something you explicitly asked it to do — something that looks like the dialog box in Figure 6-1.

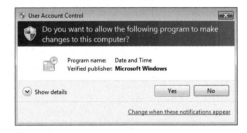

Note the title bar: User Account Control. What is that? In a nutshell, UAC keeps malicious programs that you can inadvertently or accidentally acquire from the Internet from running and ruining stuff. And although its pop-ups can be annoying, it helps keep your system clean.

Figure 6-1

How UAC works and why

The time-old assumption among operating system (OS) software developers is that the OS knows what it's doing, but people who use it are prone to mistakes. These developers created privilege levels instructing the OS to blindly permit anything that its own system software attempts to do while enabling it to deny something a human user might launch by mistake.

However, that was before the invention of computer viruses. It became insanely easy for a malicious user to create software that presents its credentials to the OS as another part of the OS prior to conducting some mischievous or destructive act, so developers changed their tune. They realized, thanks to viruses, that a human user is less likely to make something go wrong *by accident* than an unhuman, probably malicious, process is to make something go wrong *on purpose*.

And then the Web happened, and it became insanely easy to make a Web user download a program that ran with the user's credentials, making any malicious act perpetrated by the process on purpose look like something went wrong by accident. This gave a Microsoft security engineer this thought: What if every time something bad could happen, the PC halted the operating system long enough to ask the user whether this is really what he wants to happen? That's the inspiration for User Account Control — and the security checkpoints it created as a result.

REMEMBER

UAC works by obtaining administrator permission for certain actions that a standard user is about to perform. UAC creates a roadblock that only someone who can pass himself off as the administrator can cross.

LINGO

On any computer or network that uses multiple accounts, the **administrator** (admin) account has the least restrictive permissions, often no restrictions whatsoever.

Windows 7 tempered UAC somewhat by creating a new variable setting, whereby processes launched by you don't have to seek permission from you. If you're not bothered by UAC and you prefer maximum vigilance, you can turn this level back up. Or you can take the risk and turn it off entirely.

To change this setting, use a slider control in Action Center:

1. **Choose Start⇨Control Panel⇨Action Center.**

2. **In Action Center (see Figure 6-2), click Change User Account Control Settings (left pane).**

LINGO

Action Center lets you know when things need to be done with your computer. On the Action Center "tote board," you'll find messages that advise you of things you could or should do to improve the state of security.

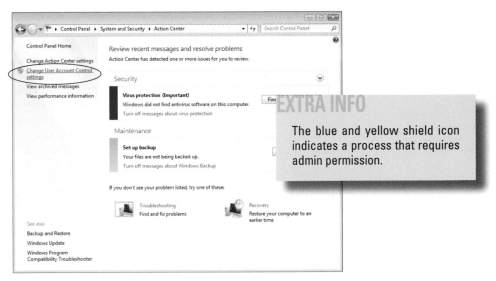

EXTRA INFO

The blue and yellow shield icon indicates a process that requires admin permission.

Figure 6-2

3. If UAC is set to Maximum, you may see the UAC permission prompt at this point. If prompted, click Yes.

4. In the User Account Control Settings dialog box that opens (see Figure 6-3), move the slider to choose the UAC option you want, and then click OK. These are your choices, from top to bottom:

- *Always Notify Me When....:* Prompts you every time Windows needs to perform an action requiring administrator permission. This includes such things as changing the system time, which is something you normally do by double-clicking the clock on the taskbar. (This setting works like Windows Vista.)

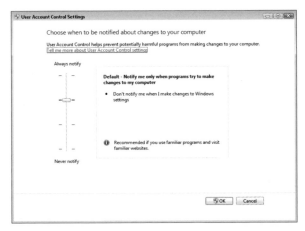

Figure 6-3

- *Notify Me Only When Programs Try to Make Changes to My Computer:* Prompts you only when a process other than one you just launched (like double-clicking the clock to change the time) starts to perform an action requiring admin permission. For instance, launching a program installer triggers one or more processes that require access to the file system, and thus admin permission. This is the default Windows 7 setting.

- *Notify Me Only When Programs...(Do Not Dim My Desktop):* Gives you the same prompts as the default setting except that it disarms the mechanism that halts running processes while the prompt is showing. If a malicious process can run while the prompt is showing, though, what's the point of the prompt? This pointless setting should be avoided.

- *Never Notify Me When...:* In effect, turns off UAC.

5. **Click Yes if prompted.**

Setting up an administrator account

If you're interested in maintaining the maximum amount of safety available, maybe even cranking up the UAC level to Always Notify Me, while at the same time leveling off the annoyance level, here's another certified way to strike a happy medium: Create a separate account on your PC (and on each PC in your homegroup) for an "administrator." (See Figure 6-4. I showed you how to do this in Lesson 1.) Let this "identity" be the one to install security programs, defragment the hard drive, run virus scans, and do PC maintenance.

EXTRA INFO

It's up to you; you could call this account "Head Honcho" if you want. I like to use "Control account." You see, there is an account in Windows called "Administrator," and it's none of the ones you see here. There are processes that might get confused if you create a second account with the same name. Of course, this doesn't have to be a different person. Let it be you, but when you need to do admin stuff, choose Start↷Switch User so you remain logged on as yourself.

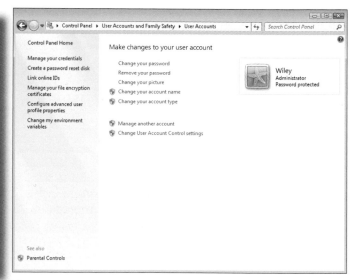

Figure 6-4

You should demote your own personal account, if necessary, to Standard User. The reason why is not to cripple your personal use of the computer: It won't. This simply disables your personal account's ability to do anything, accidental or otherwise, to folders belonging to other accounts. Creating the new admin account enables you to still be able to work with other users' folders when you need to, using an account that's much less likely to be tampered with.

WARNING!

As a security precaution for various esoteric reasons, you should name this administrator account something other than "Administrator."

After you create this "control account" (see Figure 6-5), log on to it using that account's password (from the logon screen), do the job you need to do there, log off that account, and return to your personal account.

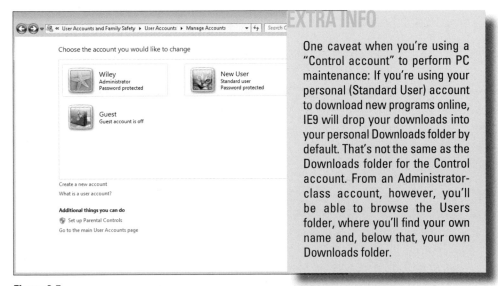

EXTRA INFO

One caveat when you're using a "Control account" to perform PC maintenance: If you're using your personal (Standard User) account to download new programs online, IE9 will drop your downloads into your personal Downloads folder by default. That's not the same as the Downloads folder for the Control account. From an Administrator-class account, however, you'll be able to browse the Users folder, where you'll find your own name and, below that, your own Downloads folder.

Figure 6-5

WARNING!

Some third-party (non-Microsoft) security programs are required to be run under an administrator account. That's silly because the limitations on the Standard User account are designed to make that class more secure. If you have one of these programs, or are forced to use one (say, your employer purchased it for you), you may have to make every account into an administrator-class account.

Taking Care of Everyday Maintenance

Face it: Programs crash. Browsers get stuck. Processes hang. Services slow down the system. Movies drag to a crawl. Applications fail to respond.

The truth about computing is that stuff fails. Windows knows that a program is running properly when it responds to a kind of "ping" sent to it, sometimes called a "heartbeat." If you've ever seen Not Responding show up in a window title bar, you know what I mean. It's the first serious indicator that something is wrong. So, you have to learn to roll with the punches when things get stuck. This section shows you the tools you use to make things that aren't working work again, or at least to get you out of being stuck.

For decades with PCs, we've used a key sequence to reset everything — the "three-finger salute" of Ctrl+Alt+Del. With Windows 7, the "salute" brings everything to a screeching halt and brings up the screen in Figure 6-6. One of the most useful functions on this screen is Cancel. If you have an application not responding to your input, clicking Cancel can bring it back.

EXTRA INFO

Pressing the key sequence Ctrl+Shift+Esc will bring up Task Manager directly, without you having to go through the "halt" screen in Figure 6-6. However, if Windows' own system processes are the cause of the problem, the system might not respond too quickly to Ctrl+Shift+Esc. Your PC's hardware is independently capable of sensing Ctrl+Alt+Del, and can literally shock Windows with a signal that its high-level processes — if they're still working — will respond to.

Figure 6-6

Getting familiar with Task Manager

If the old Cancel trick doesn't work, it's time to enlist Task Manager, which is the item listed just above Cancel in Figure 6-6. Task Manager (shown in Figure 6-7) gives you an opportunity to peek under the hood of Windows and maybe find out exactly what's causing the trouble. The thing you will use Task Manager to do most often is to stop misbehaving processes or applications that can't be stopped the normal way (that is, by invoking the Exit command, or by clicking the "X" Close button).

LINGO

In the context of Task Manager (not necessarily of the rest of Windows), a **task** is a running program.

Getting into Task Manager is a little dangerous in the sense that you can pull the plug on something that can make you lose what you're working on. It's possible, although not by accident, that you can halt a process that's doing something critical to your key storage device, such as installing new software, or defragmenting a hard drive. It's like lifting the hood of your car and just pulling on a belt that looks loose. Halting a process at this level could cause serious damage.

Figure 6-7

The first three tabs in Task Manager refer to the three categories of tasks in Windows. They're not necessarily exclusive from one another — for instance, an application is made up of processes. But here's what these classes mean.

✔ **Applications:** Programs represented on the taskbar. Anything that you launch from the Start menu, or that launches automatically at startup by virtue of being in the Startup folder of your Start menu, appears here.

✔ **Processes:** Running executable files, one or more of which may comprise an application at any one time. For example, although Internet Explorer is considered one application, a handful of separate instances of the process called `iexplore.exe` may run simultaneously.

✔ **Services:** The libraries and other executable files that provide the functionality to the operating system kernel. You can't stop the kernel from Task Manager, but you could always unplug the PC. Some of these services are device drivers, like the one that communicates with your printer or that syncs data with your smartphone or MP3 player. Unlike processes in Task Manager, not all services are running. Some are in a dormant state, or "stopped," until something you're doing requires them.

LINGO

The **kernel** is the nerve center of the operating system, and **services** are the software components to which certain functions have been delegated.

On the Processes tab shown in Figure 6-8, you can see three `iexplore.exe` processes and one instance of `wmplayer.exe` (the host process of WMP). In this snapshot, you can see (in the CPU column) that `wmplayer.exe` is registering an 02. That means that WMP really does have a heartbeat, using 2 percent of available CPU (processor) cycles.

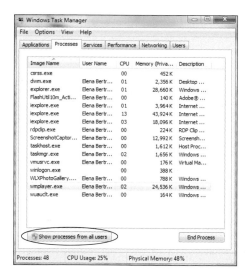

EXTRA INFO

All the processes in the list in Figure 6-8 are attributed to the current user, which is why the sum of all the numbers in the CPU column don't add up to 100. To see everything else that's going on in the system, click the Show Processes from All Users button.

Figure 6-8

However, the 00s beside the other processes don't mean these processes are dead. Task Manager updates this ticker a few times per second, and every so often, as `wmplayer.exe` slips back down to 00, one of the other processes — like `explorer.exe`, which runs the folder windows — jumps up to an 01.

To see the culprit that commands the most attention of the processor, click the CPU column header to sort the list in ascending order, as shown in Figure 6-9.

Figure 6-9

A 77 reading on the CPU count for System Idle Process is an indicator of a healthy Windows session. The one thing that's potentially worse than a process that's stuck at 00 is one that commands so much CPU time doing nothing of value that it pushes System Idle Process down the list, perhaps while registering Not Responding in the Applications list.

Removing a wayward application or process from memory

When deciding whether to terminate, or "kill," a process or application, consider the following:

- ✔ Do you have open documents that could potentially be lost if they're not saved?
- ✔ Does the process(es) belonging to the application show any kind of a heartbeat whatsoever over time, or are they settled way toward the bottom of the CPU list?

✔ Are you likely to be able to regain a normal Windows session after you killed the process, or would you be better off attempting a reboot instead?

WARNING!

For maximum safety, remove a process for your user name only. Typically, Windows prevents both a standard user and an administrative user from killing a process not assigned to that user. Technically, you should be prevented from killing a process registered to SYSTEM, LOCAL SERVICE, or NETWORK SERVICE.

EXTRA INFO

When a folder window ceases to function, the Start menu, desktop, and taskbar may no longer function properly. However, you can launch Task Manager and kill `explorer.exe`. When Windows sees that `explorer.exe` isn't running, it will try to relaunch it automatically to restore the desktop. If that's successful, then Windows can return to normal. If not, you might be stuck with having to try to use Ctrl+Alt+Del to log off and restart.

To remove the wayward application or the process from memory, start at the Applications tab.

1. **Click the application listed as Not Responding; refer to Figure 6-7.**

2. **Click the End Task button.**

   If Task Manager is successful, the application's window will disappear, and its listing will disappear from the Applications tab.

On the other hand, a particularly stubborn application might not give up quietly. The next step involves attempting a kind of "process-ectomy."

1. **Click the Processes tab in Task Manager.**

2. **Click the Image Name column if the list isn't yet sorted by the process name.**

TIP

You can tell which column the list is sorted by the arrow at the very top of the column heading.

3. **Click the process you need to stop.**

4. **Click the End Process button.**

5. **In the warning dialog box that appears (as shown in Figure 6-10), click the End Process button.**

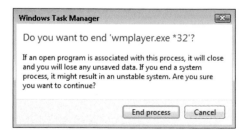

Figure 6-10

Windows discontinues the process' charter in memory, and assuming that the process is incapable of cleaning up after itself, the system tries as best it can to clear the process' local memory. The window for the process should disappear.

Seizing control of Windows Update

What's the big deal, you might have asked once or twice, about keeping Windows "up to date"? You've probably been bugged by a zillion of these little tooltips like the one in Figure 6-11.

Figure 6-11

These days, exposing your computer to the Internet is like exposing your house to a constant hailstorm. From time to time, you've got to send somebody up there to patch the roof. On the second Tuesday of every month, Microsoft releases a handful of "patches to its roof" — some to account for vulnerabilities exposed by malicious software, and others to account for deficiencies exposed by innocent users like yourself.

Of course, it's your decision whether to accept the update. On the one hand, you'd like to feel safe taking Microsoft's word for Windows' ability to patch itself automatically. On the other hand, sometimes the patch can be more of a problem than the issue it was designed to fix.

If you ever have a concern whether to accept an update, go online to the Microsoft TechNet Security Bulletin at

LINGO

A **patch** is a segment of binary code designed to replace one or more regions of a program known to cause security vulnerabilities or shown to be functionally defective.

```
http://www.microsoft.com/technet/security/current.aspx
```

to read a report as to the critical nature of a patch. If you haven't seen any warning messages on the Security Bulletin page, go ahead and accept the update.

TIP I recommend that you set Windows so that it *does* bug you about updates and patches rather than letting Windows handle them automatically.

Setting up Windows Update is a matter of wading through several warnings about what Microsoft wants you to do, and set it to do what *you* want it to do:

1. **Open Control Panel, click System and Security, then click Windows Update.**

2. **In the left pane of the Windows Update window, click Change Settings; see Figure 6-12.**

Figure 6-12

3. **In the Change Settings window shown in Figure 6-13, from the Important Updates drop-down menu, choose Check for Updates but Let Me Choose Whether to Download and Install them.**

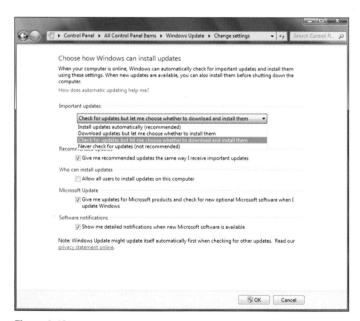

Figure 6-13

The green shield goes away.

4. **Tweak these settings if necessary:**

- *Give Me Recommended Updates the Same Way I Receive Important Updates:* Mark this check box.

A "recommended update" usually isn't a security patch, but may often be an updated device driver for your printer or network adapter, or an added feature to Windows Media Player. It's good to be informed that they're available.

- *Allow All Users to Install Updates on This Computer:* Clear this check box.

The whole point of making some people, including yourself, "standard users" is so that remote processes can't do unwarranted things with your account . . . like applying system patches.

- *Give Me Updates for Microsoft Products....:* Go for it.

This way, Windows can download security updates for Word, Excel, and Outlook in the same batch with Windows.

- *Show Me Detailed Notifications When New Microsoft Software Is Available:* Go for this one, too.

It's good to get the full report rather than the usual, "New updates are available," especially if there's a warning about one of the latest updates that you may want to hold off on deploying.

5. **Click OK.**

Almost done.

1. **Choose Start⇨Control Panel. Then from the Control Panel window, click System and Security, followed by Action Center.**

2. **In the Security section at the top of Action Center (click the down arrow to expand it, if necessary), click the Turn Off Messages about Windows Update link. See Figure 6-14.**

This does *not* turn off notifications about the existence of updates and patches for you to download but just tells Action Center to stop bugging you.

Installing updates now requires more personal attention from you. You get to see the complete report about each item that Microsoft makes available. And you use your own judgment about whether it gets downloaded onto your computer.

WARNING!

Never let anything download and install itself automatically on your computer. Whether a Windows patch from Microsoft, a replacement for Flash from Adobe, an update to Java from Oracle, or an upgrade to iTunes from Apple, don't open the back door for automatic updates.

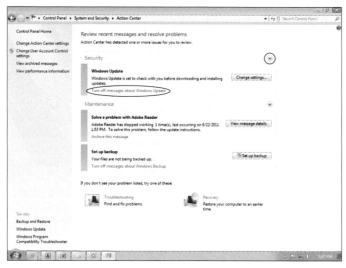

Figure 6-14

Applying updates judiciously

If you miss an update tooltip reminder, Windows will leave this notice open in the notifications area when updates become available, as shown in Figure 6-15. You might have to open the hidden notifications box to see it.

Figure 6-15

TIP

Although Windows says you can go about your work while the updates process is going on, be prepared to reboot your system as soon as the last patch has been grafted on.

1. **Click the New Updates Are Available icon in the notifications area.**

   In the Windows Update panel that appears (see Figure 6-16), you can read how many important and optional updates are available.

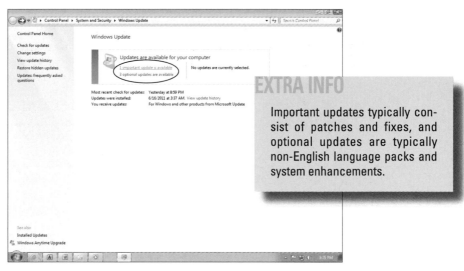

Figure 6-16

2. **Click the Important Update(s) Is (Are) Available link to bring up the Select Updates to Install window; see Figure 6-17.**

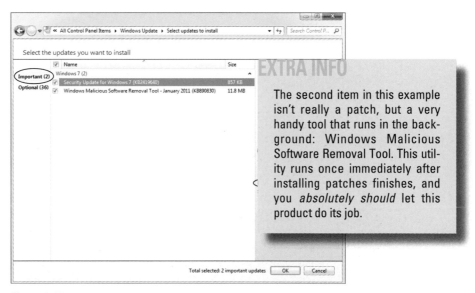

Figure 6-17

EXTRA INFO

Important updates typically consist of patches and fixes, and optional updates are typically non-English language packs and system enhancements.

EXTRA INFO

The second item in this example isn't really a patch, but a very handy tool that runs in the background: Windows Malicious Software Removal Tool. This utility runs once immediately after installing patches finishes, and you *absolutely should* let this product do its job.

3. **Click each item in the list and read the report on the right.**

   Sometimes what appears on the right pane is boilerplate text, like the example in Figure 6-17. In such a case, click the More Information link to be taken to a specific, very detailed Web page about the patch.

4. **Clear the check mark for any item you're not reasonably certain will be safe, and select any other item of which you're certain.**

5. **Click Optional (left pane) and review the choices that appear. See Figure 6-18.**

TIP

The Optional list typically contains things like language packs, updates to device drivers that are working fairly well already, and additions to Windows that aren't meant to replace something that's malfunctioning or vulnerable.

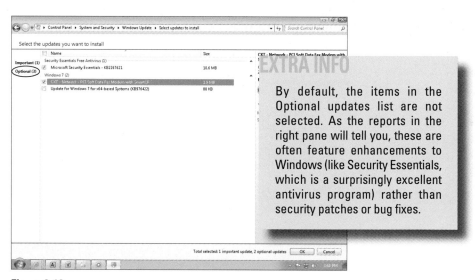

By default, the items in the Optional updates list are not selected. As the reports in the right pane will tell you, these are often feature enhancements to Windows (like Security Essentials, which is a surprisingly excellent antivirus program) rather than security patches or bug fixes.

Figure 6-18

6. **Select the check box for any optional item you feel safe installing or adding and then click OK.**

7. **Back in the Windows Update window, click the Install Updates button (see Figure 6-19).**

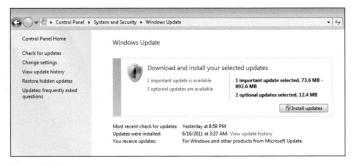

Figure 6-19

If you see a license screen like Figure 6-20 — especially if you're installing the Malicious Software Removal tool for the first time — just select the I Accept the License Terms radio button and then click Finish.

Figure 6-20

Windows shows you a downloading progress screen although it may appear only briefly before minimizing itself to the notifications area. Just click the tooltip there to bring it back.

8. **If prompted, save and close your other work and then click Restart Now.**

Not all security updates require a system restart, so when you see the message with the green shield, The updates were successfully installed, but a Restart Now button doesn't appear, just click Close to exit Windows Update.

Uninstalling faulty updates

Someday, you may need to uninstall an update. Yes, updates are presented as the first line of defense against bad software. But in addition to all the malicious software in the world is a treasure trove of benevolent software that simply has no clue about its incompatibility with other benevolent software. In simple terms, sometimes all the pieces just don't fit.

Here's what to look for: Watch how your computer acts within the first 48 hours after you install an update. If your computer severely misbehaves — for instance, it shuts down, or now applications won't start, or dialog boxes report problems — you can be pretty sure that the update is the culprit. Outside that 48-hour window, however, do *not* uninstall the update without first checking your other options: running a complete virus scan, uninstalling any third-party applications or programs you installed during the same period, and isolating any videos you downloaded during that time.

GO ONLINE

Take a minute to go read about the update. The license plate–like number beside each update to Windows, the one that starts with a KB (see Figure 6-21), is something you can use to look up more information about that update and what it purports to fix, from both Microsoft and other sources. It stands for "Knowledge Base," and refers to Microsoft's original system for cataloguing system changes, dating back to the 1980s. Enter this number into a search engine, and you're likely to find links to Microsoft and outside sources. This will help you judge whether an update has been found "in the field" (that is, outside Microsoft) to be problematic. Usually, a lack of third-party information on a knowledge base topic is a good sign.

> **Security Update for Windows 7 (KB2419640)**
>
> A security issue has been identified that could allow an unauthenticated remote attacker to compromise your system and gain control over it. You can help protect your system by installing this update from Microsoft. After you install this update, you may have to restart your system.
>
> **Published:** 1/11/2011

Figure 6-21

If you believe you need to uninstall an update, here's what you do:

1. **Open Control Panel and navigate to the Programs and Features window.**

2. **Click the View Installed Updates link in the left pane.**

   Windows presents that list in chronological order, newest items first, as shown in Figure 6-22. Updates to the operating system appear in the Microsoft Windows group.

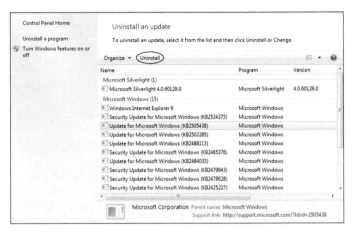

Figure 6-22

3. **In the history list of installed updates that appears, choose the update you need to uninstall.**

   If the update can be uninstalled — and most can — the Uninstall button appears in the command bar atop the list. If the update cannot be uninstalled, this button won't appear.

4. **Click the Uninstall button, and when you see a prompt asking you whether you're sure, click Yes.**

   You'll see a progress bar, and then the update disappears from the list. If prompted to restart your computer, close your work and click the Restart Now button.

After an update is uninstalled, Windows Update is likely to notice its absence, prompting you to put it back. It's your job to recognize its reappearance in later updates lists (it'll probably have an earlier release date than the others) and decide whether to try installing it again.

Backing up data

The capacities of today's hard drives are measured in terabytes (TB), or *trillions* of characters. If you're wondering how you can possibly back up trillions of characters, the good news is that you don't have to. The only things on your PC that truly matter, that would genuinely hurt you if you lost them, are your personal and work documents, family pictures, things you create with applications, and perhaps data generated by long-term games that saves your level and progress. If you lose Windows, big deal. Today, replacing a hard drive and reinstalling Windows is literally about as expensive, and about as simple, as filling up your tank with gas.

Among the many things Windows makes a point to gently bug you about until you resolve the matter is a decision on a backup strategy. For instance, Action Center puts a red "X" next to its white flag (ironic logo for a security program). When you click that flag, you see a message like in Figure 6-23.

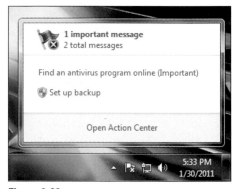

Windows comes with a convenient backup utility, appropriately called Windows Backup. To make a usable snapshot or image of your whole system disk, though, you really need

Figure 6-23

two hard disks — and you probably don't have two or three of them lying around. You could go out and buy an external hard drive.

So, backing up your Windows system image is nice, if you can do it. A more important job for you is to run a regular backup of the data and documents that you produce every day. Here's how you set up Windows Backup for that:

1. **Click the white flag in the notifications area.**

   If you've never used Windows Backup, Action Center will know this and nudge you about it.

2. **Click Set Up Backup in the pop-up menu that appears; refer to Figure 6-23.**

   Windows Backup assesses how much available storage space you have, and then shows you (in the Set Up Backup window; see Figure 6-24) a list of available storage devices for use in the backup process, including optical discs, flash memory, and external hard drives.

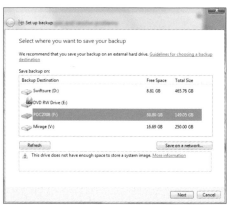

3. **Choose your backup device, under Backup Destination.**

Figure 6-24

4. **Click Next even if Windows Backup complains because the device you chose doesn't have enough storage space on it to do everything Windows wants to do.**

5. **In the first What Do You Want to Back Up? window that appears, select the Let Me Choose radio button and then click Next.**

6. **In the second What Do You Want to Back Up? window, select the check boxes of available libraries and folders you want; see Figure 6-25. Then click Next.**

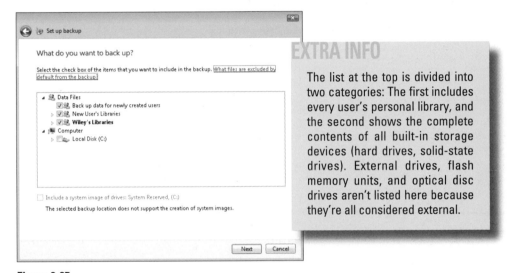

EXTRA INFO

The list at the top is divided into two categories: The first includes every user's personal library, and the second shows the complete contents of all built-in storage devices (hard drives, solid-state drives). External drives, flash memory units, and optical disc drives aren't listed here because they're all considered external.

Figure 6-25

To make a regular backup of just everyone's work files, go into each user's Libraries list and choose Documents Library.

WARNING!

Unless you can accommodate a snapshot of your system disk in the backup, leave the Include a System Image of Drives check box clear.

7. **In the Review Your Backup Settings window that appears (see Figure 6-26), set up the time(s) when backup takes place.**

TIP

You probably don't want to schedule running a backup while you're working, but if you opt for night, remember which night so you don't shut down your PC. And if you're backing up files to a DVD, like in Figure 6-26, make sure you're not backing up more than four gigabytes (4 GB) of data (because you'd need to change discs, which you can't do when you're not next to your PC), and that you have a blank DVD in your drive.

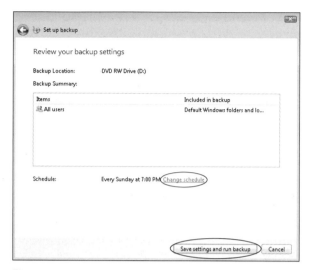

Figure 6-26

    a. Click the Change Schedule link.

    b. In the next window that opens (see Figure 6-27), set how often, the day of the week, and at what time.

    c. Click OK.

Figure 6-27

8. **Back at the previous dialog box (refer to Figure 6-26), no matter what backup period you chose, Windows Backup will want to start its first backup now, so click the Save Settings and Run Backup button.**

You'll see a progress window, and this same panel comes up when Windows Backup launches itself as you've designated.

Setting Up Security and IE9's Protections

To keep your PC as safe as possible from harmful intrusions (read: *malware*) Windows 7 ships with some anti-malware tools, and Microsoft offers a few others for free. The relative efficiency of these tools ranges from barely sufficient to surprisingly excellent. You may decide to substitute a commercial product in place of some or all these tools, and in a way, Microsoft is okay with that. Here's what you get, and what you can get:

- **Windows Firewall:** A checkpoint of sorts for software that tries to access the Internet outside your local network. It maintains a list of programs that have attempted to access the Internet since it was installed, and checks off those programs that are allowed access (Internet Explorer, obviously, yes). Other programs are blocked by default, and new programs get blocked until you say otherwise.

- **Windows Defender:** An anti-malware package that focuses on the types of stealth programs you can unknowingly download using your Web browser: perhaps not viruses *per se,* but hidden programs (or even services) that run in the background and send information without your permission or knowledge to a clandestine source.

- **Microsoft Security Essentials (SE):** A very good antivirus program, especially considering that it's free. After it's installed, it disengages Windows Defender and takes over its duties. In addition to studying the signatures of files in the system, SE tracks

LINGO

I think of **malware** as any software that tries to get you or your PC to do something you don't want to do, or turn over some private information.

LINGO

In Lesson 4, I talk a lot about **firewalls**, and in that context, I was referring to a device that listens to Internet traffic and only lets certain classes in or out. A software-based firewall, such as **Windows Firewall**, is not a substitute for one of these firewall devices, but it has a similar purpose. It monitors the Internet usage of programs in Windows, and can block Internet access from programs it doesn't yet recognize or that you haven't yet cleared.

the behavior of running applications, services, and libraries, looking deep within the system for programs that lurk in odd places, or appear to be setting up possible pitfalls such as stack overflows. So SE can detect a virus that it's never seen before, or perhaps that no one else has seen before — and then communicate that information over a network operated by Microsoft.

EXTRA INFO

A majority of malware packages detected and erased by antivirus programs today aren't actually viruses at all. Some aren't created with technically malicious intent although users still manage to acquire them without detection. Many are so-called "behavior tracking programs" crafted by Web analysis firms, and used by Web sites to determine where users go when they visit those sites, how long they stay there, and how soon they leave. By volume, there may be more of this class of malware in the field than malicious viruses.

Using Windows Firewall

The one real function that Windows Firewall (WF) performs to any appreciable degree is blocking access to the Internet from non-allowed and unknown programs. It compiles a whitelist of approved programs, starting with the obvious ones like Internet Explorer, and including newly installed programs that introduce themselves to WF during installation. This formal introduction process results in WF granting new programs a perpetual permit to cross the checkpoint.

Windows Firewall isn't the most effective program, though. A malicious application can use an already permitted service to communicate with the Internet, getting past the checkpoint.

You'll recall from Lesson 5 that Windows networking uses three separate profiles: home, office, and public. WF was created during a time when there were only two sets of policies, not three, so it can block certain programs when you're logged onto a Public network, and allow them when you're at home or at work (Private).

LINGO

A **blacklist** is any kind of list of items that are disallowed. When a security program uses a blacklist, its default policy must therefore be to allow, by default, anything not on the list to proceed normally. That's not very effective if the program doesn't know what not to trust. A stronger security program uses the reverse — a **whitelist** — and it's much less trusting. By default, it disallows behavior except for specifically cleared items on the whitelist. A relatively effective firewall is one that allows no traffic except for specific, whitelisted exceptions.

GO ONLINE

Some respectable Windows Firewall alternatives include

✔ **Comodo Firewall:** http://www.comodo.com/home/internet-security/firewall.php

✔ **PC Tools Firewall Plus:** http://www.pctools.com/firewall

✔ **ZoneAlarm Free Firewall:** http://www.zonealarm.com/security/en-us/ anti-virus-spyware-free-download.htm

When WF encounters a new program like this not on the list, you can set WF to allow it. Select the Private Networks or Public Networks check box and then click the Allow Access button. See Figure 6-28. For instance, you might not want certain instant messaging programs to be accessible or have access through public networks. Or if you don't recognize this program, you can retain WF's block on the program by clicking Cancel.

Figure 6-28

Because programs can register themselves with WF to get on the whitelist, you may find an application that slipped through without you knowing it. To be frank, the easiest way to solve this little problem is to *uninstall the application*. However, there may be some applications that you really do need for other purposes but that don't need Internet access (like to stream ads) even though they keep asking for it. You don't want to uninstall these apps, but you don't need them feeding you advertising, either.

The most effective way to handle this problem is to remove it from the whitelist:

1. **Choose Start➪Control Panel➪System and Security➪Windows Firewall.**

2. **Click the Allow a Program or Feature through Windows Firewall link (left pane); see Figure 6-29.**

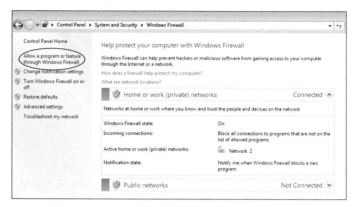

Figure 6-29

3. **In the whitelist that comes up (see Figure 6-30), click the Change Settings button.**

The items on the whitelist without check marks are disallowed.

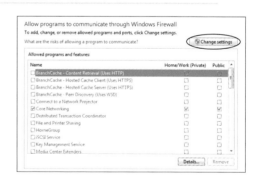

4. **Click the program that you don't want to grant network access and then click the Remove button.**

5. **When WF verifies that you want to proceed, click Yes.**

6. **Click OK, and then click Close to dismiss Windows Firewall.**

Figure 6-30

The next time the application requests Internet access from your network services, you'll see a warning message. Just click Cancel. If everything's working as it should, you shouldn't be asked again, and WF should disallow access to the app. The app may very well reappear on WF's whitelist, but it should be disallowed. (I say "should" because I've seen instances where an app got Internet access, anyway.)

Installing Security Essentials

Although the preloaded Windows Defender has some characteristics of a full antivirus package, it's not ideal. Microsoft offers a free replacement — Security Essentials — that's superior in every critical respect, and is installs just like a regular Windows update patch. I recommend switching to Security Essentials.

EXTRA INFO

Programs that you'll find (often unchecked) on the Windows Firewall whitelist fall into two categories:

Windows services that are expressly disallowed from having access until the features associated with them are officially installed, such as Connect to a Network Projector.

Programs that got access before but that you've unchecked from the Home/Work (Private) and Public columns.

Find the installation package for Security Essentials tucked on the Optional tab (left pane) of Windows Update, in the Security Essentials Free Antivirus section. Select this check box and click OK. In the Windows Update window that appears, click the Install Updates button. See Figure 6-31.

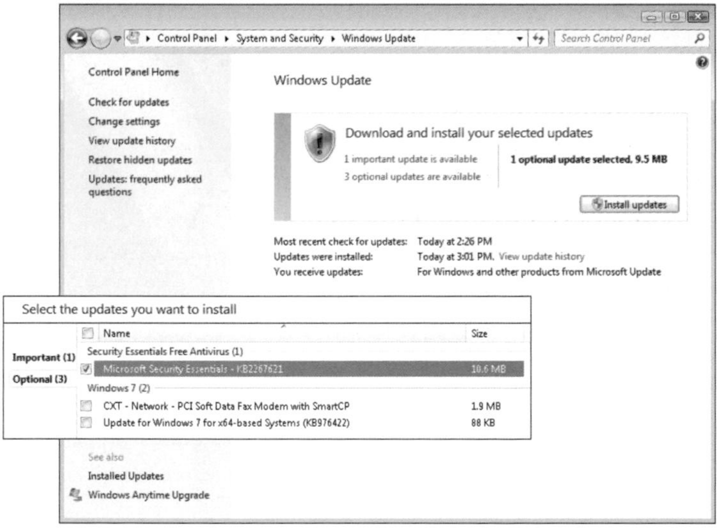

Figure 6-31

Look closely for the pop-up window in Figure 6-32, which might get tucked away as a minimized window on the taskbar. To start the installation process, click Next, followed by I Accept, then Install. Installation should take about a minute, and SE will tell you whether you need to restart your PC.

Figure 6-32

TIP

If you do have to reboot, SE may not pick up where it left off. You'll find it on the Start menu; click Microsoft Security Essentials to launch it.

LINGO

When you download SE using Windows Update, it creates a restore point after the download, but prior to the file-copying process. A **restore point** is a recording of the status of the PC at the current point in time.

SE will ask to scan your computer, and you should, so click Finish. SE begins by downloading the latest set of malware definitions. The definitions for Defender and for Security Essentials are different, so if you've downloaded Defender definitions before, they won't be used here.

When the scanning process begins, SE looks like Figure 6-33. The Quick Scan investigates the contents of memory and the most common locations for programs and services to be stored: Windows home and system folders, and the Program Files folder.

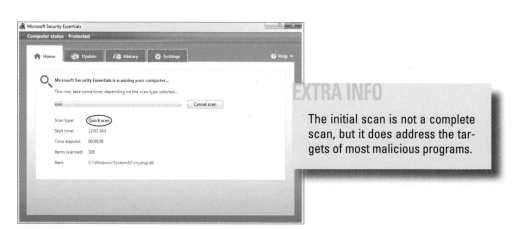

EXTRA INFO

The initial scan is not a complete scan, but it does address the targets of most malicious programs.

Figure 6-33

Security Essentials is now set to scan the contents of every file that's written to, or read from, your local storage. Everything you download, save, and open in another application passes through SE.

Using a virus scan to quarantine and remove a suspect file

When Security Essentials finds a potential threat, you'll immediately see the warning in the notifications area, as shown in Figure 6-34.

Figure 6-34

SE is one of the few Windows programs designed to act if it doesn't receive a response from you. This is a safety feature to protect your system, including if you happen to have stepped away from it. For a severe level threat, Windows 7's typical recommended action is Remove. If you want to investigate the file in question or a specific diagnosis of the virus, you'll want to stop SE from applying its default and automatic Remove action.

If you click the Clean Computer button, you're be telling SE to go ahead and do what it thinks best. That's not always optimal, though, because SE might think that an innocuous file is as a virus — for example, a compressed attachment to an e-mail message, such as a ZIP file. That's not likely, so here's a better route:

1. **Click the Show Details link in the Security Essentials notification box.**

2. **In the more descriptive dialog box window that opens, click the Show Details link.**

   Now you can see the details (as in Figure 6-35) for a more complete description of the class of malware you're (probably) dealing with, and the full scope of the problem.

3. **Choose whether to quarantine or remove the file in question.**

   • *Quarantine:* From the Recommended Action drop-down list, choose Quarantine. Then click the Apply Actions button.

LINGO

Quarantining a file allows it to continue to exist in a secure location, invisible to the regular file system as well as to the homegroup and local network. There, the file cannot be opened or executed, though. If you find the diagnosis to be false, you can go back into SE, clear the quarantine, and restore the file.

Figure 6-35

The red warning of impending doom is replaced by a green banner of honor.

- *Remove:* If you're convinced the suspect malware has been properly diagnosed, choose Remove from the Recommended Action drop-down menu and then click the Apply Actions button.

4. Click Close.

A quarantined file can be innocent. Quarantining a file gives you an opportunity to research SE's. To do your homework, choose Quarantine from the Recommended Action drop-down list. Click the Get More Information about This Item link to go to the Microsoft Malware Protection Center. Then you can safely choose to grant the file a reprieve or destroy it. Here's how you implement that choice:

EXTRA INFO

The exception to quarantining is a compressed file, such as a ZIP file. Although SE does suspend the suspect element in the ZIP file from being executed or opened, it doesn't move the ZIP file into a protected folder, so you can't restore the quarantined portion of a ZIP file.

1. Click the Security Essentials icon (lower right, notifications area).

When your computer is safe and all malware is either quarantined or blasted to bits, this icon is a green fortress wall with a flag up top and a check mark in the middle. See the top of Figure 6-36.

2. Click Open (also lower right, notifications area), as shown in the bottom of Figure 6-36.

3. On the History tab (shown in Figure 6-37), select the Quarantined Items Only radio button.

The History list shows all the files that SE identified as potential malware either since the program was installed, or since you last cleared SE's history buffer.

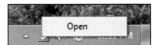

Figure 6-36

Figure 6-37

Now you see only the complete files placed under quarantine. Remember that ZIP files and portions of them are excluded.

4. **Check the box beside the quarantined file for which you've reached a verdict.**

5. **To delete the file, click Remove; or to restore the file, click Restore.**

6. **Click Yes if prompted.**

Keep out what you don't want in

Pop-up windows are a convenient, and often more visible, method for advertisers to make their messages more obvious to readers. About the only way to combat these little devices effectively is to instruct the Web browser not to open any pop-up windows, either through the ordinary methods or the lesser-known, sneakier methods. And indeed, that's what IE9 is designed to do: From moment one, its internal pop-up blocker diligently denies sites the ability to open external windows.

The problem is that not all pop-up windows are ads. Quite a few services, including Windows Live, pop up a window for logins and passwords. And countless legitimate online games are played in their own windows. So it's up to you to tell IE9 which pop-ups are legitimate and not to interfere with them.

1. **From the IE9 Command bar, choose Tools⇨Pop-up Blocker⇨Pop-up Blocker Settings. See Figure 6-38.**

Figure 6-38

If the IE9 Command bar isn't showing, right-click the top frame of the window, and choose Command Bar from the context menu.

2. **In the Pop-up Blocker Settings dialog box that appears (see Figure 6-39), type the URL you want in the Address of Website to Allow field and then click the Add button.**

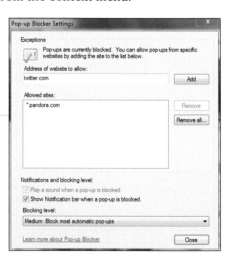

Strip the URL down to its most basic domain name.

The domain name appears in the Allowed Sites list, prefixed by an asterisk to denote that all subdomains are allowed as well.

Figure 6-39

3. **Click the Close button.**

Cookies, in the context of Web browsing, are bits of data that Web sites store on your computer in order to maintain the illusion of a connection between you and a Web site. A cookie is a Web site's way of remembering who you are and what you did last, especially if you used a username and password to log in. Not for lack of courtesy, a Web site does not clean up its cookie crumbs after itself. As a result, your browser can acquire literally hundreds of so-called *third-party cookies* deposited by servers you never thought you visited.

EXTRA INFO

Many of the world's least-wanted third-party cookies originate from a mere handful of sources. Security Essentials treats those sources the same way it treats the sources of other malware, so it suspends these cookies the way it suspends viruses.

Here's how to block cookies you don't want while allowing those that help you use the Web:

1. **Click the Gears icon in IE9, and from the pop-up menu, choose Internet Options.**
2. **On the Internet Options dialog box that appears, click the Privacy tab; see Figure 6-40.**
3. **Ignore the slider scale. Click the Advanced button.**
4. **In the Advanced Privacy Setting dialog box that appears, select the Override Automatic Cookie Handling check box; see Figure 6-41.**
5. **In the Third-Party Cookies section, select the Block radio button.**

   This makes IE9 reject all cookies whose origins are other than the Web site. If you opt for Prompt, you can make exceptions. The first time IE9 receives a cookie-saving request from a third-party

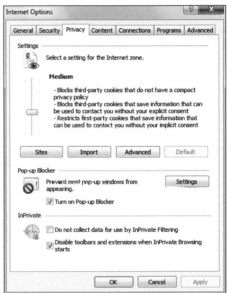

Figure 6-40

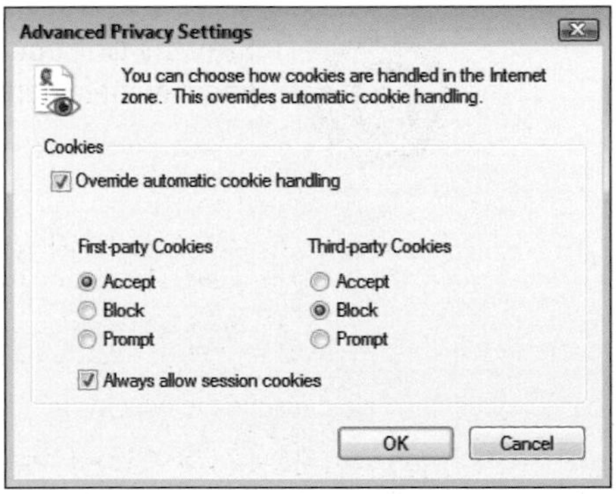

Figure 6-41

source (usually either an advertising service or an analytics service that measures traffic), you'll see a prompt like the one in Figure 6-42.

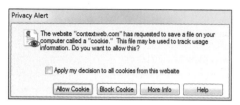

Figure 6-42

6. **To ensure that IE9 stores all cookies originating from the Web site pertaining to session state, select the Always Allow Session Cookies check box; refer to Figure 6-41.**

7. **Click OK, and then click OK again to close the Internet Options dialog box.**

Managing How Your Kids Use the PC

Microsoft markets its Windows Server operating systems on the basis of how they enable administrators to enforce the policies of their offices, businesses, and employers. Well, you have policies, too. You want to be able to restrict certain particular members of your household (often the smaller ones) from using certain programs, or from using the PC too late at night. Windows 7 gives you three specific "home policy" controls geared toward limiting how and/or when certain users can use the PC:

- ✔ Enforcing log-off times and time limits

- ✔ Restricting use of specific applications

- ✔ Limiting game play to titles rated for particular age groups

If you're an account holder on Windows Live, you can add a few more functions to this list, pertaining to their use of the IE9 Web browser: You can restrict the Web sites your kids visit, and create detailed logs that report on their activities for the sites you do allow them to visit.

You adjust these settings in Parental Controls, via Control Panel⟳User Accounts and Family Safety. There, click the Set Up Parental Controls for Any User link. Like the User Accounts dialog box, Parental Controls (see Figure 6-43) shows you a list of all the active accounts, even though individuals listed as Administrator cannot be treated like a child, as it were. You can deploy Parental Controls only on Standard users, not administrators.

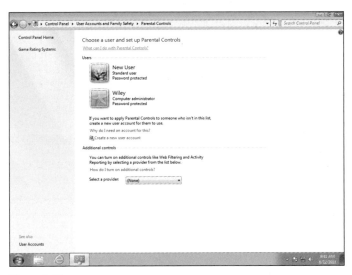

Figure 6-43

Setting strict time limits

When time limits are set for an account, Windows warns the user when that limit is near. After a bit, it effectively locks down the system, returning the system to the logon screen. The user is still logged on, just suspended until the restriction period expires. Rebooting and logging back on makes Windows responds, "Your account has time restrictions that prevent you from logging on at this time. Please check back later."

Here's how to set up time limits for a user:

1. **In Parental Controls, click the account you wish to limit.**

2. **In the User Controls window that appears (see Figure 6-44), select the On, Enforce Current Settings radio button, and then click the Time Limits link.**

   The dialog box becomes a calendar grid — a kind of whiteboard, where each box in the grid represents an hour of time on a weekly calendar. See Figure 6-45.

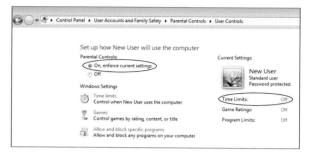

Figure 6-44

3. **Click and drag the hours you want blocked (unavailable), and then click OK.**

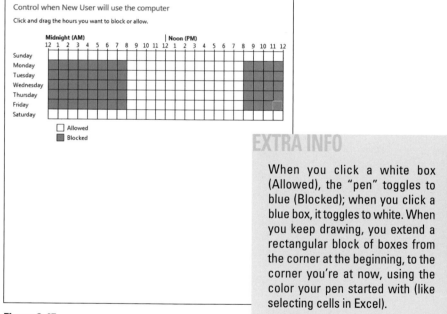

Figure 6-45

EXTRA INFO

When you click a white box (Allowed), the "pen" toggles to blue (Blocked); when you click a blue box, it toggles to white. When you keep drawing, you extend a rectangular block of boxes from the corner at the beginning, to the corner you're at now, using the color your pen started with (like selecting cells in Excel).

Restricting the use of specific programs

The strategy Windows 7 uses to enable you to choose the programs a person *can't* use is to give you the complete list of registered programs and let you check off each one. The Allow and Block Specific Programs control is great for blocking a specific program or game. To block all games by rating or content, go to the Games control.

You won't find Internet Explorer in this list. Too many other applications rely on IE for their display and connectivity capabilities, so disabling IE would probably disable them as well. And you cannot add IE to this list and then blacklist it, either.

Besides a Web browser, the other class of program most parents prefer that their kids not run are certain games. Rather than blacklist those, you'd have an easier time uninstalling them (and doing so would be more efficient, anyway) or refraining from installing them in the first place.

EXTRA INFO

Other types of programs that maybe you want certain members of your household to be able to run, but other members not include an FTP (file transfer protocol) program; programs, services, or drivers that manage the use of a built-in webcam; Skype; home accounting software; a VPN (virtual private network); and software used to uninstall an application.

After you have a strategy in mind, here's how you implement it:

1. **From Parental Controls, click the account you wish to limit.**

2. **In User Controls, make sure that On, Enforce Current Settings radio button is selected. Refer to Figure 6-44.**

3. **Click the Allow and Block Specific Programs link, also shown in Figure 6-44.**

4. **In the Application Restrictions window that opens (see Figure 6-46), mark the second radio button that restricts the user to only programs that you allow.**

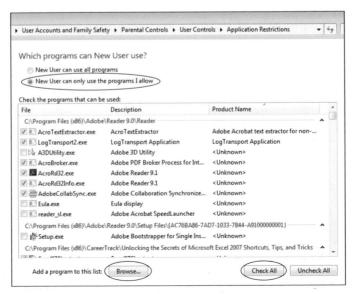

Figure 6-46

The search starts automatically, and when Windows is done searching for programs, it lists them. All checked programs are unrestricted.

5. **Because you'll want to keep the majority of the programs unrestricted, click the Check All button and then remove the check marks for those programs you want to restrict.**

If Windows didn't find a program you want to restrict, click the Browse button and go find it.

6. **To finalize your choices, click OK, and then click OK again to return to Parental Controls.**

Restricting games your kids play

To avoid the tediousness of restricting each game you installed through the Allow and Block Specific Programs screen, you can restrict the games that are already installed (or even any future games you install) by rating or type. And if you find something you didn't expect has been installed (perhaps a neighbor "loaned" your kid a disc), you can uninstall it.

Many games sold in the US are given ratings codes (inspired by the motion picture industry) by an independent bureau (the Entertainment Software Ratings Board; ESRB), such as T (suitable for teenagers but not smaller kids) or M (meant for mature adults, not for any kids at all). However, a huge chunk of the games played by young PC users are delivered not through packaged software but through Web sites — and aren't rated by the ESRB or anyone else.

1. **In the User Controls window, click the Games link.**

2. **In the Game Controls window, decide whether to allow this user to have access to any games.**

   • *No:* No means no.

   • *Yes:* If you opt for Yes, click the Set Games Ratings link, and finish this step list.

3. **In the Game Restrictions window, decide whether to allow this user to play games with no rating or which game ratings this user can play; see Figure 6-47.**

   Scroll down the page to get to the list of content types.

   Here, you can block access to games with a certain type of content so that even if a game has an approved rating, it will still be blocked if it contains content that you've blocked.

4. **Click OK to leave Game Restrictions.**

5. **Click OK to return to Parental Controls.**

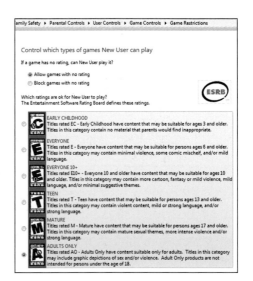

Figure 6-47

Setting up Family Safety

After you install Windows Live services on your system (refer to Lesson 3), you can extend Parental Controls using Windows Live Family Safety to control Web access and computer use for your household. Whether you opt for this depends on whether you're comfortable with the idea of a server at Microsoft maintaining a log of any family member's online activities.

It's fair to say no here. It is unlikely that anyone, anywhere in the world, is trying harm you via the Web at this exact moment. On the other hand, every point of access on the Internet is under some kind of threat at all times, not the least of which being the sanctity and integrity of your home PC or your personal network. So here's the question: Which is more important to you: something attacking Microsoft or something attacking your family?

If you do decide to use Family Safety, you don't use any of the other functions I describe in this section. Family Safety *replaces* them, in some cases with functionally identical or similar versions of these functions.

The Family Safety setup process determines which accounts you want monitored, and to what degree. You can monitor *anyone's* account, including administrator level accounts, and including your own.

1. **At the bottom of the Parental Controls window, from the Select a Provider list, choose Windows Live Family Safety. See Figure 6-48.**

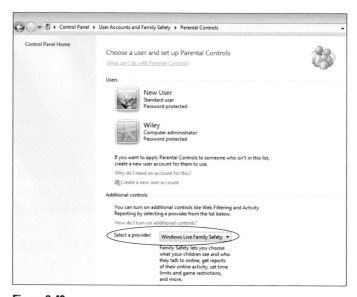

Figure 6-48

2. **If nothing happens, click the account you want Family Safety to monitor.**

   Usually, this wakes up Windows Live.

3. **Enter your Windows Live ID and password at the logon screen.**

4. **When Family Safety shows you all your accounts, like in Figure 6-49, click the account you want Family Safety to monitor.**

Standard user accounts are grouped at the top, and administrator accounts at the bottom.

Figure 6-49

5. **Click Save.**

   Family Safety takes a minute to send your choice to Microsoft. Next, you'll see a dialog box whose heading reads, "Go to the Family Safety website to customize settings."

6. **In the dialog box, click the** `familysafety.live.com` **link. See Figure 6-50.**

7. **In the Family Summary page list, click the Edit Settings link for the account you want Family Safety to monitor. See Figure 6-51.**

Figure 6-50

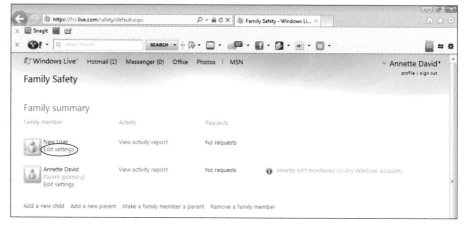

Figure 6-51

When you click this link, your Web browser appears, and you may be asked to log on to Windows Live. A settings page appears for the user you're setting up, which is where you'll see the monitoring and restriction functions that Family Safety offers:

- *Web Filtering* enables IE9 (or Mozilla Firefox or Google Chrome, if you use those browsers) to communicate to Family Safety which Web sites the account is attempting to visit.

- *Activity Reporting* generates a log of all Web addresses visited by the account, between two given dates. Although this option is listed as On, you can't turn it off.

- *Contact Management* lets you limit the other Windows Live accounts that the account can contact using Windows Live services, such as Windows Live Messenger.

EXTRA INFO

Enabling Web Filtering also instructs the browser to limit the scope of results pages from the top three search engines — Google, Bing, and Yahoo! — to the most family-friendly results available (what Google calls "SafeSearch"). However, this doesn't mean that search engines are limited to providing listings for sites that Family Safety has declared safe, or "child-friendly."

- *Requests* keeps track of those sites that the browser has blocked.

- *Time Limits* is the equivalent of the Windows 7 User Controls for your PC.

- *Game Restrictions* lets you limit game use for the account to certain age ratings provided by the ESRB (or other country's ratings service if you prefer).

- *Program Restrictions* shows the applications you're interested in restricting — not all the Windows services.

Blocking and allowing sites

Family Safety maintains a whitelist and a blacklist, but which one it chooses to use depends on the degree of filtering you choose from the Web Filtering page, shown in Figure 6-52.

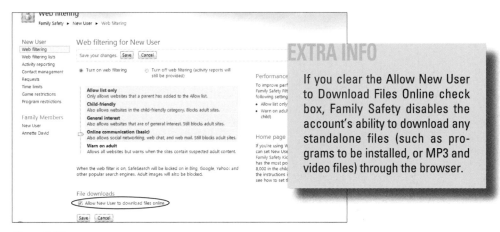

Figure 6-52

The filtering function may be turned on or off, and you adjust the slider up or down to tighten or loosen the degree of filtering. From most to least strict:

- **Allow List Only:** The account may visit only those sites you personally approved (never mind what Microsoft says).

- **Child-friendly:** Permits the account to visit sites that Family Safety has cleared as permissible and specifically geared toward children.

- **General Interest:** Permits the account to visit these regular sites, except for social networking sites like Facebook, MySpace, and Twitter.

- **Online Communication (Basic):** Permits social networking sites as well.

- **Warn on Adult:** Represents the minimum amount of filtering, and gives a warning that the site seen probably contains "adult content."

If you don't find the categories restrictive enough, or you want to ensure that specific Web sites are allowed or blocked, you can tighten things down even more:

1. **Click the Web Filtering Lists link on the Family Safety settings page for the account to which you're adding restrictions.**

2. **In the Web Filtering Lists page that appears, type the URL for the site to block (in the http:// field). See Figure 6-53.**

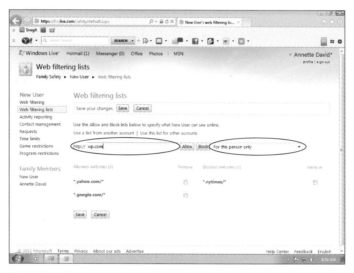

Figure 6-53

TIP

Use the most basic domain name for the URL: just *sitename*.com instead of www.*sitename*.com, for example.

3. **From the drop-down list at the far right, choose whether to block the site For This Person Only, or For Everyone.**

   "Everyone" in this case means all accounts that are being filtered.

4. **Click the Block button.**

   The name of the account is entered in the blacklist.

REMEMBER

The asterisks serve as wildcards before and after the name you entered to account for any subdomain that may appear before the DNS address (such as www.) or subdirectories after the address (such as /blogs).

5. **Click Save.**

To add a site that you like to the whitelist portion of the site (the URLs in the left column), follow the preceding steps but click the Allow button instead of Block.

When a monitored user tries to access a Web site that's blocked, he sees a page like the one in Figure 6-54:

- ✔ **Email Your Request:** Click this button to send an automated request to your Windows Live account.

- ✔ **Ask in Person:** Click this button to go directly to your child's Family Safety setting page so you can approve the site right away. A logon window appears where you log on to Family Safety (even though you're on the child's account) and grant the exception if you want.

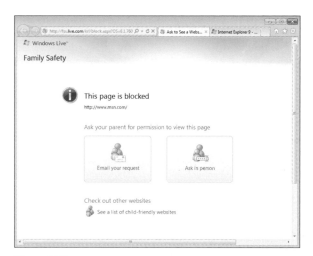

Figure 6-54

Even though you block a URL as a destination for your kids' Web browsers, that doesn't necessarily mean the server behind that URL is blocked from providing content to *other* Web sites your kids view.

A big case in point is YouTube. For any number of reasons, you may want to block your kids from visiting youtube.com. However, many Web sites, including some listed on the Family Safety Child-friendly list, use videos hosted by YouTube. That's okay if those videos are child-friendly in themselves, but perhaps you've noticed that you can view *other* videos on YouTube using the frame in which those hosted videos are presented.

This is a problem you may be able to solve only through personal monitoring — in other words, by supplementing Family Safety's filtering with your own personal involvement in your children's online activities.

Examining an activity report

To view an activity report for a monitored user, click the Activity Reporting link on the Family Safety page. Here's how to read the info on the Web Activity tab (see Figure 6-55):

- ✔ **Web Address column:** Shows a list of all Web sites that the monitored account has visited (or attempted to visit), in alphabetical order.

- ✔ **Action Taken column:** Shows whether the account was able to view the Web site or whether it was blocked.

- ✔ **Visits column:** Tells you how often the account holder accessed this Web site.

Figure 6-55

To change the status of any page to its opposite — from Allowed to Blocked, or vice versa — choose Select from the drop-down menu in the Change Setting column (on the same row as the address), and then select whether you want the change to be For This Person Only or For Everyone (that is, everyone whose account is monitored).

To see how much time the account holder has spent on the computer, click the Computer Activity tab. The amount of time the user has been logged on is listed in the Sessions category. You also get a detailed list of each computer that the account has used. See Figure 6-56.

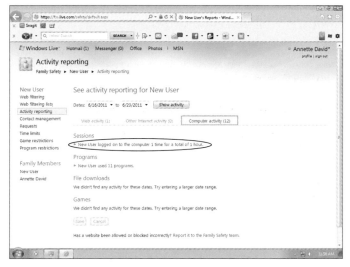

Figure 6-56

When Disaster Strikes

Maybe you've noticed once or twice already that Windows can get bogged down — and it can crash. Sometimes, though, what happens is worse than a mere crash. Maybe you encountered a power failure or power spike that disables your PC for a moment without a proper shutdown. Here are two repair mechanisms for when things go south: Safe Mode and Startup Repair.

 Save your work frequently, or make certain that your application (like Word or Excel) saves automatically for you every few minutes or so.

Running your PC in Safe Mode

When your PC boots up and you see something like Figure 6-57, that's Safe Mode: an indicator that Windows knows the last power-down sequence either didn't complete or didn't happen. It's dark and stark enough to make you think something's seriously wrong. The good news, though, is that your PC still works. And nothing you can do at this moment can accidentally make things any worse than they might already be.

You can start Safe Mode right now simply by pressing Enter. Or to access any of the other options, use the down-arrow key on your keyboard to highlight it and then press Enter.

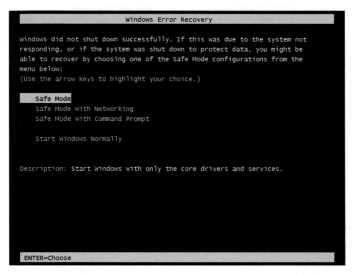

```
                      Windows Error Recovery

Windows did not shut down successfully. If this was due to the system not
responding, or if the system was shut down to protect data, you might be
able to recover by choosing one of the Safe Mode configurations from the
menu below:
(Use the arrow keys to highlight your choice.)


    Safe Mode
    Safe Mode with Networking
    Safe Mode with Command Prompt


    Start Windows Normally


Description: Start Windows with only the core drivers and services.




 ENTER=Choose
```

Figure 6-57

If you suspect a problem with your computer or one of the devices inside your computer (such as your graphics card) as opposed to with Windows itself, you can force Windows to reboot in Safe Mode. Restart your computer, but before the Windows logo appears, press the F8 key. You'll hear a series of chimes indicating that everything is okay, and then the Advanced Boot Options screen appears (see upcoming Figure 6-60). You can then choose Safe Mode.

Here are your options from the black screen of horror and terror:

LINGO

Safe Mode (a stalwart feature since Windows 95) is an alternate way of booting Windows, intentionally not loading device drivers and services beyond the ones it needs to run the screen, keyboard, and mouse. If Windows works in Safe Mode, it's likely that anything that persistently gives Windows trouble is caused by a program or service that's not part of Windows.

- ✔ **Safe Mode:** If you suspect something wrong, the first thing you should attempt is to see whether Windows will run in Safe Mode.

- ✔ **Safe Mode with Networking:** If you want to try running the Web browser to get help, try Safe Mode with Networking.

✔ **Safe Mode with Command Prompt:** Although this appears to restart Windows, it also loads a Command Prompt window in the middle of the screen. This window works like a miniaturized DOS environment, and if you're not familiar with DOS, you'll be lost here.

✔ **Start Windows Normally:** If you just suffered a power failure and you're pretty sure your PC is okay, try this. Then watch carefully to see whether your PC starts the usual way. If it doesn't, it may reboot itself, or it may appear to do nothing after a very long while (15 minutes is way too long), in which case you may manually reboot it yourself. And in either event, you'll see the screen in Figure 6-57 again.

When Safe Mode begins, Windows lists all the files it loads into memory and begins executing: a list that looks something like Figure 6-58. The boot process will be somewhat slower than usual, and that's fine. That's not a sign that your PC is ill or malfunctioning. Safe Mode just runs slower than normal mode.

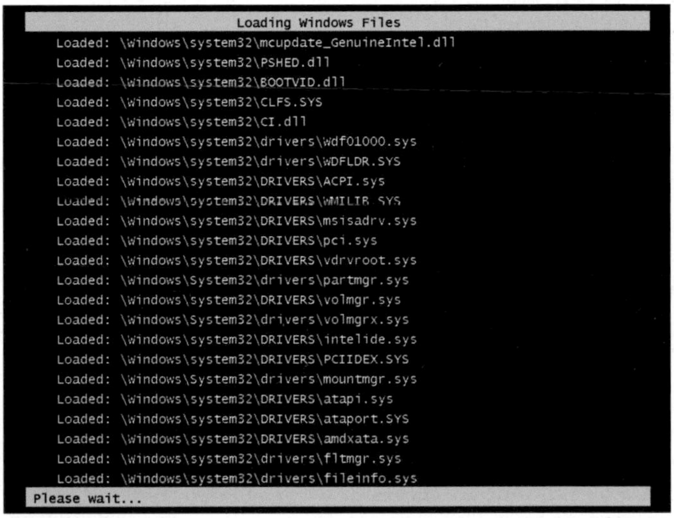

```
                    Loading Windows Files
   Loaded: \Windows\system32\mcupdate_GenuineIntel.dll
   Loaded: \Windows\system32\PSHED.dll
   Loaded: \Windows\system32\BOOTVID.dll
   Loaded: \Windows\system32\CLFS.SYS
   Loaded: \Windows\system32\CI.dll
   Loaded: \Windows\system32\drivers\Wdf01000.sys
   Loaded: \Windows\system32\drivers\WDFLDR.SYS
   Loaded: \Windows\system32\DRIVERS\ACPI.sys
   Loaded: \Windows\system32\DRIVERS\WMILIB.SYS
   Loaded: \Windows\system32\DRIVERS\msisadrv.sys
   Loaded: \Windows\system32\DRIVERS\pci.sys
   Loaded: \Windows\system32\DRIVERS\vdrvroot.sys
   Loaded: \Windows\System32\drivers\partmgr.sys
   Loaded: \Windows\system32\DRIVERS\volmgr.sys
   Loaded: \Windows\system32\drivers\volmgrx.sys
   Loaded: \Windows\system32\DRIVERS\intelide.sys
   Loaded: \Windows\system32\DRIVERS\PCIIDEX.SYS
   Loaded: \Windows\System32\drivers\mountmgr.sys
   Loaded: \Windows\System32\DRIVERS\atapi.sys
   Loaded: \Windows\system32\DRIVERS\ataport.SYS
   Loaded: \Windows\system32\DRIVERS\amdxata.sys
   Loaded: \Windows\system32\drivers\fltmgr.sys
   Loaded: \Windows\system32\drivers\fileinfo.sys
Please wait...
```

Figure 6-58

COURSEWORK

So that you'll feel confident diagnosing a Windows 7 system problem, try booting your PC in Safe Mode with Networking and doing a "dry run." With Safe Mode started, see whether anything is in your Startup folder. If so, launch each program there individually. Then bring up Control Panel. In the Troubleshooting panel (where you find diagnostic tools that evaluate your system's performance), run one of the tools there. Run them all if you like. They probably won't find anything wrong. But, if one of them does find something wrong, let it run its course. Maybe it'll fix a problem you never knew you had! Then try bringing up the Recovery panel, and stop short of doing a System Restore. This way you'll know where it is, and you'll be ready to use it if you need it.

If this list stops scrolling for a very long time without your system coming up, something is wrong with Windows. Actually, that's good news because now you know the problem, and there's probably a solution. I'll tell you how to handle that in a bit.

When Windows does start up, you'll see the very familiar logon screen with all your regular accounts. You click one (preferably an administrator account this time) and enter its password just like you usually do. In a minute or so (a little longer than normal), you'll see a stark, black desktop that looks something like Figure 6-59. You still have your applications icons, and Safe Mode indicators appear in all four corners. The taskbar along the bottom isn't the usual color, the Start button looks like older versions of Windows, and the Help window on Safe Mode opens automatically.

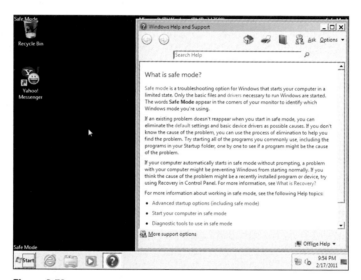

Figure 6-59

Repairing Windows 7 Startup

If you've been a Windows user for a while, you might have reinstalled Windows to fix it. Windows 7 has a much safer, and extremely welcome, option — Startup Repair — which uses the installation files that come with Windows. If you couldn't diagnose what's wrong while running your PC in Safe Mode, the next step is running Startup Repair.

Startup Repair runs a separate version of Windows, so even if your Windows 7 truly is damaged, you can still run Startup Repair. However, running Startup

Repair should be your last option before taking the drastic step of re-installing Windows 7. System Repair should keep all your files safe, but for safety reasons, back up anything you can't easily replace.

You'll need your Windows 7 DVD that you should have received from your PC's manufacturer. Here's how to get Startup Repair started:

1. **Power-down your computer or reset it.**

   Preferably, power it off totally first, if you can. If your PC is stuck and you don't have any control over the screen, or it appears frozen solid, press and hold your Power button down for three seconds. When it shuts off, count to five and switch it back on.

2. **Wait for the system beep and immediately press F8 on your keyboard.**

   If you get a wailing noise or several beeps instead of just one, your PC's hardware has a problem. Stop now because you need a repairperson.

If your PC does power up properly and your keyboard is working, you'll see the Advanced Boot Options menu shown in Figure 6-60.

```
                    Advanced Boot Options

Choose Advanced Options for: Windows 7
(Use the arrow keys to highlight your choice.)

    Repair Your Computer

    Safe Mode
    Safe Mode with Networking
    Safe Mode with Command Prompt

    Enable Boot Logging
    Enable low-resolution video (640x480)
    Last Known Good Configuration (advanced)
    Directory Services Restore Mode
    Debugging Mode
    Disable automatic restart on system failure
    Disable Driver Signature Enforcement

    Start Windows Normally

Description: View a list of system recovery tools you can use to repair
            startup problems, run diagnostics, or restore your system.


ENTER=Choose                                          ESC=Cancel
```

Figure 6-60

3. **Highlight the Repair Your Computer option (use the down-arrow key) and then press Enter.**

   This may take a few minutes, but you'll see a startup indicator that suspiciously looks more like Vista than Windows 7. Later, you'll see the System Recovery Options dialog box in Figure 6-61.

4. **Click Next.**

5. **In the system logon prompt that appears, choose an account from the User Name list, enter the password, and then click OK. See Figure 6-62.**

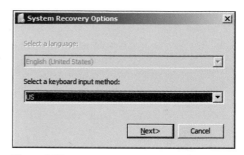

Figure 6-61

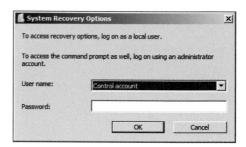

Figure 6-62

TIP

Opt for an administrator account so that you have all the restoration privileges you need.

6. **In the System Recovery Options window that opens, click Startup Repair. See Figure 6-63.**

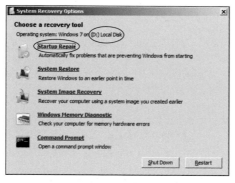

Figure 6-63

EXTRA INFO

The system disk might show a different letter here than it normally uses; for example, if it's usually C:, then it'll be shown at the top as D:. This is normal; don't worry about it.

Startup Repair begins to search your Windows system files for anomalies. (It shows a basic progress indicator while it's running.) If it finds a problem, it may begin repairing them automatically. If it needs your Windows 7 DVD, it will ask you for it. Best case scenario is that nothing is wrong with your Windows system files; if so, Startup Repair reports this, without making any changes to your system.

 Summing Up

User Account Control is a tool to halt system processes that could be commandeered by remote programs. You get the opportunity to let Windows 7 know that a human being is the one in control of this PC.

Task Manager lets you see what programs and services are running on your PC, and gives you clues as to whether they're actually running at all. If it's vital that you regain control of your PC so you can save or recover your work, you can use Task Manager to "kill" a stalled application.

Keeping your PC up to date with patches that account for system vulnerabilities is important. Because an update can be problematic, though, don't let your PC update automatically, either for Windows 7 or for your applications. You should manage updates yourself and monitor them.

Windows does have a backup utility, of sorts. It may not be suitable if the volume of data you need to back up requires using a huge backup device. You can try Windows Backup and see whether it works.

Windows Firewall can help keep certain programs from accessing the Internet when they don't need to, and other programs you've never seen from accessing the Internet, either. It's semi-effective, and you'll be much happier replacing it.

For Web servers, cookies serve a fundamental purpose. Sadly, this purpose is abused by services that use these state-storage mechanisms to examine how you use your browser. There's a complex system for filtering cookies in IE9.

In lieu of using Windows Defender, go for Microsoft Security Essentials. This free and wonderful download does a number on malware. It's so effective that many safeguards built into other parts of Windows and IE become useless.

Periodically, have Security Essentials (which, unlike Windows Firewall, is good) scan your system for possible malware. Anything SE suspects as dangerous will be moved into a safekeeping area called "quarantine." It's like a jail for suspects awaiting sentencing, but SE may not wait long for you to pass judgment before it sends quarantined malware to the gallows.

Use Parental Controls system to limit the hours that your kids use their accounts. If you need to watch what they're doing and where online, use Windows Live to set up a monitoring system.

If a program or application or third-party driver is making Windows crash, boot Windows into Safe Mode to assure yourself first that it's not Windows at fault. If the Windows system files are damaged, run Startup Repair to bring up another version of Windows: a safe and undamaged version exclusively for the purpose of restoring damaged files to health.

Know This Tech Talk

administrator account: The account within any networked computer presumed to have the greatest amount of privilege, or the least amount of restrictions

compressed file: A file composed of one or more other files that have been mathematically reduced in size, to enable their portability

cookie: A small element of data stored by a Web server on the client, to assist it in recalling information such as data you may have typed into forms, or the number of times you've visited a certain site

FTP (File Transfer Protocol): The principal means for sending and receiving files between remote computers over the Internet

impersonation: A remotely launched program to assume the credentials of the human user, which is sometimes necessary for processes to run within a Web browser

Live Messenger: An instant messaging system offered by Microsoft for users of Windows and mobile phones

Parental Controls: A system of restrictions and policies that use whitelists and blacklists to determine which resources a young user may be allowed to access within the homegroup

patch: A fragment of binary code intended to replace existing code in an operating system, which may upgrade or repair that code

ping: A program, typically called from a command line, used to detect the existence of a server at a designated IP address

process: The encoded sequence of instructions with which a task is carried out

restore point: A backup copy of the System Registry and other system files that enables Windows to undo possible damage that an application or service may cause to the system, if that application cannot be uninstalled or that service stopped properly

Safe Mode: A provision for running Windows so that programs and services other than Windows' own do not run automatically, and services that do run are confined to the most basic available, enabling the user to determine whether Windows or some other process is responsible for bad system behavior

script: A set of encoded instructions meant for the Web browser's interpreter, embedded alongside or within the HTML code of a Web page

Security Essentials: The replacement for Windows Defender; a free antivirus program offered by Microsoft capable of detecting malware almost immediately upon discovery

service: A component of an OS that usually runs without notifying the user; provides critical functionality to the OS: for instance, network access

third-party cookies: Data files stored on a Web browser user's PC whose sources are other than the Web site's servers, and whose purpose is probably to track browser usage

User Account Control (UAC): A safeguard system built into Windows that is triggered prior to the changing of a system setting that may impact the PC's operation, which disables programs' ability to make these changes automatically or remotely, and proceeds only after the human user has given his or her approval

VPN (Virtual Private Network): One means of enabling remote access to a secured network

Windows Backup: A tool offered in Windows 7 for the periodic replication of files to secure (usually external) storage devices

Windows Defender: The anti-malware tool shipped with Windows 7, which Microsoft itself should replace with Security Essentials

Windows Firewall: The software-based firewall tool, shipped with Windows 7, that restricts certain programs' and services' access to the Internet

Windows Live Family Safety: An online service offered by Microsoft to replace the Parental Controls system in Windows 7 with an extended service that also monitors use of IE by multiple accounts in a homegroup

Windows Update: Microsoft's delivery channel for patches to Windows and other Microsoft programs

About the CD

This README file contains information to help you get started using Dummies eLearning. This course requires no installation.

System Requirements

Dummies eLearning will provide all required functionality on the following Microsoft operating systems: Windows 7, Windows Vista, Windows XP, Windows 2000, and Windows 2003 Server.

The following browsers will be supported under Windows: Microsoft Internet Explorer 6.0 or higher, and Mozilla Firefox 2.x or higher.

To run a QS3 CD-ROM, the system should have the following additional hardware/software minimums:

- Adobe Flash Player 8
- A Pentium III, 500 MHz processor
- 256 MB of RAM
- A CD-ROM or DVD-ROM drive

A negligible amount of disk space must be available for tracking data. Less than 1 MB will typically be used.

Launch Instructions

Setup instructions for Windows machines:

1. **Put CD in CD drive.**
2. **Double-click on the My Computer icon to view the contents of the My Computer window.**
3. **Double-click the CD-ROM drive icon to view the contents of the Dummies eLearning CD.**

4. Double-click the start.bat file to start the Dummies eLearning CBT.

Your computer may warn you about active content. Click Yes to continue starting the CD. The CD may create new tabs in your browser. Click the tab to see the content.

The browser offers the option of using the lessons from the CD or from the website:

- ✔ To use the web version, click that option and follow the instructions. The web version may require a registration code from the book.

- ✔ To use the CD, click that option and follow the instructions. Agree to the EULA and install Flash Player, if prompted. Allow disk space usage by clicking the allow button, if prompted.

Operation

After you enter your user name, the eLearning course displays a list of topics. Select any topic from the list by clicking its Launch button. When the topic opens, it plays an introductory animation. To watch more animations on the topic, click the Next button (the arrow pointing right) at the bottom of the screen to play the next one.

If you want to switch to another lesson or another topic, use the list on the left side of the topic window to open a lesson and select a topic.

Some topics have a hands-on activity section that lets you perform a task on your own. To see the activity from start to finish, click Show Me Full Demo. If you want to try the tasks for yourself, click Guide Me Through to see the animation in sections and repeat it yourself. If you're ready to solo, click Let Me Try to work through all the steps yourself without coaching. (If you need a helping hand to finish, just click Hint at the bottom of the window, then click Show Me Clue in the dialog box.) When you perform the activity, be sure to position the cursor directly over the subject you want to click; your computer may not respond the first time you click. To end the activity, click the X at the bottom of the Milestone box.

Some topics have an active tab for resources on the right side of the window. By default, Windows opens this content in a new window. If you have another compressed file manager installed, such as WinZip, your system may behave differently.

Troubleshooting

What do I do if the page does not load?

It is possible that you have a security setting enabled that is not allowing the needed Flash file to run. Be sure that pop up blockers are off, ActiveX content is enabled, and the correct version of Shockwave and Flash are on the system you are using.

Please contact your system administrator or technical support group for assistance.

What do I do if the Add User window appears when the course loads and there are no names in the Learner Name list, but I have previously created a user account?

The course stores your information on the machine on which you create your account, so first make sure that you are using the eLearning For Dummies course on the same machine on which you created your Learner account. If you are using the course on a network and use a different machine than the one on which you created your account, the software will not be able to access your Learner record.

If you are on the machine on which you created your account, close the course browser window. Depending on the configuration of your machine, sometimes a course will load before accessing the user data.

If this still does not work, contact your network administrator for more assistance.

What do I do if I click on a Launch button but nothing happens?

This may occur on machines that have AOL installed. If you are using the course from a CD-ROM and you are an AOL subscriber, follow the following steps:

1. **Exit the course.**
2. **Log on to AOL.**
3. **Restart the course.**

What do I do if the Shockwave installer on the ROM says that I have a more recent version of the plugin, but the software still says that I need to install version 8.5 or higher?

Download the latest version of the Shockwave plugin directly from Adobe's website:

```
http://www.adobe.com/downloads/
```

If prompted to install Flash Player to view the CD's content, you can download the latest version from the same URL.

Index

• X •

• Y •

• Z •

Notes

Notes

End-User License Agreement

READ THIS. You should carefully read these terms and conditions before opening the software packet(s) included with this book "Book". This is a license agreement "Agreement" between you and John Wiley & Sons, Inc. "WILEY". By opening the accompanying software packet(s), you acknowledge that you have read and accept the following terms and conditions. If you do not agree and do not want to be bound by such terms and conditions, promptly return the Book and the unopened software packet(s) to the place you obtained them for a full refund.

1. **License Grant.** WILEY grants to you (either an individual or entity) a nonexclusive license to use one copy of the enclosed software program(s) (collectively, the "Software") solely for your own personal or business purposes on a single computer (whether a standard computer or a workstation component of a multi-user network). The Software is in use on a computer when it is loaded into temporary memory (RAM) or installed into permanent memory (hard disk, CD-ROM, or other storage device). WILEY reserves all rights not expressly granted herein.

2. **Ownership.** WILEY is the owner of all right, title, and interest, including copyright, in and to the compilation of the Software recorded on the physical packet included with this Book "Software Media". Copyright to the individual programs recorded on the Software Media is owned by the author or other authorized copyright owner of each program. Ownership of the Software and all proprietary rights relating thereto remain with WILEY and its licensers.

3. **Restrictions on Use and Transfer.**

    (a) You may only (i) make one copy of the Software for backup or archival purposes, or (ii) transfer the Software to a single hard disk, provided that you keep the original for backup or archival purposes. You may not (i) rent or lease the Software, (ii) copy or reproduce the Software through a LAN or other network system or through any computer subscriber system or bulletin-board system, or (iii) modify, adapt, or create derivative works based on the Software.

    (b) You may not reverse engineer, decompile, or disassemble the Software. You may transfer the Software and user documentation on a permanent basis, provided that the transferee agrees to accept the terms and conditions of this Agreement and you retain no copies. If the Software is an update or has been updated, any transfer must include the most recent update and all prior versions.

4. **Restrictions on Use of Individual Programs.** You must follow the individual requirements and restrictions detailed for each individual program in the "About the CD" appendix of this Book or on the Software Media. These limitations are also contained in the individual license agreements recorded on the Software Media. These limitations may include a requirement that after using the program for a specified period of time, the user must pay a registration fee or discontinue use. By opening the Software packet(s), you agree to abide by the licenses and restrictions for these individual programs that are detailed in the "About the CD" appendix and/or on the Software Media. None of the material on this Software Media or listed in this Book may ever be redistributed, in original or modified form, for commercial purposes.

5. **Limited Warranty.**

    (a) WILEY warrants that the Software Media is free from defects in materials and workmanship under normal use for a period of sixty (60) days from the date of purchase of this Book. If WILEY receives notification within the warranty period of defects in materials or workmanship, WILEY will replace the defective Software Media.

(b) WILEY AND THE AUTHOR(S) OF THE BOOK DISCLAIM ALL OTHER WARRANTIES, EXPRESS OR IMPLIED, INCLUDING WITHOUT LIMITATION IMPLIED WARRANTIES OF MERCHANTABILITY AND FITNESS FOR A PARTICULAR PURPOSE, WITH RESPECT TO THE SOFTWARE, THE PROGRAMS, THE SOURCE CODE CONTAINED THEREIN, AND/ OR THE TECHNIQUES DESCRIBED IN THIS BOOK. WILEY DOES NOT WARRANT THAT THE FUNCTIONS CONTAINED IN THE SOFTWARE WILL MEET YOUR REQUIREMENTS OR THAT THE OPERATION OF THE SOFTWARE WILL BE ERROR FREE.

(c) This limited warranty gives you specific legal rights, and you may have other rights that vary from jurisdiction to jurisdiction.

6. Remedies.

(a) WILEY's entire liability and your exclusive remedy for defects in materials and workmanship shall be limited to replacement of the Software Media, which may be returned to WILEY with a copy of your receipt at the following address: Software Media Fulfillment Department, Attn.: *Windows 7 For Dummies eLearning Kit,* John Wiley & Sons, Inc., 10475 Crosspoint Blvd., Indianapolis, IN 46256, or call 1-800-762-2974. Please allow four to six weeks for delivery. This Limited Warranty is void if failure of the Software Media has resulted from accident, abuse, or misapplication. Any replacement Software Media will be warranted for the remainder of the original warranty period or thirty (30) days, whichever is longer.

(b) In no event shall WILEY or the author be liable for any damages whatsoever (including without limitation damages for loss of business profits, business interruption, loss of business information, or any other pecuniary loss) arising from the use of or inability to use the Book or the Software, even if WILEY has been advised of the possibility of such damages.

(c) Because some jurisdictions do not allow the exclusion or limitation of liability for consequential or incidental damages, the above limitation or exclusion may not apply to you.

7. U.S. Government Restricted Rights. Use, duplication, or disclosure of the Software for or on behalf of the United States of America, its agencies and/or instrumentalities "U.S. Government" is subject to restrictions as stated in paragraph (c)(1)(ii) of the Rights in Technical Data and Computer Software clause of DFARS 252.227-7013, or subparagraphs (c)(1) and (2) of the Commercial Computer Software - Restricted Rights clause at FAR 52.227-19, and in similar clauses in the NASA FAR supplement, as applicable.

8. General. This Agreement constitutes the entire understanding of the parties and revokes and supersedes all prior agreements, oral or written, between them and may not be modified or amended except in a writing signed by both parties hereto that specifically refers to this Agreement. This Agreement shall take precedence over any other documents that may be in conflict herewith. If any one or more provisions contained in this Agreement are held by any court or tribunal to be invalid, illegal, or otherwise unenforceable, each and every other provision shall remain in full force and effect.